Shakespeare and the Revolution of the Times

James Joyce: A Critical Introduction (1941, 1960)

The Overreacher: A Study of Christopher Marlowe (1952)

Contexts of Criticism (1957)

The Power of Blackness: Hawthorne, Melville, Poe (1958)

The Question of Hamlet (1959)

The Gates of Horn: A Study of Five French Realists (1963)

Refractions: Essays in Comparative Literature (1966)

The Myth of the Golden Age in the Renaissance (1969)

Grounds for Comparison (1972)

Selected Works of Ben Jonson (1938)

Rochester: A Satire against Mankind, and Other Poems (1942)

The Viking Portable Joyce (1947)

Perspectives of Criticism (1950)

Shakespeare: Coriolanus (Pelican Edition, 1956)

Hawthorne: The Scarlet Letter,
   and Other Tales of the Puritans (1960, 1961)

Shakespeare: The Comedy of Errors (Signet Edition, 1965)

Veins of Humor (1972)

The Riverside Shakespeare (with G. B. Evans and others, 1974)

Shakespeare
and
the Revolution of the Times

PERSPECTIVES AND COMMENTARIES

HARRY LEVIN

OXFORD UNIVERSITY PRESS
Oxford   London   New York

OXFORD UNIVERSITY PRESS
Oxford London Glasgow
New York Toronto Melbourne Wellington
Ibadan Nairobi Dar es Salaam Lusaka Cape Town
Kuala Lumpur Singapore Jakarta Hong Kong Tokyo
Delhi Bombay Calcutta Madras Karachi

Library of Congress Cataloging in Publication Data

Levin, Harry, 1912-
Shakespeare and the revolution of the times.

Includes bibliographical references and index.
1. Shakespeare, William, 1564-1616—Criticism
and interpretation—Addresses, essays, lectures.
I. Title.
PR2890.L46   1978   822.3'3   77-13660
ISBN 0-19-502362-5 pbk.

Printed in the United States of America

For

HERSCHEL BAKER

GWYNNE EVANS

WALTER KAISER

Note

This volume comprises a series of sixteen essays, plus two appendages, most of them written and published during the decade that began with the Shakespeare Quadricentennial in 1964. Their object of common concern has been the central thread in my teaching for thirty-five years, though I have divagated as often as not, and it is largely the divagations that have been reflected through my previous publications. These Shakespearean pieces have emerged under various conditions; consequently they vary in mode and in method. Since very few of them appeared in the same periodical and the rest have been more or less widely scattered, there may be some warrant for gathering them in here. At the beginning of each paper I have tried to indicate the auspices under which it was first prompted and printed. Together with those indications go my warmest thanks for the original stimulus and the permission to reprint. Minimal revision has been carried out, mainly in the interests of stylistic uniformity and occasional updating. I am gratefully indebted to the Joseph H. Clark Bequest for sponsorship in preparing the manuscript. Here again I must express my gratitude for invaluable help from Elizabeth Ann Farmer, Marina Levin Frederiksen, and Anna-Maria Kovacs. I have not reprinted my commemorative paper, "Shakespeare Today"—from *Proceedings of the American Philosophical Society*, CVI, 5 (October 11, 1962)—because I have made two subsequent attempts at presenting the subject in breadth to the general reader: with due brevity in *Atlantic Brief Lives*, ed. Louis Kronenberger (Boston, 1971), and rather more comprehensively in my General Introduction to the new *Riverside Shakespeare* (Boston, 1974). However, I have plagiarized a few paragraphs from my omitted essay, and have reintroduced them in other contexts. It is from the Riverside text that Shakespeare has been quoted and cited throughout, with one indicated exception. I am additionally grateful to G. Blakemore Evans, the textual editor, for generously permitting me to reprint, by way of appendix, an article on which we collaborated. I must thank my wife for suggesting the title, not to mention the many other ideas that I perennially owe her. It had been my intention to dedicate this book to the four colleagues who have shared with me, during the last few years, the responsibility for and the privilege of teaching Shakespeare at Harvard. It has been sad to see that number reduced by the recent death of Reuben Brower.

Cambridge, Massachusetts   H. L.
May 13, 1975

Contents

Induction,   1

I   PERSPECTIVES
      Shakespeare and "The Revolution of the Times,"   29
      Shakespeare's Nomenclature,   51
      The Shakespearean Overplot,   78
      Evangelizing Shakespeare,   90

II   COMMENTARIES
      Form and Formality in *Romeo and Juliet,*   103
      Falstaff Uncolted,   121
      The Underplot of *Twelfth Night,*   131
      Othello and the Motive-Hunters,   143
      The Heights and the Depths: A Scene from *King
          Lear,*   162
      An Introduction to *Coriolanus,*   187
      Shakespeare's Misanthrope,   197
      Two Magian Comedies: *The Tempest* and *The
          Alchemist,*   210

III   FURTHER PERSPECTIVES
      The Primacy of Shakespeare,   235
      Reconsidering Marlowe,   261
      The End of Elizabethan Drama,   274
      Dramatic Auspices: The Playwright and His
          Audience,   284

      APPENDIX: Shakespeare as Shakespeare,   315
      INDEX,   327

Shakespeare and the Revolution of the Times

Induction

While I hope my running title carries some distance beyond the scope of my titular essay, I should make it clear at once that Shakespeare was not speaking of *revolution* in the immediate sense that catches our headlines today. For political rebellion, which was one of the innumerable phases of human interaction that concerned him deeply, he employed a shorter and sharper cognate, *revolt*. Revolution, in the sense of changes wrought by time itself, is a major theme in the *Sonnets* (59.12). The ultimate change is signalized ironically when Hamlet picks up a skull: "Here's fine revolution . . ." (V.i.90). When Antony foresees his fate prefigured, "by revolution low'ring" from the topmost point to the very bottom after half a cycle of Fortune's symbolic wheel, he adumbrates the medieval conception of tragic downfall (I.ii.125). Truly, Shakespeare's imagination was—even if the talent of Holofernes was not—"full of forms, figures, shapes, objects, ideas, apprehensions, motions, revolutions" (*Love's Labor's Lost,* IV.ii.66-8). "The revolution of the times" is destiny—and, in this larger sense, it refers to his own (2 *Henry IV,* III.i.46).

1

Now time is of the essence in any approach to Shakespeare. It has kept revolving since his day, faster and ever faster we sometimes think, and he has continued to span it and to abridge it, much as Ben Jonson prophesied. Shakespeare's appeal to our age seems no less great than it was to his own, or to many of the intervening periods. Perhaps it is all the greater because its tokens and trophies have meanwhile been accumulated so massively and disseminated so widely. Fortune is indeed another theme on which he had every reason to meditate. The very circumstances of that continuance have come to play a part in the picture he has spread before us. Strictly speaking, we ourselves are time-bound to our twentieth century—or rather, we would be, if it were not for such emancipating influences as those he has exerted upon us. He in turn, as the child of a different and increasingly distant century, could but work with materials it had provided. The chain of continuity from then to now, moreover, extends across three other centuries, each with its interlinking vicissitudes.

We are thus confronted with three temporal dimensions, if they may be so described: first the contemporaneous (Shakespeare in his time), second the traditional (Shakespeare as handed down from then to now), and third the contemporary (Shakespeare in our time). Such, at all events, has been the chronological sequence. Logic would reverse this order, since perforce we must start wherever we are and find our way to him. We would not be minded to make the attempt if he had not already reached us to a certain extent, if we had not been touched by the spell of his poetry or felt the force of situations transcending those historical particulars in which they happen to be temporarily clothed. But we cannot laugh with much spontaneity at a joke which requires a philological footnote, or sympathize profoundly with the claims of contending rulers whose genealogies have not heretofore been inscribed in our memories. If only, by some imaginative leap from the contemporary (ours) to the contemporaneous (his), we could put ourselves in the ideal position of a pristine spectator!

Estheticians like to posit their theories on the unviolated sensibility, the unmediated response. To his fellow Structuralists, who have so ingeniously been generating subtexts and supertexts, pretexts and post-texts, Roland Barthes has lately been recommending *Le Plaisir du texte*. Susan Sontag has headed a volume of interpretative essays with an anti-intellectual manifesto *Against Interpretation*. There has always been an underlying suspicion that the role of the interpreter was officious and *de trop*, and this may be quite true when an esthetic experience can be fully and directly communicated without him. But if the communication is in a language which differs considerably from that of its recipient, or if it is presented through an idiom which has to be transposed to another medium, then the interpreter's services are necessary and vital. If he is discreet, he will subordinate himself as much as possible to the work, simply trying to bridge the distance between it and its latter-day audience. If he is an egotist, like most orchestral conductors and even some Shakespearean directors, he will interpose his personality.

The foregoing distinctions are, admittedly, too categorical. The heterogeneous nature of Shakespeare's original public is one of my premises; the differing trends of reaction must therefore have begun with his earliest performances. Furthermore, no middleman can attain invisibility; perhaps the best he can do is to bear in mind the Elizabethan convention for it, a neutralizing black cloak. Shakespeare would not be of such compelling interest if his works did not bristle with problems to be faced and alternatives to be explored. Any consistent version is bound, in some measure, to reflect the outlook of its exponent. In the theater generations of actors and producers have vied with their predecessors and their contemporaries to bring forth fresh and novel interpretations of every play. Their productions have varied extremely, both in style and in quality. The quest for novelty and the pressure for adaptation have often strained the texts to the limits of recognition. Yet the record, taken as a whole, attests the triumphs of infinite variety over withering age and staling custom.

In the classroom or the library there is ampler freedom to interpret, since no single reading need be adopted to the exclusion of all the rest. There is room and leisure to consider the ambiguities and to entertain conflicting views. This does not mean that the stage should no longer be the framework for our understanding of Shakespeare. On the contrary: if the scholarship of the last two generations has taught us anything, we have learned the lesson that nineteenth-century critics so hazardously neglected. What it means—according to Granville-Barker, an authoritative figure in that connection, since he had been an actor-manager as well as a moderately successful playwright—is that we should cultivate the habit of "reading score." Just as a trained musician can look at the notes and hear the music, so we can train ourselves to read the script and project the dramatic action into the mind's eye. Similarly, our studies should help us to make a projection into the past, whenever we are invited to do so, responding to archaic phrases or playing with half-forgotten ideas.

The scholar is essentially a conservationist. It is his continual endeavor to preserve the monuments, to remove the encrustations of time, to restore the fading colors to freshness. These can be technical matters, and our age has not been behindhand in developing techniques: notably those textual and bibliographical methods which have brought us closer to what Shakespeare actually wrote than his readers have ever been. Theatrical history has been showing us how his plays may originally have been staged, while the history of ideas has made us feel more at home in their climate of opinion. Historicism leads, of course, toward approximation at best; the decisive line of intercommunication is not the one that leads us back to Shakespeare but the one that brings him back to us. Here we reach the uneven ground where criticism plods away at its Sisyphian task of unending reinterpretation. This is not the same thing as revaluation, for esthetic criteria have proved to be more subject to fluctuation than has Shakespeare's standing. He once stood supreme as a natural genius; now we tend to admire him as a consummate artist.

Shakespeare must by now be surrounded with a larger array of books and articles, monographs and periodicals, not to mention editions and translations, than any other writer who ever lived. One who has read much in them, oftentimes with profit, who has added a little to them and is about to add a little more, and who has for the most part been employed to talk about Shakespeare with congenial and intelligent young people, can hardly afford to deprecate what has been termed "the Shakespeare industry." It would be surprising if, after so much prior industriousness in so overworked an area, actual contributions to knowledge were not getting fewer and slighter or else more far-fetched every year. Yet the outpouring does not seem to diminish; each generation, it seems, must discover Shakespeare for itself and offer the testimonials of minds he has newly enkindled. He is less the basis of an industry than he is a sort of lay religion, a humanistic source of precepts and parables, whose rites we celebrate in a time-honored liturgy. And liturgy, though repetitious, has been known to change.

The annual pilgrimage to the hallowed shrines at the birthplace, the cenotaphic Stratfords in Ontario and Connecticut, the mysteries and cults of Bardolatry have been counteracted by heresies—which have not been unproductive when they pointed back, as Bernard Shaw did, from the chancel to the stage. My personal concern has been fixed on the far less Orphic plane of the lecture platform. Though the papers that follow were not addressed to classes, eleven of them were delivered orally on various occasions. One was an introduction, another a review-article, still another an expanded stage-direction; and two others were written for symposia. My opening section, "Perspectives," deals with questions both structural and ideological that apply to Shakespeare's work as a whole. "Commentaries," the central section, mostly consists of explications, each essay dealing with a single play—except for the last, which involves a comparison, and is thereby linked to the final section. This is "Further Perspectives," which concerns itself with Shakespeare's relations to other writers and to the drama in general.

The present apologia is titled by a word that has several meanings in this context. It has certain logical connotations, which—I trust—are not altogether irrelevant. However, the Elizabethans used *induction* to designate a kind of framing prologue. Though Shakespeare did not use the term that way, Pope supplied it for the Sly episode in *The Taming of the Shrew,* and it has counterparts in Kyd and Jonson. I should like it to serve not only for the process of introduction into the subject-matter before us, but for the problem of initiation in its passive and active aspects. I should like to write briefly, candidly, and informally about my own induction to Shakespeare. And I shall try to recollect and summarize a few impressions gained while initiating students to Shakespeare. This has been an opportunity which I cannot be too grateful for. Frequently I have told them that I ought not to be paid, and they ought not to receive academic credit, for so purely pleasurable a form of activity. I cannot say we have followed that altruistic impulse, but it had an exhilarating air which our subject has never ceased to excite.

I can hardly remember a time when Shakespeare did not loom large on my horizon. Whether such early access was an advantage or a handicap I cannot be sure. Certainly it opened up a world beyond one's own, but how far could one appreciate the enrichment? And was there not the countervailing danger that appreciation, as it developed, might be blocked by stock responses and stereotypes? Probably *Julius Caesar* is the single play to which most of my generation were introduced at the grammar school level, and commonly our impression of it was blurred by the rigid insecurities of our teachers. To see it performed—and it must have been the first play I ever saw in theatrical performance—was like the awe and mystery of a church service after the copybook didacticism of Sunday school. But the turbulent struggle for power behind the tense rhetoric did not really come to life for me until the nineteen-thirties, with the dynamic production of Orson Welles and John Houseman, where Caesar's Rome was transformed into Mussolini's and the atmosphere was charged with the menace of Fascism.

I was eleven years old when my father first gave me a

Shakespeare of my own: a single volume bound in crimson leatherette, apocryphally edited and printed on tenuous paper, its crowded text containing many misprints which I could hardly tell from the other strange and alluring words. I took it along to camp, and it colored my memories of that summer more than the woods or lakes or my more athletic companions. My father was a self-educated man, and seldom read for pleasure; but he had also been exposed as a boy to Shakespeare in the theater, and he enjoyed the experience throughout his life. He had stood in line and sat in the gallery, as he liked to relate, for Irving and Forbes-Robertson on their American tours. Our middlewestern city, Minneapolis, still had an opera-house, which rather ambitiously called itself the Metropolitan. Though its late Victorian glitter had somewhat faded by my day, it was there with my father that I attended my earliest matinées. There, as an adolescent, I sometimes had a chance to usher or to carry the spear of a supernumerary.

Those first impressions must have come at the very end of a tradition which had encircled the country with roadshows performing the standard Shakespearean repertory. Thus, when I beheld Robert B. Mantell, he was literally tottering, appropriately enough for Lear if less so for Hamlet. E. H. Sothern and Julia Marlowe, though picturesquely costumed, made a mature pair of Shakespearean lovers. Yet their enunciation had a resonance which I had not heard before, and which contrasted with the nasal intonations of our most frequent trooper, Fritz Leiber. Leiber, as a frankly provincial actor whose province was primarily the midwest, honestly earned the admiration of his constituents for services energetically rendered. The tradition of bringing Shakespeare to the people, harking back to river-boats and caravans, is an integral part of

American culture, like the circuit-riding of judges and preachers. What I witnessed of it seemed to be a last flickering; but it held more magic than television would bring; and who could have foreseen that, after a moribund interlude, Tyrone Guthrie would wave his wand and create a brave new playhouse and a resident company at—of all places—Minneapolis?

I remember certain big productions which toured the road during my teens, starring famous actors whose credentials were not particularly Shakespearean. One of these affairs was billed as Gordon Craig's *Macbeth*. Craig had stayed in Rapallo, but the producer had attempted to construct the sets from his impressionistic designs (Lee Simonson would later argue that this was quite impossible). At all events, the platforms and pylons got in the way of the actors, and pieces of scenery had to be left behind in local warehouses at every stop. Even more spectacular was *The Merchant of Venice,* as produced by David Belasco and acted by David Warfield in their common vein of naturalistic melodrama. Venice itself was rebuilt upon an enormous revolving stage, and Shylock's padded part was drenched with *Judenschmerz.* More to my taste was a version which starred George Arliss, better known through those films in which he impersonated historical characters. His technique was based on underplaying, and his Shylock was crisp and ironic, realizing some of the grimly comic overtones that too often have been emotionalized out of the portrayal.

It was part of Harvard's lure, for me, that Boston was still a theatrical center. When I was an undergraduate, it had two repertory companies (one of which played Shakespeare not infrequently), a first-class opera-house, and half a dozen legitimate theaters, regularly filled by touring companies or pre-Broadway openings. The attrition since has been sad to watch, though to some extent the losses have been offset by dramatic activities on university campuses and by occasional little-theater groups. Over the years, I might parenthetically say, I have been a trustee of three theatrical ventures in the community; the most durable of them lasted just three seasons. Some would judge that our New England capital, distinguished for its patronage of music and the fine arts, turns a cold puritanical shoulder to drama. The monument of its ambivalence—now, alas, burned down—was the Old Howard. Originally this had been called the Howard Athenaeum, no mere playhouse but a place where proper Bostonians could be elevated by the wisdom of Shakespeare. By the time my classmates and I knew it, its raked stage and ornate proscenium framed the more bacchantic ecstasies of burlesque.

Boston was then a port of call for the original Stratford troupe, competently performing under the regime of Bridges-Adams, yet far less vivid than the Abbey company, which brought Sarah Allgood and Barry Fitzgerald. New York was never far away, and London was getting nearer. Shakespeare had his innings with Eva Le Gallienne's Civic Repertory, but significantly did not figure with O'Neill or Shaw in the increasingly commercialized record of the Theatre Guild, while the subsequent development of the Group Theater moved in an anti-classical direction. Indeed I can recall a strained evening with Clifford Odets, who waxed indignant over some of us Harvard amateurs because we were striving to resurrect Shakespeare. Small wonder that, in the heyday of the Actors' Studio, American audiences looked to Britain again for their supply of Shakespeareans. Hamlet, as interpreted by John Gielgud, refined his romantic introspection to a final Proustian nuance. It was left for

Maurice Evans to restore all the cuts and to give a lyrical but less sharply defined performance—not exactly *Hamlet* without the Prince, but a realization of how much we usually miss by concentrating upon the star.

After I graduated, a *Wanderjahr,* largely divided between London and Paris, offered me my first opportunity to live in theatrical capitals. In spite of a slender fellowship and a declining dollar, I managed to celebrate two or three evenings a week at the theater. Guthrie was then the emergent genius of the Old Vic, and his brilliant casts included Flora Robson, Athene Seyler, Lydia Lopokova, Ralph Richardson, and Charles Laughton. I was in a crowd that braved the drizzle of Regent's Park when John Drinkwater was Prospero and again when Robert Atkins was Bottom. The Parisian stage, of course, proved more sophisticated on the scenic plane. *Richard III,* directed by Charles Dullin at the Théâtre de l'Atelier, exhibited a series of miniatures from a medieval book of hours. The metallic clangor of *Coriolanus* lent itself to the full-scale heroics of the Comédie Française. At the *représentation* that I happened to attend, as I have had occasion to mention elsewhere, a political riot broke out. It turned out to be a small milestone in the history of the Third Republic, and a very large one in my induction to the relationship between drama and life.

My first recollection of the Memorial Theatre at Stratford is Theodore Komisarjevsky's *Macbeth,* a modernization which neutralized the supernatural elements, and heralded a recurrent policy of arbitrary direction. The playhouse, recently built, was—and remains, despite continued tinkering—a model of the intractable, both in its stage and its auditorium. As such it has challenged the brightest talents in acting and direction, and their responses have been lively if not always convincing. The official mandate to run through the same familiar repertory once in every few years, playing to full houses for a lengthy season, has been met as an annual invitation to "make it new." This may stand in wholesome contrast to the sclerotic *mise en scène* that haunts more traditional theaters, but it likewise prompts the director to overwhelm Shakespeare's texts with his own improvisations. The Savoy operettas must go on forever as Gilbert staged them; Guthrie encountered bitter opposition when he tried to restage *Pinafore*. Yet at the theater dedicated to Shakespeare there are no ground rules for staging his plays. Possibly the comparison tells us something about complexity and flexibility in dramatic material.

In 1958, while lecturing at the Stratford Summer School, I was keenly struck by Michael Redgrave's Hamlet. In my Alexander Lectures at the University of Toronto that spring (subsequently published as *The Question of Hamlet*), I had argued for a less neurotic, more heroic sense of the role. Circumstances reinforced that conception; for Redgrave—though himself an intellectual—looked and acted every inch a Viking hero, and the production of Glenn Byam Shaw was straightforward and powerful. I have kept in intermittent touch with Stratford-upon-Avon through the Shakespeare Institute, graciously conducted by Terence Spencer of Birmingham University. I have spent less time at the cisatlantic Stratfords, though the Canadian festival has impressed me most of all three: by its highly adaptable playhouse, by the quality and consistency of its standards, by the talented actors trained in so brief a period and in a country with such sparse theatrical traditions. As for Stratford-on-the Housatonic, it started with some promise, but has drifted for lack of intelligent· guidance, and its policies have been aligned to the magnetic fields of Broadway.

Succeeding generations will clearly be more dependent upon the cinema than mine has been. Erwin Panofsky, on the esthetics of film, holds that it is predominantly a visual medium. Where does that leave Shakespeare, the animator of language *par excellence?* What more need for flights of imagery, conventions of local color, narratives of offstage action, when everything can be photographed and projected? If the cameraman can simply pan to the bank whereon the wild thyme grows, Oberon can be spared the trouble of describing it. If a picture can convey the idea, the words are redundant. They must be severely cut in any case; yet the director, especially if his background is the stage, fears to pare away too many recognizable lines; and the result is likely to be an uneasy compromise, such as Laurence Olivier's *Hamlet.* The Russian director Grigori Kozintsev, at a farther remove from Shakespeare's diction, reconceived the play more successfully in pictorial and cinematic vistas. Olivier eclipsed his other films in *Henry V,* where he departs from theatrical confines—as licensed by the Chorus—and seeks an epic range. But this *Henry V* comes nearer to Eisenstein than to Shakespeare—notably to *Alexander Nevsky.*

I have mentioned that my first induction to Shakespeare at grade school was a blurring experience. High school brought a happier situation; an enthusiastic teacher, who had graduated from Wellesley College, doubled as dramatic coach; and during our junior year she set us mainly to reading scenes aloud, confining her interventions to explanations of words and necessary help with the pronunciation and rhythm. Then, when I came to Harvard, I had the privilege of enrolling under the most famous American teacher of Shakespeare, George Lyman Kittredge. This was one of my deepest disappointments.

Kitty, as we called him behind his back, was unquestionably a man of outstanding presence. But presence depends on the others who are also present, and Kitty's attitude toward them—toward us—was absolute in its despotism. He must have been just past seventy, in full vigor, and nearing an involuntary retirement which was to dismantle what Irving Babbitt termed "the Philological Syndicate." His Olympian features were dignified by a noble white beard and a high bald dome. Uniformly he wore a whitish salt-and-pepper suit, which emphasized the uniqueness of the role he acted.

He had come back to teach English at Harvard after having taught Latin for several years at Phillips Exeter Academy, and the old-fashioned style he had perfected was that of the classroom martinet. His class was limited to 150, the number of students that could be seated at the long initial-carved desks in the middle-sized lecture room on the second floor of Harvard Hall. He would enter at the last moment, and would conclude his remarks while walking down the aisle, escaping through the doorway as the bell tolled. None of us would have dared to ask him a question. Occasionally he went through the motions of asking someone to recite—some unlucky undergraduate who would rise only to be put down. (He was said to be particularly gruff with Radcliffe students, at a time when their classes were held separately from ours.) If anybody coughed, the interruption was protracted by a much reiterated diatribe against coughing. In fairness it should be added that, with his graduate seminars, he was more relaxed and comparatively benign. Afterward, when I was working on Ben Jonson, I found him helpfully interested—as did his doctoral candidates almost invariably.

The two-semester course was based upon six typical plays, taking up a different six in alternate years. These he explicated line by line, with frequent digressions, beginning wherever he had broken off at the previous session, and seldom completing the sixth play by the end of the second semester. The texts we brought to class had been badly edited, ineptly glossed, and inexcusably bowdlerized by the Cambridge (Massachusetts) schoolmaster, W. J. Rolfe, not long after the Civil War. Kittredge, whose assignments kept them belatedly in print, was well aware of their inadequacies and exploited them as a pedagogical device: Rolfe, as it were, played the Fool to Kittredge's Lear. We were advised to interleave our copies for the purposes of taking notes. It is boggling to think of the hundreds of derivative courses in Shakespeare, given over and over in schools and colleges all across the land, on the basis of those interleavings. Kittredge's own editions, both the one comprehensive volume and the selected individual plays, which were finally published during his retirement, were of as high a quality as any single editor could at that stage have achieved.

His pedagogy lent itself to editorial preparation. He had approached the task before Greg, McKerrow, and his own former pupil Fredson Bowers had made a demi-science out of it; but his eclectic readings were consistently sensible and knowledgeable, even though his textual apparatus remained minimal. He was a great glossarist; his forte was the capacity, not unlike Dr. Johnson's, to paraphrase a difficult passage aptly, precisely, and lucidly; one must be eternally grateful to him for a fluent acquaintance with Elizabethan English. He had little interest in the theater, or in those accumulating studies which consider Shakespeare through its perspective. Though he was eager to pursue any antiquarian or folk-loristic allusion, he paid scant attention to the history of ideas. He had been preceded in all of his interests, both in teaching and research, by the pioneering Francis James Child. A thoroughly erudite—if not an original—scholar, Kittredge had comprehensively scanned the available criticism and reached a kind of interpretative consensus. Yet the Romantic critics had been so preponderant that we heard this shrewd Yankee from Cape Cod echoing Maurice Morgann and insisting, with habitual dogmatism, on the misconstrued bravery of Falstaff.

Otherwise common sense—so proverbially rare, and therefore so peculiarly welcome within the Shakespearean sphere—did as well as it could in utter default of imagination. The mechanics of the course were indeed mechanical. The examination consisted of numerous short quotations to be identified and explained, plus no essay questions but a number of memorized passages to be written out. Memorization is a habit which, to my sincere regret, we seem to be losing. When I started to teach, I too required a certain amount of it, inviting the student to make his own selections and listening to him recite them. But that exercise, designed to justify his choice and to illustrate the oral character of blank verse, showed up such disparities between rote and any feeling for poetry that I abandoned it as a problem which should have been tackled at an earlier level. I did keep the pattern of six plays, filling in more briefly on a dozen others, but proceeding by explication from scene to scene if not from line to line. This procedure enabled me to walk through each play, commenting on whatever seemed to come next, and not excluding a concern for the stage, the verse, and the intellectual background.

Kittredge had the local ascendancy and a strong influence over the field at large. Indeed I seldom enter a classroom today without feeling the cold breath of his ghost, stalking like the elder Hamlet just behind my shoulder. On the other hand I cannot say that, except for the all-important matter of language, I learned much else from him which helped me to understand Shakespeare. The scholar from whom I learned most, Elmer Edgar Stoll, I was to encounter personally through a happy accident. By then I had read his *Shakespeare Studies: Historical and Comparative in Method*, which demonstrated not only that Shakespeare belonged on the stage (for a student of Kittredge's this was by no means self-evident), but that he was best understood in the tradition of its prototypes, modes, and conventions, and that he belonged to a world which included Greek drama, Commedia dell' Arte, Molière, Racine, Goethe, Ibsen, and Shaw. Stoll's articles and monographs, converging with the work of Levin Schücking in Germany, and a little later on with the emergence of Granville-Barker as critic, brought about a breakthrough in that romanticized character-study which had reached its limits with A. C. Bradley.

In view of the fact that Stoll spent his teaching career at the University of Minnesota, which was located in my native city, our occasion for meeting was somewhat round-about. Upon revisiting my family, I was given a letter of introduction to him from Fernand Baldensperger—who, after retiring from the Sorbonne, had assumed the chair of Comparative Literature at Harvard. It is not without significance that the link was established through a visiting European *savant*, and not through Kittredge. Once I took my courage in both hands and asked the latter what he thought of Stoll. "The trouble with him," said Kitty, "is that he thinks he's superior to Shakespeare." It was a revealing diagnosis for the doctor as well as the patient. Stoll had been audacious enough to resist the tug of Shakespearolatry and the Arnoldian evasion of the critic's task in this crucial case. He had demanded that Shakespeare, along with others, abide our question. And it was by placing Shakespeare in context, by studying the evolution of genres to the point where he could elaborate upon them, by comparing him with his contemporaries and with playwrights from other cultures, that we could better appreciate his superiority.

Stoll had attended Harvard College, but had proceeded—following a precedent set by earlier American scholars—to obtain his doctorate at the University of Munich, with a dissertation on John Webster. Although a middlewesterner, he was culturally oriented toward Great Britain and the Continent, and seemed to look upon the middle west as a place of Gothic banishment. Accordingly, he lived in a weathered and rambling gingerbread house near the east bank of the Mississippi River, close to the university and far from the rest of the town. There he would receive me for tea on my visits home, a tall, thin, bookish, austerely courteous figure. He never seemed to be on very friendly terms with his colleagues, though he reciprocated the special devotion of certain advanced students. Most of his spare time must have been passed in reading foreign periodicals and writing letters to remote correspondents. We corresponded with some regularity, and I have a thick file of the articles he continued to write and send long after he retired. But he had increasing difficulty in getting his books published. When he died in 1959 at the age of eighty-five, his complaint about being forgotten had become almost justified.

He had kindly offered to nominate me as his successor at Minnesota, but in the very same letter he advised me to stay in the east if I could, and even hinted that his nomination might prove a kiss of death. He expressed displeasure at what he considered a serious defection, when I strayed from the Elizabethans to bring out a small book on Joyce. Though his tastes were cosmopolitan, they did not include most of the moderns, and his crotchety conservatism—in a progressive state—made politics a theme to be avoided. At an early stage he had undertaken fresh and intellectually challenging positions on an over-written subject all too commonly sentimentalized or rationalized. The ensuing controversies had left him lonely and bristling. He had trenchantly undermined the pseudo-problems of Shakespearean criticism—Falstaff's courage, Hamlet's hesitation, Iago's motivelessness—with polemical pungency and far-ranging documentation, and with gusto that had not been lessened by a distance from his frame of reference, the stage. More broadly and rather frequently, he returned to the dynamic relations between literature and life. Drama kept him well aware that art requires artifice and that the representation of reality is an artful illusion.

I realize how fortunate I was in knowing Kittredge, in taking some of his courses, and in never quite having to study under his direct supervision; for his chilling distrust of all interpretation, save what he chose to echo from his forerunners, frightened most of his graduate students into becoming editors, collectors, compilers, and writers of notes and queries. Not that I would disparage such useful roles. But, as a pontiff of the establishment, he might have taken more responsibility for the central business of reconsidering our greatest author. As it often happens in such situations, the initiative was taken by a man who stood nearer the margin. Granted that the academy is bound to be academic, some of its most striking contributions are made by its loneliest dissenters: Thorstein Veblen, Charles Sanders Peirce, V. L. Parrington, E. E. Stoll. Shakespeare, as a stock item in the curriculum, could have been just too easy, too respectable, too platitudinous. Stoll, although he wrote with wit and learning, had to insist, to resist, to fight his way toward reinterpretation. We should remember that the university and the theater were far apart when he began to write, and that he did as much as anyone to bring those two worlds together.

Kittredge had taken over English 2 from Child and taught it some forty years. When he retired, he was generally conceded to be irreplaceable, for better or for worse. Shakespeare was taught afterward in other ways at Harvard by a succession of lecturers, most notably for a brief term by Granville-Barker, who was then formulating his *Preface* to *Othello* and whose lectures were rich in recollections of famous performances. Theodore Spencer's memorable readings and critical insights were cut short by his untimely death. In 1950 I was asked to teach the undergraduate course and, on a biennial basis, I have done so ever since (alternating with Alfred Harbage through much of that period). My principal assignment for the previous years, my first decade of teaching, had been a course in English drama from its ritual origins to the closing of the theaters in 1642. Its incitement was not merely to trace the train of cultural development, to watch how conditions and accretions had led from the starkest rites to the most elaborate forms of dramatic art, but to note as closely as possible what Shakespeare owed to that organic process and what in turn he had contributed to it.

To concentrate wholly on Shakespeare, and mainly on six of his plays, called for some change of focus, particularly in dealing with a larger group of students, most of whom were not concentrating in literature. We were addressing, as my teaching assistants used to say, an Elizabethan audience, a gallimaufry or mingle-mangle of interests and backgrounds. There was no question about the attractiveness of the subject-matter or the motivation of those who chose to pursue it. What we had to work hardest for with them, at the introductory stages, was a certain amount of style-consciousness. No one had any trouble in following plots or in recognizing the *dramatis personae*. It is easy enough to empathize with a series of case-histories about passion, power, or frolic. What we tried to inculcate was an awareness of why those characters spoke as they did, the cadences and shadings of the language in verse and prose, the extent and precision of that enormous and subtle vocabulary, the relation of words to images and of images to ideas. This, of course, was intrinsically related to a sense of the theatrical medium. We likewise tried to account, wherever we could, for the ongoing dimension of history.

We likewise had to face the Shakespearean problem of shuttling from the Blackfriars to the Globe Playhouse. Not limited to 150 seats in Harvard Hall, as were Kittredge's classes, mine expanded to more than 500 at the Lowell Lecture Hall. I regarded that expansion with mixed feelings, and feel relieved that it has since diminished by about half, though I shall never be altogether happy in an electronic classroom. For a few breathless years, in any case, Shakespeare preempted the largest optional course in the college. President Pusey once commented upon that circumstance. As a classicist by training, he believed in curricular "greats," and he suggested that—what with the erosion of Greek and Latin—Shakespeare was supplying a modern corpus. I would like to agree with his comment, and I think it was true at the moment. Yet, judging from my subsequent experience, I must report that Shakespeare's position has been eroded too. Interest in his work continues to be substantial, but not quite as central as it has been. He stands farther from the core of the curriculum, if indeed it still has one, and by implication farther from the center of our culture, wherever that may be.

At all events, the pedagogical situation has changed. As a matter of principle, I have always avoided talking down to students; I would rather lose a dozen mediocre ones, who might find the lecture above their heads, than the more occasional brilliant one, who would properly look down at any condescension on my part. Though I differed from Kittredge on most points, I also asked my pupils to bring their books to class (often his editions), and moved through the texts by explication. This is a method which makes considerable use of cross-reference. It presupposes that one's listeners' minds are stored with a fairly wide range of cultural data, such as names from the Bible or classical myth. If these go unrecognized, the explicator cannot make his connections; each allusion must either be spelled out or lost; and critical commentary is reduced to footnoting or paraphrase. Background of this sort can no longer be taken for granted, any more than I can now assign the serried reading-lists of thirty-five years ago. Students may not be less bright, but they require more demonstration and simplification, more synthesis and spoon-feeding. I have had reluctantly to hedge my explications.

If there has been some retreat, there has been some compensation in more active interplay between education and drama. Our studies led toward performance from time to time, such as a series of scenes from *Coriolanus* on the steps of Widener Library. During most of the period I am remembering, Harvard was notorious for providing no official acting space, having lost the playwriting workshop of George Pierce Baker to Yale, which was willing to build him a playhouse. But there was never any lack of dramatic activities, carried on in courtyards and dining-halls or wherever two boards could conjoin with a passion. Eliot House, for its first twenty years, cultivated an Elizabethan tradition of Christmas comedy. Roger Merriman, our stalwart master, acted Mistress Quickly in a farthingale like a circus-tent, appealing to the transvestite humors of the occasion with the line that he had never been called a woman in his own house before. In a later year, on the verge of retirement, he enacted the King in the Second Part of *Henry IV;* and, though I had sharply cut the farewell speech, he kept recalling more and more lines, as he had memorized them in college under "Stubby" Child. It was a Frazerian ceremonial.

My production of Jonson's *Volpone* was honored by being mentioned in the monumental edition of Herford and Simpson. Being rather shy, I enjoyed directing more than acting, though I took bit-parts now and then. Direction is—or should be—a mode of teaching, and involves the same preliminaries in the way of interpreting the text. It has been a particular satisfaction to follow the many talents that have emerged through our undergraduate rehearsals. The group to which I served as adviser just after the War had split off from the Harvard Dramatic Club; slightly more experienced and vastly more ambitious, they called themselves the Veterans' Theatre Workshop; and after graduation they acquired the small Brattle Theater, where for five years they gave Cambridge a splendid repertory, replete with Shakespeare and Shaw. A number of them have since pursued active careers in the professional theater. With William Devlin as guest star, they managed to produce an impressive *King Lear* on a minuscule stage—a practical refutation of those who deem it unplayable. They scored a reverberating success in persuading Paul Robeson to enact *Othello* with them, at a point when he had been discouraged from attempting the part in New York.

What is known as Sanders Theatre at Harvard is actually a convocation hall, a Victorian version of the Sheldonian Theatre at Oxford, a shabby old auditorium designed for oratory primarily and for music secondarily. Yet such a locale, with its amphitheatrical seating and its lack of a proscenium, is not at all unsuitable to the mode of staging used in Shakespeare's day—or among imaginative practitioners today. Professor Baker seems to have staged productions there in a more or less Elizabethan manner, as we tried to do when *Henry V* was directed by Douglas Seale for the Cambridge Drama Festival. I recall from long ago the appearance of Ben Greet and his company on that stage, where the cutting of *Hamlet* was simplified by using the bad First Quarto—and, more memorably, the visit of the Piccolo Teatro from Milan, with their pyrotechnical presentation of Goldoni's *Arlecchino servitore di due padroni*. In the central pit, with its seats removed, a later generation of undergraduates put Greet and his fellow actors to retrospective shame with a four-hour uncut version of *Hamlet,* very ably directed by Stephen Aaron, now a director and teacher at the Juilliard Institute.

Once I took Lincoln Kirstein to see *Richard II,* when it was performed at Sanders by our Workshop group, under the direction of Albert Marre with Jerome Kilty in the title role. My guest responded, with characteristic sensitivity, by remarking that these youthful students seemed to know what it felt like to be warring peers of a medieval realm. This, he said, was the kind of imagination that his collaborator, George Balanchine, sought to evoke in their pupils at the New York School of American Ballet. That remark, for me, threw light on the value of student dramatics, and of Shakespearean study as well. Perhaps the most important lesson we learn, if we can, is what it feels like to be someone else. Self is too much with us, particularly when young. We mature, we rise to the possibilities of life, by entering into the existence of others. We become educated by learning how they met the circumstances of other cultures and periods than our own. If the human consciousness can be expanded, it is not by drugs or mystical incantations but by such exercises in empathy. And it may well be Shakespeare who offers us our best program for such psychological enlargement.

To return to local matters and complete my anecdotal ramblings: after long years of concerted pleading for the support of the administration and the generosity of alumni, Harvard was enabled to erect a fine playhouse, which opened in 1960 with *Troilus and Cressida*. The Loeb Drama Center is truly so up-to-date, so ingeniously planned, and so efficiently managed that sometimes the perfection of the machinery shows up the all-too-human imperfections of those who man it from play to play. There are some older Cambridge playgoers who believe, nostalgically, that we had more passion when we had only two boards, so to speak—that, in Arnold Toynbee's terms, the challenge of a poorer physical situation elicited a livelier response. But, though the zest for improvisation has a basic importance in drama, so has the great, good, glamorous place; mobility is kept alive by interacting with stability. The stage door of the Center (which we cannot designate as a theater because that designation would affront its proper Brattle Street neighbors) opens—by an interesting irony—just across the street from the house where Professor Kittredge lived, now the residence of the gifted composer, Leon Kirchner.

Apprenticeship—we like to think, as we bungle along, in getting up our subject or keeping up with it—is a precondition which leads toward mastery. It should not be less so when that subject is the literary journeyman who achieved the ultimate in mastering his craft. Shakespeare was a professional to his fingertips, and he frequently invites us to look at life *sub specie theatri,* as Bergson would put it. He was rather a generalist than a specialist, though the very richness of his conversance with so many areas of knowledge (for example, the law) has prompted many specialists to claim him as one of their own. One of the ironies is that some of us now endeavor to specialize in Shakespeare. Such professionalism can be justified principally by what it does for the amateur; and I use the word to signify, in the positive and literal sense, not a novice but a devotee. The indulgent comment of Theseus, on the bad acting of Bottom and his fellows, should be a source of encouragement to the rest of us: "The best in this kind are but shadows; and the worst are no worse, if imagination amend them" (*Midsummer Night's Dream,* V.i.211-2). It is no mere metaphor in Shakespeare when shadow turns into actor, dream into drama, and world into stage.

I

PERSPECTIVES

Shakespeare and
"The Revolution of the Times"

It is Henry IV, in his insomniac monologue on the burdens of the kingship ("Uneasy lies the head that wears a crown"), who longs to "read the book of fate" and thereby to learn how "the revolution of the times" works out its endless round of permutation, erosion, and leveling (2 *Henry IV*, III.i.31, 45–6). Henry IV is not our favorite among Shakespeare's kings. We may well prefer his son; and, significantly, most of us prefer the latter in his role as Prince Hal, before he parted from Falstaff to become King Henry V, Shakespeare's nationalist hero whom some of the critics have regarded as a prig and a jingo. All those sovereigns fascinated Shakespeare even as they continue to fascinate us—not least the very worst of them, Richard III, whose dramatized rule was notably less responsible or legitimate than that of Henry IV. We

----

First delivered at Southern Illinois University on an occasion celebrating the publication of *The London Stage* by the university press (October 12, 1971); published in *TriQuarterly*, 23/24 (Fall, 1972)—an issue republished as *Literature in Revolution*, ed. G. A. White and Charles Newman (New York: Holt, Rinehart and Winston, 1972).

should also note in passing that it is still another usurper, Claudius, King of Denmark, who voices so ardent a fervor for the divine right of kings: "There's such divinity doth hedge a king . . ." (*Hamlet*, IV.v.124). Rulers at best are ambivalent figures to Shakespeare, as they are to themselves in their moments of soliloquy. We sympathize with Henry IV so long as he is the injured Bolingbroke, but our sympathies shift to Richard II when Henry ascends the throne and turns into a cold-blooded politician, while Richard becomes a victim in his turn.

Henry's desire to read the book of fate is characteristic of this ambivalence, for he concludes his speculation by predicting that any reader so privileged "would shut the book, and sit him down and die" (2 *Henry IV*, III.i.56). Well, either we are made of sterner stuff, or we have been hardened through recent years by watching the revolution of the times every evening in our living rooms. From where we sit, there is even a kind of romantic escape in the glimpse of a defunct heroism that we get from contemplating conflicts which are settled by alarums and excursions rather than by mass bombing or international hijacking. Truly, we have witnessed more than our share, as Macbeth did, of "Bloody instructions, which, being taught, return / To plague th'inventor" (I.vii.9). Yet, stripped of their knightly armor, their heraldic trappings, and their patriotic rhetoric, Shakespeare's monarchs act out a sorry record of turbulence and treachery, of arrogant wrongs and smoldering revenges all too often fated to reach their grim *dénouement* at the Tower of London. It is rather cold comfort for us to be noting the precedents they set. But, since the spacious mirror he sets before us has already reflected so many topical problems of the eventful interval between his time and ours, we should not be surprised to see it now flashing back images which are more recognizable than reassuring.

"The times are wild," we hear at the outset of the Second Part of *Henry IV* (I.i.9). The somber king will prophesy "rotten times," though the ebullient Pistol will herald the "golden times" promised by the enthronement of Henry V (IV.iv.60; V.iii.96). The new regime will usher in a triumphant interlude, from a nationalistic point of view; but that triumph will be brief; and Shakespeare sustains it only by cutting off the play at Henry's betrothal, just two years before his premature death. The melancholy trilogy that covers his son's reign does indeed treat of "heavy times." "O bloody times!" the King himself cries out, when on the battlefield he encounters a son who has slain his father. Then, in a parallel casualty of war, a father who has slain his son appears, exclaiming: "O pity, God, this miserable age!" (*3 Henry VI*, II.v.63, 73, 88). When the royal uncle, Humphrey, Duke of Gloucester, warns the King, "Ah, gracious lord, these days are dangerous," Humphrey is already doomed to death; but so, before too long, is Henry VI (*2 Henry VI*, III.i.142). The backdrop for the major sequence of Shakespeare's dramatic histories is civil war at home—the Wars of the Roses between the houses of York and Lancaster—and imperial war abroad—the Hundred Years' War between England and France. The Yorkist tyrant that emerged from the struggle, Richard III, selfishly thinks of the age as his "golden time," but publicly professes it "this troublous time"; and it was, of course, a reign of terror (*3 Henry VI*, III.ii.127; II.i.159).

Golden ages are by definition either Edens or Utopias, taking place either long ago or not yet. During the stormy moment we tend to look backward or forward toward some vista of tranquility. As the Archbishop of York complains, in the Second Part of Henry IV, "Past and to come seems best; things present worst" (I.iii.108). Shakespeare's extended historical pageant, with all its assassinations and executions, has recently been summed up by Jan Kott as a "succession of kings climbing and pushing one another off the grand staircase of history." These plays are described as representing a "naked struggle for power," in which the only values involved are "hate, lust, and violence." Mr. Kott, a Polish dramatic critic who has lately been promulgating his interpretations in this country, seems to have derived his inspiration not so much from a knowledge of Elizabethan drama as from the so-called Poor Theater of Jerzy Grotowski, Antonin Artaud's Theater of Cruelty, and the Theater of Beckett, Ionesco, and the Absurd. Mr. Kott has been writing in justified revulsion from a political situation which he has seen doubly overridden by the Nazis and the Soviets. Consequently, he discerns no meaning whatsoever in history. Like some of the most disaffected among us, he can descry no alternative to violence in life, and he attempts to draw Shakespeare into his anarchistic camp. But, if I were permitted the Shakespearean license of a pun, I would add that "camp" is the *mot juste*.

Thus, a few years ago, the Royal Shakespeare Company revived *Titus Andronicus*—that early experiment which most of us are content to regard as a gory reduction to melodramatic absurdity, so crude that some devoted critics have sought to exonerate Shakespeare from its authorship. When this grotesque revival came to play in Poland, Mr. Kott hailed it as a naturalistic slice of life, telling things precisely the way they were. Not long thereafter, the British director Peter Brook returned the compliment with a production of *King Lear,* stressing its similarity—which no one before Mr. Kott had ever thought of—to Samuel Beckett's *Endgame*. Now, updating Shakespeare has been a continual and an inevitable process in the living theater. Jonathan Miller has directed a London production of *The Tempest* in which both Caliban and Ariel were exploited Africans and Prospero was a colonial despot. Given the widespread assumption that the successful director is a man who can compose the wildest variations on the themes with which Shakespeare provides him, there would seem to be no limits to the display of such ingenuity. We might well expect an up-to-date version of *The Taming of the Shrew* to be restaged as a parable of Women's Liberation. Yet after nearly four centuries of garbling, piracy, adaptation, emendation, and bowdlerization, readers of today have closer access to Shakespeare's text than perhaps they have ever had.

Naturally, they are bound to read it in the variable context of their lives—our lives. Mr. Kott introduces his book by declaring:

> Shakespeare is like the world or life itself. Every historical period finds in him what it is looking for and what it wants to see. A reader or spectator in the mid-twentieth century interprets Richard III through his own experience. He cannot do otherwise. And that is why he is not terrified—or rather, not amazed—at Shakespeare's cruelty. He views the struggle for power and mutual slaughter of the characters far more calmly than did many generations of spectators and critics in the nineteenth century. More calmly, or, at any rate, more rationally.

One might conceivably question those last two adverbs. Calmness and rationality are not among the attributes of Mr. Kott's approach. But it is their conspicuous absence that has keyed his voice to the irrational frenzies of our epoch. The appealing title of his provocative study is *Shakespeare Our Contemporary*. The endeavor of scholars

33

and commentators or of teachers and students, moving in the opposite direction, is to make ourselves contemporaries of Shakespeare. Ben Jonson, who first put a classical stamp upon his immediate contemporary through a much quoted eulogy, declared that Shakespeare "was not of an age, but for all time." All time, however, comprises a succession of different ages, and we count a dozen generations from Shakespeare's to our own, each of which has had its own modes of apprehending him. To be contemporary, after all, simply means being temporary together. Some of our younger contemporaries may not remember that the passing instant has always been *now* until it has passed. On the other hand, nowness—like newness—is subject to wear and tear and change and decay. The rock-and-roll production of *Twelfth Night* that played off Broadway only yesterday will some day seem as dated as Dryden's and Purcell's operatic improvements on *The Tempest* during the Restoration. Mr. Kott and Mr. Brook—like ourselves—will pass along in the procession, and Shakespeare will remain to be reinterpreted by future generations.

And yet "there is a history in all men's lives," as the Earl of Warwick tells the moribund Henry IV (III.i.80). Jonson also hailed Shakespeare as the "Soul of the Age." Timely as well as timeless, he was not without his own consciousness of the ever-changing *Zeitgeist*. He even anticipated that German term which modern historians use, when the Bastard speaks in *King John* of "the spirit of the time" (IV.ii.176). To be sure, the pedants have accused him of anachronisms, such as citing Aristotle in the midst of the Trojan War. But though he may not have distinguished very clearly between Achaean and Alexandrian Greeks, contrary to what some critics would maintain, he recognized the distance and the difference between the

Romans and the Elizabethans. The single authentic sketch that we possess of his drama in Elizabethan production depicts the cast of *Titus Andronicus* in something like Roman dress. What is more to the point, his ancients and moderns differ sharply in their ethical outlook. The pagan suicides of Brutus and Cleopatra, judged by the Stoic creed, are noble ends; whereas Hamlet is precluded from, and Ophelia is attainted by, such a death, because of the Christian canon against self-slaughter. Shakespeare, then, was working between two temporal dimensions: the legendary and the contemporaneous, the old unhappy far-off times about which he wrote and the epoch during which he wrote—a time-conscious epoch, highly conscious of the portentous transition it was making from the Elizabethan to the Jacobean era, through the *fin du siècle* of the sixteenth into the dawn of the seventeenth century.

This diachronic attitude toward history, the sense of a vital interrelationship between past and present, comes out most expressly in the mature historical plays. For example, the choric allusion to the troops of the Earl of Essex returning from Ireland in *Henry V* carries an almost journalistic vibration of topicality. When the Lord Chief Justice alludes to "th' unquiet time" in the Second Part of *Henry IV*, Shakespeare is actually quoting a chapter-heading from one of his sources, the chronicle of Edward Hall (I.ii.150). As a propagandist for the house of Tudor, Hall's grand design had been to trace its claims and fortunes from the dynasty of Lancaster, which he presented in a eulogistic light. Does it follow that Shakespeare was a sycophant of the Tudors? He was presumably a loyal and discreet Englishman at a time when the monarchy was popular, and his plays are not without their flattering salutes to royalty. Yet he indirectly got into serious trouble when his company revived *Richard II* at the height of the Essex Conspiracy. The Earl, whom he had gone out of his way to salute through the Chorus of *Henry V,* was the hope of many to supplant the aging Queen. To reenact the spectacle of Richard stepping down from his throne and giving up his crown, it was felt, would fan the flames of revolt. The Deposition Scene could not be printed in the earlier quartos of the play.

This revival was linked with an all-too-timely book, focusing upon the dethronement of Richard and suggestively dedicated to Essex by its seditious author, John Hayward. When the Star Chamber censured Shakespeare's actors, Queen Elizabeth is reported to have angrily asked: "Know ye not that I am Richard?" At the present distance, it is hard to detect much resemblance between the two rulers or their respective situations and political styles. Later poets would hark back wistfully toward what Tennyson designated "the spacious times of Queen Elizabeth"; and it is true that the Elizabethans enshrined their Virgin Queen in all the aura of courtly compliment; yet her greatest literary glorifier, Spenser, even while addressing her directly, expressly states that hers is not a golden but a stony age. His poetic monument to her, *The Faerie Queene,* was left hardly more than half-finished; the Seventh Book, with which it tapers off, was to have celebrated the virtue of constancy; it is significant that the surviving two cantos are wholly preoccupied with the antithetical characteristic, namely mutability. Here we are not very far from the fragmented vision of Donne's *Anniversaries.* A strong authoritarian emphasis upon stability, as we gather from those who talk so loudly about law and order today, can indeed express deep basic emotions of anxiety and insecurity.

Twentieth-century scholars who have reconstructed a picture of the Elizabethan world view, such as Hardin

Craig, Theodore Spencer, and E. M. W. Tillyard, emphasize its elements of tradition, hierarchy, and fixity. But here their Elizabethan witnesses may have been protesting overmuch out of a distrust of innovation, alienation, and disruption. *Terra firma* had its abysses for them, as it would have for Pascal, as it has for us. Hence, like Hamlet in Queen Gertrude's closet, they display two contrasting pictures of the human condition. Naturally the new subjects of Elizabeth had their trepidations when they beheld a young girl crowned as a ruler, after a period of dynastic and religious turmoil when Protestants and Catholics had successively been burned at the stake and royal claimants beheaded in the Tower. Fortunately, she proved to be both long-lived and strong-willed. She presided over England for forty-five crucial years—years which saw its emergence from the status of an island off the coast of Europe to a world power, having wrested the hegemony of the seas from Spain. This was predestined to be accompanied by magnificent fanfares in literature and the arts. But it also caused accelerating tensions, particularly in her later years, when the question of a successor was so much in the air. Then the succession itself, which brought in the Stuarts, and with them a mounting series of economic and social crises, scarcely succeeded in staving off by much more than a generation the formidable revolution ahead.

Meanwhile, at the turn of the century, while Shakespeare was transposing his interests from history and comedy to tragedy, there seems to have been a more general crisis of belief. Scientific skepticism had something to do with this creative unrest at the intellectual level—that New Philosophy which, as Donne served notice, was calling all in doubt. So Shakespeare, in the little metaphysical poem addressed by Hamlet to Ophelia, could echo the

37

heretical observations of his exact contemporary, Galileo, with a single monosyllabic line: "Doubt that the sun doth move" (II.ii.117). So Yeats's anguished cry for lost authority, "the center cannot hold," has its prophetic counterpart in Donne's lament for "all coherence gone." That could not be the prevalent mood for long, yet the undertone was heard and voiced by more serious spirits. Behind the gorgeous pageantry and the official mythology looms an apparition of chaos. The image of man in his ideal dignity is loftily sketched by Hamlet, even while he is denouncing man's bestial corruptibility: "How like an angel in apprehension; how like a god!" (II.ii.306-7). Perfection of brain and body is attuned to the commonweal, the body politic; nature is in harmony with the supernatural, which is providential and benign. (I am following Shakespeare by indulging in musical metaphors.) The universe is designed to revolve so harmoniously that its reverberations constitute the music of the spheres, and man is so much at the center of things that his acts have planetary significance—or, conversely, astrological determination.

A deviance from these ideals is the basis of tragedy. The future Richard III foresees his villainous destiny in his own deformity; his twisted body is "like to a chaos" (*3 Henry VI,* III.ii.161). An old conception shared by Shakespeare held that the artist was a demiurge, a second creator after God, who by his artistic creation imposed cosmic form upon chaotic matter. Romeo's first inkling of tragic disillusionment evokes the exclamation: "Misshapen chaos of well-seeming forms" (I.i.179). Similarly but much more explicitly, Othello's protestation makes it clear that everything is staked on his relation with Desdemona (III.iii.90-2):

> Perdition catch my soul
> But I do love thee! and when I love thee not,
> Chaos is come again.

The Moorish hero in the service of Venice has just brought about, as the Herald announced, "the mere perdition"—the total loss, and here the usage is literal—"of the Turkish fleet" (II.ii.3). Othello soon will be warning Desdemona that the loss of his talismanic handkerchief would entail terrible consequences (III.iv.67-8):

> To lose't or give't away were such perdition
> As nothing else could match.

It would prefigure nothing less than the lost world of their love, and so it turns out. Victimized by Iago's plot, he victimizes her and finds himself facing the ultimate perdition, loss of soul. Seldom can a word that would be forbidden by the Victorians have been bandied so roundly back and forth across the stage. "Damn'd Iago" is "a damned slave," a "damned villain" who has told "an odious damned lie" (V.i.62; ii.243, 316, 180). But it is Othello who damns himself "beneath all depth in hell" (V.ii.137). He has sworn a premonitory oath in the tense scene where Iago opens up the abyss: "Death and damnation, O!" (III.iii.396). Chaos, in fulfillment, has come again.

It is easy to understand why a rage for order seizes upon Shakespeare's characters when they are confronted by menacing circumstances.

> All form is formless, order orderless,
> Save what is opposite to England's love,

says the papal legate Pandulph in *King John* (III.i.253-4). Since he is plotting with the King of France against England, his argument must be taken with some degree of ironic reservation. More regularly, it is England's well-being which is threatened by decomposition. When the Earl of Northumberland receives the bad news about the death of his son Hotspur, he calls for universal dissolution. "Let order die!" he exclaims (2 *Henry IV*, I.i.154-6),

> And let this world no longer be a stage
> To feed contention in a ling'ring act.

Pursuing a familiar train of Shakespearean imagery, he envisions the whole of life as a drama which now has come to its dark and murderous catastrophe. The routing of the Lancastrians by the Yorkists in the Second Part of *Henry VI* prompts the loyal young Clifford to voice the same sort of reaction. "Shame and confusion!" he cries (V.ii.31-3),

> all is on the rout.
> Fear frames disorder, and disorder wounds
> Where it should guard.

Then, when he discovers the body of his father slain in battle, he utters his apocalyptic apostrophe (40-2):

> O, let the vile world end,
> And the premised flames of the last day
> Knit earth and heaven together!

The atmosphere in tragedy is normally heavy with doom, but in Shakespeare the very language reechoes that word. An individual doom signifies a judgment, such as a sentence of death or exile, often arbitrarily handed down, as in the case of *King Lear*. But inevitably the individual tends to associate his personal fate with the last judgment of mankind. Condemned to die on All Souls' Day in *Richard III*, the Duke of Buckingham responds: "Why, then All-Souls' day is my body's doomsday" (V.i.12). Romeo enlarges the malediction, seeing his banishment from the presence of Juliet as—worse than death—a *dies irae*. "What less than dooms-day is the Prince's doom?" (III.iii.9). After the parley before the Battle of Shrewsbury, in which he will be killed, Hotspur closes upon a gallant note of foreboding: "Doomsday is near, die all, die merrily" (*1 Henry IV*, IV.i.134).

Hamlet is likewise ready to recognize the imminence of the world's end; but for him the recognition comes as part of a sardonic interchange, when Rosencrantz tells him the news "that the world's grown honest," and he rejoins: "Then is doomsday near" (II.ii.237-8). A graver portent of impending fatality is Horatio's introductory description of the omens that preceded the death of Julius Caesar, when the moon was "sick almost to doomsday with eclipse" (I.i.120). Dreams, ghosts, and other portents admonish the tragic protagonist that he is standing at the verge of a cataclysm. When Macduff proclaims the murder of Duncan, he exhorts the sleepers in Glamis Castle to rise up as from their graves (*Macbeth*, II.iii.77-8):

> Up, up, and see
> The great doom's image!

In much the same emblematic vein, when the blinded Gloucester is reunited with Lear, he hails the mad old man as a prefiguration of the final disaster (IV.vi.134-5):

> O ruin'd piece of nature! This great world
> Shall so wear out to nought.

Just as Shakespearean tragedy may be said to reenact the Fall of Man, so it may be said to anticipate the Day of Judgment. Thence its unremitting quest for justice—not legal justice, which is constantly being challenged, nor poetic justice, which too neatly balances sufferings with re-

41

wards and villainies with punishments, but the problematic sanction of a higher morality, a tragic ethos, an insight into the *rerum natura*. Where Shakespeare's histories deal with "time misord'red" (2 *Henry IV*, IV.ii.33) largely upon the plane of politics, his tragedies and comedies have their divergent ways of dealing with disorder. Gloucester may have been right in his superstitious warning: "Machinations, hollowness, treachery, and all ruinous disorders follow us disquietly to our graves" (*King Lear*, I.ii.112-4).

Moralizing over the fall of Richard II, his gardener puns and attributes it to his "disordered spring" (III.iv.48). Richard, in his last soliloquy, uses a phrase which curiously rhymes, when he compares his kingly negligence to the "disordered string" of an instrument (V.v.46). The word *disorder* does not seem to have been used by Shakespeare for disease, although the latter figuratively comes to stand for the former, as students of his imagery have shown. In comedy, disorder is misrule in the sense of prankishness, confusion, or revelry, as with those disorders of Sir Toby Belch which Malvolio vainly seeks to curb in *Twelfth Night* (II.iii.88ff.). Ultimately these must be set straight. Bachelors must get married; deceivers must be exposed; and poor old Falstaff, who by his own confession lives "out of all order," must be dropped by his erstwhile companion now destined to rule (*1 Henry IV*, III.iii.19-20). Approaching our terminology from the more positive side, we observe that the word *order* is employed more frequently in *Measure for Measure* than in any other Shakespearean play—and rather more equivocally, as is hinted by the self-balancing title. The drastic measures of the law-and-order governor, Angelo, against those citizens who live out of all order, elicit countermeasures which prove him to be a hypocrite and a reprobate. Municipal corruption is weighed against civic reform, permissiveness against repressiveness.

All drama oscillates between order and disorder, as the defeated French do at Agincourt, the Constable of France embracing the cause of disorder, the Duke of Bourbon cursing: "The devil take order now!" (*Henry V*, IV.v.17, 22). Shakespeare's ideas of *order* can be glossed as a command at the very simplest (to give or take orders), then as a compact like the "threefold order ta'en" by the enemies of Henry IV (Part One, III.i.70), still again as a protocol like Lady Macbeth's "Stand not upon the order of your going" (III.iv.118), and not least as a vocation (taking orders, holy or chivalric). More broadly, actions may be scaled to a moral order, incidents be framed within a world-order. Every drama must terminate, in effect, with the kind of resolution that Augustus Caesar formulates in the tag-line of *Antony and Cleopatra* (V.ii.365-6):

> Come, Dolabella, see
> High order in this great solemnity.

Furthermore, Shakespeare not infrequently moralizes the scene with a set speech or homily or *exemplum,* placed in the mouth of an elderly character such as the gardener in *Richard II.* His instructions to his assistant constitute a little allegory and act out, as in a morality play, the deathbed forebodings of John of Gaunt—his fears for "this blessed plot, this earth, this realm, this England" (II.i.50). In each case, the ideal of commonweal is held up as a model in order to stress its current violation. The King's garden,—and gardens were a most congenial analogy for the man from Stratford—"the whole land" was "full of weeds" (III.iv.43-4). Why, then, "should we . . ./ Keep law and form and due proportion?" (40-1). Under

43

a more fortunate dispensation, when Henry V would be attaining "the world's best garden," France, the Archbishop of Canterbury spells out a sociological lesson with a fable of the honeybees (I.ii.188-9),

> Creatures that by a rule in nature teach
> The act of order to a peopled kingdom.

The passage that is invariably cited, when Shakespeare's conceptions of order are discussed, consists of some sixty lines from the longer speech delivered by Ulysses to the Greek council of war in *Troilus and Cressida:* "The specialty of rule hath been neglected" (I.ii.78). Now this is neither an everlasting gospel nor an eternal verity; nor does the speaker represent Shakespeare himself, any more than do his other personages. This is a diagnosis, which leads to a strategy. Ulysses is not really a *raisonneur* like those neutral moralists of Molière: he is the wily strategist of the Greeks; and they, we should recall, were much less sympathetic to Western Europe than were the Trojans from whom it claimed descent. Against the contextual background, the eloquence dwindles into semiscandalous questions of personality, notoriously the unheroic mockeries of Achilles, before it is interrupted by the challenging mission of Aeneas. The other purple passage of Ulysses, the argument with which he works on the vanity of Achilles, whom Shakespeare presents as an effeminate brute, is devoted to the topic of opportunity and the spirit of opportunism, "emulation" or competitiveness. The line of thought that is amplified and illustrated by Ulysses' oratorical exposition had been propounded by Sir Thomas Elyot, the authoritarian apologist for the ruling house, in his book of *The Governor.* "Take away order from all things, what should then remain?" Elyot rhetorically inquires, and his answer to his inquiry begins: "Certes nothing finally, except some men would imagine eftsoons chaos. . . ."

Ulysses takes a more affirmative tone when he appeals to the heavens, and instances the well-regulated movement of the sun and the planets around the earth according to the old Ptolemaic astronomy—which, a generation before Shakespeare's birth, had been all but discredited by the more open and less anthropocentric system of Copernicus. For the Trojan War, as for the Middle Ages, it could still exemplify a pattern of office and custom, hierarchies and priorities, functioning together "in all line of order" (88). This is what the more orthodox commentators have stressed. But we have already noted that Hamlet, as a man of the Renaissance, registered some doubt about the traditional worldview; and the central part of Ulysses' picture dwells upon its negative aspect, not the ideal but the *status quo*. It is a harrowing evocation of plagues and portents and the ensuing disintegration of nature when the cosmic machinery grinds to a halt. "O, when degree is shak'd, / Which is the ladder of all high designs," the sequel is earth-shaking (101-2). Thereupon institutions fall apart and anarchy prevails. And it is here that Shakespeare takes up Elyot's point (109-11):

> Take but degree away, untune that string,
> And hark what discord follows. Each thing meets
> In mere oppugnancy.

Notice that, as the usual Shakespearean harmonics give way to cacophony, the discordant images are orchestrated to a strained and crackling diction. If there were no bounds, if everything were utterly unbounded (111-13),

> The bounded waters
> Should lift their bosoms higher than the shores,
> And make a sop of all this solid globe.

This solid globe! One cannot imagine Shakespeare writing that line without hinting at some cross-reference from the world to the stage in his habitual fashion, and from the Trojan War to that artistic microcosm known as the Globe Playhouse. The climax of the conjuration is a view of life conceived as a lawless struggle for naked power, *homo homini lupus,* and emblematized by the figure of a son who strikes his father dead. Shakespeare had displayed an early tableau of parricide in the Third Part of *Henry VI,* and would go on to dramatize its motivation in depth with *King Lear. Troilus and Cressida* has been unfavorably compared with Chaucer's *Troilus and Criseyde,* possibly because Chaucer sympathized more with the lovers. Though their love perforce is bittersweet, he brought out much of its sweetness, whereas Shakespeare gave equal stress to the war, and thereby clouded the drama with bitterness. Everyone is exacerbated in the mutual suspicion of the disunited allies and the protracted stalemate of the two superpowers. The attitude that finds its scurrilous vent in the cynical curses of Thersites makes the play as powerful a disavowal of war as the *agitprop* of Bertolt Brecht.

Another famous attempt to reaffirm the conservative norms of society is the fable of the belly and the members, as told by Menenius Agrippa in *Coriolanus.* Here again the story had been previously recounted by the archconservative Elyot; but, though Menenius goes even farther in his patrician bias than Ulysses, Shakespeare utilizes dialogue rather than monologue and allows the heckling plebs to lodge a strong counterargument. Under any thoughtful scrutiny, the identification of the Senate with the stomach is as questionable in logic as it is in physiology. The quick-witted First Citizen, whom Menenius does not altogether refute by branding as "the great toe of this assembly," has a case to make for the leg, the arm, the head, the heart, the eye—in short, for the other social estates (I.i.155). If the Citizens are incited by the demagoguery of the Tribunes, they have a genuine grievance in the "dearth" (67). Probably their protests reflect a concern for the famines and riots that had broken out in the Midlands shortly before Shakespeare wrote his play. The antidemocratic tirades of Coriolanus himself have made him the most controversial among Shakespeare's heroes. The ideological conflict between him and the populace becomes so strongly polarized that, on various occasions, it has inflamed its audiences. As a student in Paris during the nineteen-thirties, I myself witnessed a performance at the Comédie Française which prompted rioting and contributed to a general strike and the fall of a government.

One of the reasons why Shakespeare turned from the English histories to his Roman tragedies, I suspect, was that the setting of a model republic in the distant past accorded him freer scope for dramatizing politics than did the thornier issues he encountered closer to home. There, too, he could shift his focus from kingship to citizenship. He could balance, as he does in *Julius Caesar,* democracy against dictatorship, the rabble-rousing Mark Antony against the liberal Brutus. The latter, brought reluctantly to engage in an act of violence, brings down upon his head and that of Rome the retributive forces of counterviolence. In his troubled hesitation he likens his mind to a country undergoing a revolt (II.i.67-9):

> the state of a man,
> Like to a little kingdom, suffers then
> The nature of an insurrection.

The term *revolution,* for Shakespeare, retained its mechanical connotation and its medieval application, the cycle of Fortune's wheel. *Revolt* was the catchword; and Shakespearean dramaturgy abounds in what King Lear terms "images of revolt," some of which I have been trying to relate and elucidate (II.iv.90). If it celebrates rebellious barons on the battlefield, it can also envisage disgruntled mobs fighting in the streets. Because of such an episode, which may have been written by Shakespeare himself, the collaborative play of *Sir Thomas More* was banned (albeit the hero is shown rebuking the unruly populace). Nonetheless Shakespeare's treatment of Jack Cade's rebellion forms a seriocomic underplot to the Second Part of *Henry VI,* and the author virtually appends his signature when he shows the rebel run to earth in a Kentish garden rather than a London street. Even on Prospero's enchanted island, the threat of revolution is raised by Caliban and the two drunken clowns.

Nor should we forget, amid the many counterclaims to our attention in *Hamlet,* that climactic scene where the mob breaks into the palace, revolting against the regime of Claudius. Something is rotten, we know; the state is disjoint and out of frame; the time is out of joint, and Hamlet has been born to set it right, to set his father's house in order. Can he be considered to have fulfilled that resolve? In seeking to redress the regicide, he has embarked upon a course of incident and accident which results in his death and seven more deaths, and which leaves the state of Denmark under the rule of its hereditary enemy. Tragedy always culminates when the survivor takes over with an appeal for the restoration of order—or, at least, for the reestablishment of continuity. Inevitably, its final couplets try to modulate its funeral eulogies with brave words about carrying on and with whatever silver linings can be dimly discerned among the still lowering clouds. All this can place the tragic events in perspective, but it cannot palliate them for us, insofar as we have truly felt them. I see very little point in pretending, through some Hegelian exercise in cosmic optimism, that tragedy is other than pessimistic. Scotland has been turned into a chaos by Macbeth. Deliberately he curses: ". . . let the frame of things disjoint" (III.ii.16). When Macduff reenters with his severed head and announces that "the time is free" (V.ix.21), we rejoice with Malcolm and the rest. But the line of future kings that stretches out is not to end so happily with the Stuarts as Shakespeare implies. History can outdo even tragedy in its reversals.

Tragedy does not pretend to encompass the totality of experience, in any case, and Shakespeare had an especially poignant feeling for its intermixtures with comedy, not to mention his feelings for the happier spheres of the purely comic or the lyrically romantic. The ills that flesh is heir to—he knew well—have their compensations, and he might have ruefully smiled at this sentence from a recent editorial commentary in *The New York Times:* "It is a Shakespearean irony that new prospects for peace exist precisely because all industrial societies, Communist and capitalist, are in the process of tearing themselves apart." Shakespeare's name is justly invoked in that immediate and momentous connection, since he had so comprehensive an overview, so keen a sense of the long run. Life itself was so much larger than people, he realized, that their best intentions were more likely than not to go astray. He was also fully aware that destruction was the underlying precondition of renewal, and that any person who understood this had found his identity even while losing it, had earned—like Enobarbus—"a place i' th' story" (*Antony and Cleopatra*, III.xiii.46). Heretofore most Americans have had no difficulty in dwelling, with Wil-

49

liam Dean Howells, upon the smiling aspects of life. Shakespeare becomes increasingly meaningful as, at his profoundest, he habituates us to learning the worst; as he initiates us into the mystery of evil, the *mysterium iniquitatis;* as he offers us, through the tragic catharsis, a retrospect of life and a foretaste of death; as he heartens us, by our momentary survival, to take an ethical stance against overwhelming odds.

Shakespeare's Nomenclature

When Juliet asks, "What's in a name?," she assumes that the question is rhetorical. Her implicit answer, if it were voiced, would be "Little or nothing." But her concrete example is ambiguous (II.ii.43-4):

> That which we call a rose
> By any other name would smell as sweet.

It may be a case in point that the sweetest of all names, for Romeo up to a few moments before, has been Rosaline. Now he is quite willing to forget it in favor of the sweeter Juliet. Shakespeare had made earlier amends for this neglect when he gave the name of Rosaline to the sprightly heroine of *Love's Labor's Lost;* and, in the slightly modified form of Rosalind, he glorified it with the irresistible heroine of *As You Like It.* Even she, however, has her detractors. "I do not like her name," says the melancholy Jaques (III.ii.265-7). To which the lover Orlando

---

Delivered at the University of Denver, May 25, 1963; published in *Essays on Shakespeare,* ed. G. W. Chapman (Princeton: Princeton University Press, 1965).

wryly retorts, "There was no thought of pleasing you when she was christen'd." Names, then, are matters of personal taste to which reactions can vary. Romeo sounds propitious to Juliet's nurse because it alliterates with rosemary—rosemary for remembrance, if not for Rosaline— even though it is also the dog's letter, a snarling omen, *rrr!* To Mercutio the lovelorn Romeo seems as lank as a herring without its roe; what is left of him can be no more than a lover's sigh: *-meo, -meo,* O me! (That wordplay, such as it is, would have been spoiled if Shakespeare had not Italianized the Latin ending of the original Romeus in Arthur Brooke's poem, through which he had acquainted himself with the tale.) To "be some other name" is to be a stranger. So, in *King John,* the newly knighted Bastard resolves to snub his former cronies (I.i.186):

> And if his name be George, I'll call him Peter.

Would Romeo retain his dear perfection without his existing name, as Juliet affirms? "I doubt it," Wilson Knight has succinctly commented. "Try Iachimo." Professor Knight's suggestion is worth the experiment:

> O Iachimo, Iachimo! wherefore art thou Iachimo?

We need not presume that there is something innate in certain vocables which makes the villain of *Cymbeline* a fitting companion for Iago; but Romeo has a sound, for Professor Knight, which is simultaneously Roman, romantic, and suggestive of roaming. Within a few moments Juliet comes to adore the repetition of the name, and within a day Romeo comes to believe that it can have a murderous impact. Yet the really dangerous appellation, after all, is not his forename but his surname. "What's Montague?" (II.ii.40). One of the noblest families in Verona, to its members and to some of their fellow citizens. To others, especially to the Capulets, it is a rallying cry for tribal antagonisms. Shakespeare balances the rival claims with symmetry and objectivity by making them metrically equivalent: *Montague/Capulet, Romeo Montague/Juliet Capulet,* double dactyls. Similarly, he plays no favorites as between the two complaisant school friends of Hamlet. Each has his interchangeable amphimacer (II.ii.33-4).

> Thanks, Rosencrantz and gentle Guildenstern,

says the King, to which the Queen adds:

> Thanks, Guildenstern and gentle Rosencrantz.

Juliet—on that night in the orchard, at any rate, before the lovers are overtaken by the swift fatalities they have challenged—is a nominalist. That is to say, she believes in the immediacy of experience and the uniqueness of individuals rather than in classes, categories, or generalizations.

So is Falstaff: he is the very nominalist of nominalists when he reduces honor to a word, and that word to a breath of air. Since that word is a fighting word for Hotspur, it is a transcendent reality by which men live and die. Insofar as words can be realities, Juliet was wrong; there can be all too much in a name, as she will find out all too soon. Good name means considerably more than an illusory image to Cassio, to Desdemona, and finally to Othello; it is a jewel of the soul, the loss of which spells tragedy. What becomes there involved is social repute, not simple denomination. Yet how much of the atmosphere in Shakespeare's plays is already conveyed to us when we scan his *dramatis personae!* True, he is not so erudite a philologist as many of his commentators. John Ruskin, who had more Greek, paused in the midst of his unfinished treatise on political economy, *Munera Pulveris,* to hold an etymological inquest over Ophelia and other Greek-rooted names. Thereupon Matthew Arnold took exception to Ruskin's digression for its "note of provinciality," its lack of moderation and proportion. It is not clear at this distance, a century afterward, just who was being provincial. Ruskin felt that he had made a discovery, to which he kept returning in side remarks, but Arnold's counterthrust was sharp enough to deter him from the special investigation he promised.

Arnold, surprisingly for a major English critic, has no light to shed upon Shakespeare, and not much sweetness. Others abode Arnold's question; Shakespeare, in Arnold's obscurantist phrase, overtopped knowledge; and their conjunction leaves us where the Romantics stood, gazing in uncritical awe at the inscrutable handiwork of a natural genius. During the last hundred years we have been learning to examine Shakespeare more and more closely. On the whole he has withstood that scrutiny, and rewarded it with a renewed awareness of his insight and technique. Today we think of him as a highly conscious artist. Being only human and writing for set occasions, he had his lapses and he made his compromises; but he nods far less frequently than his critics, whose principal activity has been to catch one another napping; and we are likely to understand him better if we assume that he knew what he was doing every minute, even at the risk of an occasional exercise in overingenuity on our part. Professor Knight may be considering too curiously when he suggests that Alonso connotes aloneness, or that the Prince of Aragon is designated *ex officio* as arrogant, or that the pirates Menas and Menecrates are threatening figures because they have minatory names. But his intensive kind of curiosity has done much to underline the patterns and highlight the details of Shakespeare's artistry, and we should feel indebted to him for reviving Juliet's question in his volume of essays, *The Sovereign Flame.*

It should have been a secure assumption that names, like most of the other components in language and life, meant a great deal to Shakespeare. Yet criticism was set back by Arnold's caveat. Except for one or two German dissertations, which are hardly more than annotated listings, plus a few articles on specific lines of derivation, the field of Shakespearean nomenclature is wide open, and constitutes an inviting pasture to browse in. Meanwhile there has been wider realization that the naming of characters is a serious—albeit subordinate—feature of literary art, and that it is susceptible to analysis by linguistic science—more specifically, by that branch of it which bears the name of onomatology, and which, if it does not intimidate us, can illuminate our concern. Nothing is ever completely random in the artistic process. Providence, as Ruskin put it, is tempered by "cunning purpose." Much may be unconscious, to be sure; and some of it, being inherent in the material, may not express the artist himself. But, to state it categorically, the *persona* begins with the name; it is as much part of character as the mask—which is what the Latin word meant—in ancient drama; and when it is not handed down from a myth or some other source, it may be taken as the expression of a writer's own intention. Hence a realistic novelist, like Flaubert, would take the same sort of care with names that he did with dress or milieu. They had to be real names, characteristic only in that they sounded right for the people who bore them.

At the other and older extreme, which goes back at least as far as to Homer, we have the name that stands by itself as a characterization. Though we have no vernacular phrase for this device of language, such as the German *sprechende Namen,* "speaking names," a technical term has been coined, so that we may talk of charactonyms. Such are the abstract labels of the moralities, which Shakespeare was not above recalling, like the Vice Iniquity and Lady Vanity. Such usages were reinforced by the Puritan habit of deriving Christian names from moral qualities. Temperance, sneers Antonio in *The Tempest,* "Temperance was a delicate wench" (II.i.44). It takes a Bunyan to confer flesh and blood upon a Mr. Greatheart or a Mr. Badman, but the "Mr." always helps to humanize the situation. In the long comic tradition where the charactonym flourished, it gradually evolved from the sphere of morals to that of manners, and by way of Ben Jonson to the Restoration and eighteenth century. Knights are in particular evidence here, since they have the privilege of sporting double-barreled names: Sir Politick Wouldbe, Sir Fopling Flutter, Sir Benjamin Backbite. But the ladies hold their own: Lady Sneerwell, Lady Wishfort (in words of one syllable, "Wish for't"). And Mrs Malaprop's name, so neatly adapted from *mal à propos,* is no less inspired than her classic abuse of the King's English.

The resourceful namer tends to use metonymy rather than personification: in other words, to single out the vivid attribute rather than to fall back on the pallid abstraction. Thus Tom Jones's tutor is named Thwackum, since he so roundly exerts his tutorial prerogative. Tom's own name embodies straightforward typicality, as deliberately contrasted with Sir Charles Grandison, where the pretentious note is sounded by the first syllable of the surname. With the increase of realism and the decline of allegory, there is a tendency to leave the meaning somewhat latent, so that it seems to be rather a marginal comment than a heraldic flourish. Heathcliff, for instance, has the air of a perfectly plausible cognomen; yet what more compelling designation could we hit upon for the forces unleashed in *Wuthering Heights?* The author of *Vanity Fair*, not surprisingly in view of his title, hints at the personalities of his puppets: Becky Sharp, Lord Steyne (stain). He even indulges in a caricaturist's dalliance with such eighteenth-century appellatives as Bareacres, for a penniless lord, and Yellowplush, for a strutting lackey. Yet Thackeray held, among his many reservations on Dickens, that "Micawber appears to me an exaggeration of a man, as his name is of a name."

Now many of Dickens' names are self-characterizing: Pecksniff, Veneering, Bounderby. We could not, by any stretch of the nomenclatorial license, call Scrooge Cheeryble or the Cheeryble brothers the Scrooges. Others, like Micawber itself or Pickwick, are merely odd; yet they serve, in spite of Thackeray's cavil, to bring out individual eccentricities; and some of those inventions have become eponyms, in the sense that the name has become a by-word for a peculiar pattern of behavior. Commonly we speak of persons or actions as Pickwickian or Micawberish. Shakespeare made such a joke over Benedick in *Much Ado about Nothing* that this recalcitrant bachelor, normalized into Benedict, ended by becoming the eponymous patron of all married men. Comparably, Romeo became the generic lover, Shylock the extortionist, Falstaff the roisterer, Puck the jokester, and so on. Dickens borrowed his Pickwick from a sign on a passing vehicle; other names he jotted down from placards and tombstones, keeping those lists which have been reprinted in Forster's biography. Henry James moreover worked with lists culled from his daily reading of the London *Times*, seeking in them—as in everything else—a certain style, an Anglo-American tone; but there are some occasions on which he was more explicit, as with Mr. Newman on the one hand or Prince Amerigo on the other. Yet James grew impatient with the otherwise sober Trollope over such "fantastic names" as that of the philoprogenitive parson, Mr. Quiverful.

The perfect name could be defined as combining a literal authenticity with a symbolic purport. However, the gamut ranges widely between those extremes, and Shakespeare ranges up and down the gamut. Certainly he inherited as much as he invented, and here the interest lies in his handling of the conventional associations. Melville employed the scriptural names well sanctioned by Yankee custom—Ishmael, Ahab—to convey the effect of prefiguration, the feeling that all this has happened before and will inevitably happen again. Joyce, by christening his spokesman Stephen Dedalus, provided him with both a patron saint and a classical prototype. So the virgin goddess Diana, whose cult is celebrated in *Pericles,* has an Elizabethan godchild in the maiden whose maidenhood was so precariously preserved, Diana (Capilet!) of *All's Well That Ends Well;* and the Roman Portia—Cato's daughter, Brutus' wife in *Julius Caesar*—has a civic-minded namesake in *The Merchant of Venice,* whom Ruskin, with the casket scenes in mind, would connect with "portion." Later characterizations, in like fashion, have been prefigured by Shakespeare's. Hamlet's jester Yorick is the legendary ancestor of Parson Yorick in *Tristram Shandy,* while in turn Trollope's Mr. Slope will claim descent from Sterne's Dr. Slop. "Of Yorick," remarks Professor Knight, "all I can say is that it fits." That impression of fitness, which begs the question somewhat, is a testimonial to Shakespeare's aptness for making names fit, for using them as keys to memorable characters.

They must be chosen out of the available vocabulary in order to be fitted into the dramatic context. Yet, since form follows function here as elsewhere, perhaps I should discuss some of their uses before discussing some of Shakespeare's choices. It should almost go without saying that his word-conscious world is a name-conscious world, where conflict is fought out by name-calling and status is conferred by name-dropping. In that respect, its logical culmination is the account of Princess Elizabeth's baptism at the end of *Henry VIII*. This name-consciousness manifests itself in the usual habits of paronomasia. To judge from Falstaff's recollection, John of Gaunt has been destined to go through life hearing puns on his name; and he himself, by punning on his deathbed, invites the sarcasm of Richard II (II.i.84):

> Can sick men play so nicely with their names?

In *The Merry Wives of Windsor* the camouflaged Master Ford appropriately masks himself as Master Brook; and Falstaff, whose immersion in a ford will be a further chance to quibble, responds to a draught of sack from his visitor: "Such Brooks are welcome to me, that o'erflows such liquor" (II.ii.150-1). Inasmuch as punning is a triumph of sheer material circumstance over the reason, it may be a grim reduction to existential absurdity, as in the Second Part of *Henry VI* where York pronounces (I.i.124):

> For Suffolk's duke, may he be suffocate.

The prophecy that the Duke of Suffolk will meet his death by water turns out to be an equivocation on the forename of his assassin, Walter Whitmore. The foreordained malefactor in *Richard III,* whose name starts with a G, turns out to be not George, Duke of Clarence, but Richard, Duke of Gloucester. Oracles, like charades, take delight in such unexpected confrontations and unlikely materializations.

Satire, when it presents real characters and events, usually changes their names in the interests of discretion. When Hamlet presents a dramatization of his father's murder, he calls the victim Gonzago and implies that any resemblance to actual persons, living or dead, is purely coincidental. In comedy, which thrives upon confusions, to mistake a person is to get his name wrong. The pairs of identical twins in *The Comedy of Errors* could not be confounded for very long, if there were not two Dromios and two Antipholuses. But mistaken identity can be tragic as well as comic. There is no grimmer scene in *Julius Caesar* than the one in which a certain Cinna—an innocent man, in fact a poet—is confused with Cinna the conspirator and found guilty by nominal association. "I am Cinna the poet," he plaintively cries, but it makes no difference to the angry plebeians. "Tear him for his bad verses," then they shout, and hustle him away to his death (III.iii.29-30). What's in a name indeed! It can operate as a disguise, when a character is engaged in eluding identification, such as Cesario, Bellario, or Sebastian. It can thereby show a sense of decorum, as with Florizel, the flowery prince of *The Winter's Tale,* who is addressed as Doricles in the pastoral episodes. Again it can show a sense of humor, as with Feste, the festive clown of *Twelfth Night,* whose mock-priest is addressed as Sir Topas, presumably after the mock-knight of Chaucer.

When Celia flees to the forest in *As You Like It,* she announces that her *nom de guerre* will be

Something that hath a reference to my state (I.iii.127).

Accordingly she becomes Aliena, the alien one, the fair stranger. Rosalind, her fellow traveller, still rather girlish though disguised as a boy, is accordingly known as Ganymede after Jupiter's epicene favorite. In *Cymbeline,* when Imogen is forced to disguise herself, she emerges as the semi-allegorical Fidele. "Thy name well fits thy faith," she is told, "thy faith thy name" (IV.ii.381). The moral posture can be pushed too far, as everything is in *Titus Andronicus,* where Tamora and her two sons introduce themselves to the demented Titus as Revenge and Rape and Murder respectively *in propria persona,* a troop of pale shades from the older moralities. Of much greater significance is the agnomen, the honorific name of Caius Martius, who is hailed as Coriolanus by virtue of his bravery at Corioles; for it is at Corioles that, with a hollow reverberation, Coriolanus is fated to die. Through the other two Roman plays we watch the private name of Caesar becoming a synonym for emperor, and the root for *kaiser* or *tsar*. It is more than a verbal transference when a country is personified by its monarch, when Cleopatra herself is saluted as Egypt. Whereas to speak of the Dane is to underscore one of the innumerable questions raised by *Hamlet:* who is the Dane? is it the King or the Prince or the Ghost?

Worldly preferment is often signalized, in Shakespearean parlance, by "addition," as when the hierarchic ascent of Macbeth is heralded by the tantalizing salute of the Witches: Thane of Glamis, Thane of Cawdor, King of Scotland. In the course of that ascent Macbeth itself becomes "a hotter name/ Than any is in hell" (V.vii.6-7). The transitoriness of such ambitions comes out strongly

in the First Part of *Henry VI* with the prolonged and son-
orous inquiry (IV.vii.60-71):

> But where's the great Alcides of the field,
> Valiant Lord Talbot, Earl of Shrewsbury,
> Created, for his rare success in arms
> Great Earl of Washford, Waterford, and Valence,
> Lord Talbot of Goodrig and Urchinfield,
> Lord Strange of Blackmere, Lord Verdun of Alton,
> Lord Cromwell of Wingfield, Lord Furnival of Sheffield,
> The thrice-victorious Lord of Falconbridge,
> Knight of the noble Order of Saint George,
> Worthy Saint Michael, and the Golden Fleece,
> Great Marshal to Henry the Sixt
> Of all his wars within the realm of France?

Where indeed? where is he now? *ubi est?* Joan of Arc—or
Joan la Pucelle, as Shakespeare styles her, with innuendos
on Pucelle or virgin—levels the feudal hierarchies with
her vulgar retort (72-6):

> Here's a silly stately style indeed!
> The Turk, that two and fifty kingdoms hath,
> Writes not so tedious a style as this.
> Him that thou magnifi'st with all these titles
> Stinking and fly-blown lies here at our feet.

Falstaff is well nigh out-Falstaffed in Joan's reduction of
honor to a breath. The magniloquence of the Turk, the
exotic coloring of the Levant, the distant place-names of
Asia and Africa had contributed to the geographic impetus of Marlowe's tragedies. Shakespeare could ridicule
those effects in the fustian of Ancient Pistol: "Have we
not Hiren here?" (*2 Henry IV,* II.iv.175) He could likewise cultivate them at need, as in *Antony and Cleopatra*
when the potentates of the East are mustered out in full
panoply (III.vi.69-76):

> Bocchus, the King of Libya; Archelaus
> Of Cappadocia; Philadelphos, King

> Of Paphlagonia; the Thracian king, Adallas;
> King Manchus of Arabia; King of Pont;
> Herod of Jewry, Mithridates, King
> Of Comagena; Polemon and Amyntas,
> The Kings of Mede and Lycaonia,
> With a more larger list of sceptres.

Roll-calls and casualty lists, like the catalogues of epic, set the scene and dramatize the issues, whether in Mediterranean antiquity or in the British past.

> I had an Edward, till a Richard kill'd him;
> I had a Henry, till a Richard kill'd him:
> Thou hadst an Edward, till a Richard kill'd him;
> Thou hadst a Richard, till a Richard kill'd him,

laments the dowager Queen Margaret to the dowager Queen Elizabeth in *Richard III;* and the litany, with its familiar and repeated names, suggests that—though dynasties pass—there will always be an England (IV.iv.40-3). The implication becomes an affirmation, suggesting as it does firm dynastic stability, when the new King Henry reassures his brothers (2 *Henry IV,* V.ii.47-9):

> This is the English, not the Turkish court;
> Not Amurath an Amurath succeeds,
> But Harry Harry.

There the shift from Islamic to Christian names brings matters home directly to Shakespeare's audience, as he so frequently liked to do.

Whether he drew upon foreign or domestic history, history converging on mythology or legend at all events, he had to play the game with traditional counters. Tragedy, to a larger degree, and comedy, almost wholly, offered him the freedom to characterize and to coin. We turn, then, from the functional aspect of names to the problem of selection, a terrain no less broad and vague than Shakespeare's European geography, with its Bohemian seacoast and Danish cliffs. Its general flavor is more or less Italianate, as the Elizabethans conceived of Italy, glamorous and sinister by turns. Verona furnishes the setting for both a comedy and a tragedy. Its prince is Escalus, which is a Latinized variant of the ruling family's name, della Scala. Its two gentlemen are Valentine, whose connotations are those of the perennially faithful lover, and Proteus, who is assuredly protean in the moods and changes of his heart. Neither sounds especially Veronese—any more than that model of Old French courtliness, Sir Eglamour. Some of Shakespeare's Italian names are the standard ones accorded to minor parts in grand opera (Claudio for the juvenile lead in both *Much Ado about Nothing* and *Measure for Measure*). Others have undeniably English overtones. Mercutio is nothing if not mercurial; and Romeo's confidant, Benvolio, is his tried and true well-wisher. The antithesis of the latter is Malvolio, an envious detractor with a jaundiced outlook, nominally resembling Malevole, the satiric revenger in Marston's *Malcontent*.

The riddle of Maria's forged love letter—M.O.A.I.— seems to be based upon certain key letters in Malvolio's name. It also comes alphabetically close to the names of the two heroines in *Twelfth Night:* if you play anagrams, add one letter to Viola, scramble, and you get Olivia; add two more letters, allow one substitution, and you get Malvolio. Sir Toby Belch, the apostle of cakes and ale, whose name is too often interpreted as a stage direction, and Sir Andrew Aguecheek, the knight of the quaking countenance,—not to mention the vicar of *As You Like It,* Sir Oliver Martext—take their stand in the staunch old English humorous tradition. Ben Jonson strengthened that tradition decisively when he Anglicized *Every Man in His Humour,* shifting the locale from Florence to London and renaming his Italian characters. Shakespeare juxtaposes the two backgrounds in *The Taming of the Shrew*, where Christopher (or Christophero) Sly, the tinker of the Induction, is more in his element with Marian Hacket, the fat alewife of Wincot, than in watching the play-within-the-play. This performance is all the more theatrical because it is supposed to occur in Padua, yet Petruchio's servants seem to be Sly's compatriots: Curtis and Ralph and Sugarsop and the rest. One of them, Grumio, seems to be an Anglo-Italian groom.

The comic servant in *The Merchant of Venice*, too, has an Italian name with an English undertone. Launcelot is a romantic improvement on its naive predecessor, Launce in *The Two Gentlemen of Verona*. Gobbo might be Venetian; but it also approximates "gobble," along with Shylock's epithet for his servingman, "a huge feeder" (II.v.46). Shakespeare found an Old Testament name for Tubal, the Venetian Jew, as well as for Aaron, the Moor of *Titus Andronicus*. As for Shylock, he has been traced to Shalach, one of the minor progeny of Shem. The Hebrew meaning, cormorant, is apt if obscure; but Shakespeare makes the sound convey a meaning of its own, compounded of sharpness and harshness, so that the name evokes the character by a kind of psychological onomatopoeia. Shakespeare smattered a number of languages, quoted Latin freely, and knew French well enough to perpetrate some outrageous *double-entendres*. Jack Cade can ribaldly allude to Monsieur Basimecu, Pistol blasphemously take in vain the name of Signor Dew, and Princess Katherine be shocked by mistaking "foot" and "gown" for *foutre* and *con*. The cast of *All's Well That Ends Well* includes the clown Lavache—cow being a contemptuous metaphor—and the boastful man of words, Parolles (*paroles*). The former refers to a papist as Poysam (*poisson*) and to a puritan as Charbon (*chair bonne*). Among the aristocratic French names in *Love's Labor's Lost,* Moth (pronounced "mote") would pass for an Anglicization of La Motte, while likening its bearer, the diminutive page, to both a delicate insect and a particle of dust. The constable, Goodman Dull, needs no translation.

The Forest of Arden, where *As You Like It* takes place, is evidently the border region between Belgium and France, the Ardennes; but at the same time it takes us back to the heart of England, Shakespeare's Warwickshire; for Arden was his mother's family name. The denizens of this forest are bucolic shepherds: Corin, Silvius, Phoebe. The hero and his brother are named after two of Charlemagne's doughtiest paladins: an Orlando (*gallice* Roland) for an Oliver. The eccentric Jaques, invoked monosyllabically, echoes a somewhat malodorous pun vented by Sir John Harington in his notorious pamphlet on the introduction of the water-closet, *The Metamorphosis of Ajax,* where the mythic allusion plays on the word for privy, a jakes. There may be a fainter echo in the Ajax of *Troilus and Cressida.* Hence drama involves catharsis in its most literal sense, when Jaques proposes to administer an ethical purge (II.vii.58-61):

> Give me leave
> To speak my mind, and I will through and through
> Cleanse the foul body of th'infected world,
> If they will patiently receive my medicine.

If names can localize and lend concreteness, they can equally well etherealize, as they do by abetting the fantasy of *A Midsummer Night's Dream.* There the principal characters are Greek; the presiding couple are mythological figures, Theseus and Hippolyta. The fairy pair, Titania and Oberon, may well be uneasy in their mixed marriage; for one of them was an Ovidian enchantress, the other an elf-king of medieval romance (Alberich). Their factotum, Puck or Robin Goodfellow, could scarcely be more English; nor could the names of their more exquisite followers, Mustardseed, Peaseblossom, Cobweb, and Moth. Even less probable is the relationship that precipitates Nick Bottom, the Weaver, into the arms of the Fairy Queen. His name, with its standing invitation to punsters, actually denotes a tool of his trade, a weaver's skein. The other rude mechanicals—Peter Quince, Francis Flute, Tom Snout, Robin Starveling, and Snug the Joiner—assist in the transposition from Athens to London.

If we compare *King Lear* with the old play that Shakespeare adapted, we can see that he made a fairly consistent attempt to historicize his fairy-tale subject-matter. The Celtic names of the main plot were largely given; the Anglo-Saxon names were interpolated with the underplot. The jingling juxtaposition of Edgar and Edmund emphasizes the polarity of the half-brothers. The obsequious Oswald seems to have more than an opening syllable in common with the affected Osric in *Hamlet*. The same repetition imposes a uniformity on two walking gentlemen in *The Merchant of Venice:* Salanio and Salarino; variant spellings of their names have sometimes conjured up a ghostly third, Salerio. There are only three women in *Coriolanus,* and they are further limited by sharing the same initial: Volumnia, Virgilia, and Valeria. Latin names seem to predominate over Greek even in *Timon of Athens;* yet even in the Greco-Roman sphere of *The Comedy of Errors* there is a Dr. Pinch; while the maids answer to "Maud, Bridget, Marian, Cic'ly, Gillian, Ginn" (III.i.31). The Roman Caius seems to be both a plausible alias for Kent and a suitable patronymic for the French doctor in *The Merry Wives of Windsor,* pronounced like "keys" and doubtless influenced by the Queen's physician of Cambridge fame, Dr. John Caius. National terminations are subject to change for metrical reasons: Antony, Antonio, Antonius. The Latinism Polonius reminds us of the Polish question, moot throughout *Hamlet,* where the onomastics are polyglot. If Marcellus and Claudius are Latin, Bernardo and Horatio are Italian, and Fortinbras signifies "strong arm" not in Norwegian but in French (*fort-en-bras*).

On the other hand, the son of Polonius has a Greek godfather in Laertes, the father of Odysseus. The Scandinavian names, at least the Germanic Gertrude, stand out because they are in the minority. The authentic Norse of the titular name could not have been very meaningful to Shakespeare. Yet it may be the crowning irony that Hamlet, our sobriquet for an intellectual, derives from *Amlothi,* meaning a simpleton and alluding to the feigned madness of the Prince. Shakespeare manipulates the ironies consciously with Angelo in *Measure for Measure,* who realizes that he is no angel; with Prospero in *The Tempest,* who rounds out a cycle of prosperity and adversity; and with Bianca, the courtesan in *Othello,* who casts her own reflection on the interplay between whiteness and blackness. Failure to live up to one's name results in an anticlimax which Shakespeare coarsely exploits with the clown in *Measure for Measure,* whose first name is Pompey and whose last name is Bum. Like Costard, the clown in *Love's Labor's Lost,* whose name is slang for the other end of the body, he is imperfect in the role of Pompey the Great; he is, as Costard puts it of himself, "a little o'erparted"; the part is a little too big for him (V.ii.584). On a serious level, Shakespeare sometimes found himself constrained by his *donnée,* when the roles had been too often enacted before.

Thus the air of cynical fatalism that hangs over *Troilus and Cressida* is due to the fact that the lovers and their go-between, given their names, could not behave otherwise. Since their names are proverbial, their actions are predestined; for Troilus has already become an eponym: in Rosalind's phraseology, "one of the patterns of love" (*As You Like It,* IV.i.99-100). As Pandarus puts the oath that is foresworn: "Let all constant men be Troiluses, all false women Cressids, and all brokers-between Pandars!" (III.ii.202-4). Since *Troilus and Cressida* contains a hound named Brambler, it is worthy of notice that Petruchio has a spaniel named Troilus, in contradistinction to the English names of the hunting dogs in *The Taming of the Shrew*—or, for that matter, the phantom pack of Ariel in *The Tempest*. There is one hound in both packs which answers to the name of Silver. Unquestionably Launce's Crab in *The Two Gentlemen of Verona* is the greatest scene-stealer among Shakespeare's animals. But the dogs that move us to heartbreak do not exist, except in the delirious imagination of King Lear (III.vi.62-3):

> The little dogs and all,
> Trey, Blanch, and Sweetheart, see, they bark at me.

Shakespeare seems to refer to horses generically, by their condition or breed as in Cut, Dobbin, or roan Barbary. Such accepted names as Graymalkin for cat and Paddock for toad acquire a grotesque inflection when the Witches invoke them as their familiar spirits.

Through a curiously memorable trick of pseudo-reference, seldom more than the merest passing mention, Shakespeare manages to project a vivid impression of characters who never appear on the stage: poor Robin Ostler, by the road from London to Gadshill, who died when the price of oats rose; Jane Smile, who received the bashful attentions of the youthful Touchstone; Alice Shortcake, who once borrowed a book of riddles from whom but Master Abraham Slender? All our lives are the richer for having heard about them. Mistress Quickly, who has a dubious talent for total recall, peoples the wings with such neighbors: the silk-man, Master Smooth; the butcher's wife, Goodwife Keech (keech being a lump of fat); and, less happily, the minister, Master Dumbe, and the deputy, Master Tisick (pthisic?). Sometimes a type is individualized by a courtesy title: *e.g.,* Sir Smile for a hypocrite (*The Winter's Tale*) or Sir Oracle for a pundit (*The Merchant of Venice*)—or, more exotically, Signior Smooth for a flatterer (*Pericles*). The honorific belittles the abstraction when Ulysses deprecates Achilles as Sir Valor or Antonio disposes of Gonzalo as Sir Prudence. Orlando is Signior Love to Jaques, and Jaques is Monsieur Melancholy to Orlando. Benedick's wit transforms Beatrice into Lady Disdain and Claudio into Lord Lackbeard. Falstaff is the target of many such bynames (Monsieur Remorse), and the Host in *The Merry Wives of Windsor* is an expert at devising them (Monsieur Mock-water).

Whenever the cast is prescribed by an anterior plot, it is axiomatic that invention has a freer hand with the lesser parts: Neighbor Mugs, the carrier, for instance, or the shouting tradesmen who follow Jack Cade's rebellion. Servants, wherever they are, have English names more often than not, common enough for the most part but now and then more expressive, like Grindstone and Potpan and the timorous Sampson in *Romeo and Juliet,* where the three musicians vibrate to their stringed instruments: Simon Catling, Hugh Rebeck, and James Soundpost. Rather less sympathetically, it is "Sneak's noise" which furnishes incidental music for the Second Part of *Henry*

IV (II.iv.11). In the Messina of *Much Ado about Nothing,* where the redoubtable constable and his compartner are Dogberry (the fruit of the dogwood tree) and Verges (rods of office), the stout souls of their watch are Hugh Oatcake and George—or is it Francis?—Seacoal. In the Vienna of *Measure for Measure,* the ultimate guardian of the law is the executioner Abhorson—a portmanteau name with two ill-conditioned compartments, "abhor" and "whoreson." The list of his prisoners is virtually a reckoning of their misdemeanors: Rash, Caper, Dizzy, Starve-lackey, Drop-heir, Shoe-tie, Half-can. Several of Shakespeare's Viennese are recognizable by their un-Austrian charactonyms: Froth, Elbow, Thomas Tapster. Nor should we forget Mistress Overdone, whose profession as bawd would be obvious to contemporaries from the specialized nuance of the verb "to do," and who is more elaborately characterized as Madam Mitigation.

None of Shakespeare's capitals is vaguer or more remote than Pentapolis; yet the shipwrecked Pericles is greeted there by homely fishermen, Patchbreech and Pilch (a crude coat). The names of the Morris-dancing villagers in *The Two Noble Kinsmen* ("Friz and Maudline . . . And little Luce with the white legs, and bouncing Barbary . . . And freckled Nell") are about as Athenian as those of the hempen homespuns in *A Midsummer Night's Dream* (III.v.25-7). When Coriolanus discharges his scorn upon the Roman populace, he specifies them by the commonest of denominators, the nicknames Hob and Dick. Shakespeare can be depended upon to out-English himself upon the home ground of the histories when he is dealing with the little people, like Peter Thump the apprentice, who gives his master a sound thumping in the Second Part of *Henry VI.* But English becomes fully British when Henry V is served by three captains: the Welsh Fluellen, the Irish McMorris, and the Scottish Jamy. On the eve of the Battle of Agincourt, Shakespeare envisions

A little touch of Harry in the night,

when the King fraternizes on the battlefield with three common soldiers: John Bates, Alexander Court, and Michael Williams (IV.Chorus.47). He goes incognito as "Harry Leroy," which Pistol thinks must be a Cornish name. As the language expresses an upsurging patriotism, so the names assert an underlying democracy. King Henry, when he was plain Prince Hal, had learned to drink with the good lads of Eastcheap and to "call them all by their christen names, as Tom, Dick, and Francis" (*1 Henry IV*, II.iv.8). We might have expected a Harry to be the third in that convivial trio; but Francis was the tavern boy with whom the Prince had been jesting; and Tilley's *Dictionary of Sixteenth-Century Proverbs* makes clear that "Tom, Dick, and Harry" was not yet the standard expression for indiscriminate camaraderie. Shakespeare may have helped to crystallize it with his King Harry.

The popularity of the royal nickname was confirmed by the Tudors; Henry VII and Henry VIII were linked with the most popular of the Lancaster Henries, the former Prince Hal. Whereas King Henry IV is referred to as Bolingbroke from the name of his castle, the Prince of Wales was Harry Monmouth from his birthplace in Wales, and was therewith differentiated from his heroic rival, Harry Percy, surnamed Hotspur for his splenetic valor. It is even fancied, by Henry Bolingbroke, that those two younger Harries might have been exchanged in their cradles. Ultimately they must fight it out in an alliterative duel to the death (IV.i.122-3):

Harry to Harry shall, hot horse to horse,
Meet and ne'er part till one drop down a corse.

It was predictable that the victorious Harry would wed a woman whom he could address by that most Shakespearean of feminine nicknames, Kate. She is the French Princess Katherine, of course; but Petruchio insists on making a Kate out of his Italian Katherina, "Kate of Kate-Hall," despite her emphatic objections (II.i.188). Katherine of Aragon may retain her formal dignity, though she is once apostrophized as Kate behind her back. That other Harry, Hotspur, has a wife who is rechristened Kate by Shakespeare—even though, historically speaking, Lady Percy's maiden name was Elizabeth (Mortimer). Shakespeare's heroes are fond of punning on "cates," meaning delicacies; some of them may imply a less flattering jingle on "cats," meaning prostitutes. Of such is Kate Keepdown in *Measure for Measure* or the tailors' Kate to whom the sailors preferred Moll, Meg, Marian, and Margery in the sea-chanty of *The Tempest*.

Nell is not much less basic, as applied to the Duchess Eleanor in the Second Part of *Henry VI* or—most informally—to Helen of Troy by Paris in *Troilus and Cressida*. It seems more suitable for the offstage slattern (alternatively Luce) described by the out-of-town Dromio in *The Comedy of Errors*. Yet the hostess, Mistress Quickly, who appears to be an Ursula in the Second Part of *Henry IV*, somehow becomes a Nell in *Henry V*. She has become a more respectable figure to us, as the advance of years has muffled the bawdy pun on "quick-lie." Nor, while we are citing occupational names, should we overlook her friend and *protégée*, Doll Tearsheet. Coleridge, who was constantly trying to purify Shakespeare's mind, tried to emend the metonym to Tearstreet. It is a far cry, which demonstrates Shakespeare's range, to the innocent wide-eyed girls of the later romances with their lyrical names: Marina, child of the sea, in *Pericles;* Perdita, the lost one, in *The Winter's Tale;* and the wondrous and wondering, the admiring and admirable Miranda of *The Tempest.* In contrast with their poetic remoteness, nothing could be simpler or more downright than plain Joan. When the Bastard Faulconbridge is dubbed by King John, he declares (I.i.184):

> Well, now can I make any Joan a lady.

And when Berowne confesses his love and denounces his luck, in *Love's Labor's Lost,* he repeats the antithesis (III.i.205):

> Some men must love my lady, and some Joan.

And in the refrain of the song that closes the play, as the elegant French ladies are departing, we are accorded a glimpse of that rustic creature, "greasy Joan," stirring the pot at a wintry hearth. These simplicities may have some bearing on Shakespeare's reductive attitude toward Joan of Arc, whose anti-heroic vein we have already sampled.

Nor does he hesitate to draw upon folklore, while he is exemplifying the way of a maid with a man: of Tib with Tom or of Jill with Jack. Jack appears ordinarily as a term of contempt; but for us it has the friendliest connotations; for we cannot but associate it with Jack Falstaff to his familiars, John to his brothers and sisters, and Sir John to all Europe. Here we encounter a coinage brightly minted by genius in the mold of circumstance. We are aware that Shakespeare's supreme comic figure was originally known as Sir John Oldcastle, after a historic personage, indeed an unseasonably austere Protestant leader, and that Shakespeare—apparently responding to a Puritan protest—saw fit to withdraw the allusion and to hint an apology in the epilogue to the Second Part of *Henry IV*. The substitution has no exact counterpart any-where, but it does recall Sir John Fastolfe, who is re-ported to have played the coward in the First Part of *King Henry VI*. Furthermore the metathesis, from Fastolfe to Falstaff, has an enlarging significance. A writer named Shakespeare, whose contemporaries jested about his name and whose incomparable sensitivity to words might have been intensified for that reason, must have been quite conscious of what he was doing when he renamed his fat knight Falstaff. *Shake spear . . . Fall staff . . .* A metaphorical staff is flourished and dropped at Gadshill, Eastcheap, and Shrewsbury. Just as Cleopatra mourns, "The soldier's pole is fall'n," so "Falstaff" accentuates the detumescence of the mock-heroic theme (IV.xv.65).

His raffish subalterns are calculated to fit in well with it: Pistol, who is so noisily self-explanatory; Peto, who may have something to do with *pétard* and its uncouth etymology; Nym, who conforms to his synonym for filch; Gadshill, who picked up his alias at the scene of the high-way robbery; and Bardolph, who seems to have pinched his from Lord Bardolph. Bardolph's ragged conscripts rate an honorable listing in the chronicles of realism: Ralph Mouldy, Simon Shadow, Thomas Wart, Francis Feeble, and Peter Bullcalf. Perhaps the most remarkable *tour de force* is the evocation of personalities not simply ab-sent but long dead, like old Double, through the nostalgic recollections of Justice Shallow. These, we gather from Falstaff (who at first mistakes Justice Silence for Master Surecard), are much livelier than his youthful escapades ever were: swaggering at the Inns of Court with Francis Pickbone and Will Squele, a Cotswold man (Shakespeare's Williams tend to be slightly comic); fighting with one Sampson Stockfish, who—oddly enough—seems to have been a fruiterer, not a fishmonger; and teasing that *bona roba,* Jane Nightwork, who had Robin Nightwork by old Nightwork some fifty-five years ago. Robert Shallow, Esquire, for all his name, adds a dimension with his reminiscence. Yet the fondest of memories fade. Not long afterward Mistress Page cannot hit upon Falstaff's name, and even the conscientious Fluellen has forgotten it. Would they have remembered Oldcastle, we wonder?

Shakespeare's overt fools—above all, Touchstone—bear names as sententious as they are. Yet the profoundest of them, like the unnameable spokesman of Samuel Beckett, is the nameless fool of *King Lear.* The Quarto text of *Love's Labor's Lost* has a way of introducing characters as if they were types in the Commedia dell'Arte, referring to the Braggart for Don Armado and to the Pedant for Holofernes. Shakespeare particularizes by naming his Spaniard for the vainglorious Armada and his schoolmaster for Gargantua's tutor in Rabelais. In the universe of the pedantic Holofernes, everything has its appropriate label. Why was Ovid's family name identical with the Latin word for nose? "And why indeed 'Naso,' but for smelling out the odoriferous flowers of fancy, the jerks of invention?" (IV.ii.123-5). Life is not always so ingeniously tagged by literature; that is one of the points scored by *Love's Labor's Lost.* Yet man's command over his environment hinges upon that faculty exerted by Adam and Eve when they named the beasts in the garden, or by Prospero when he endowed Caliban's purposes with words, and taught him how to tell the sun from the moon (*The Tempest,* I.ii.334-6),

> To name the bigger light, and how the less,
> That burn by day and night.

Caliban, whose name is an imperfect anagram of *cannibal,* making mischief with the sodden Stephano and with Trinculo, whose name is a clinking toast, cannot be considered an apt pupil. But through the ministrations of Ariel, whose name betokens his ethereal flights, and through the consequent magic of Prospero's art, Shakespeare conjures and creates with words. It is no mere superstition that prompts Glendower to seek the control of nature by reckoning up the names of the several devils—devils whom mine Host of the Garter swears by, and against whose torments Edgar cries out. Their demonic potency, figuratively construed, is nothing less than the control of nature. For the power of naming is intimately allied to the gift of characterization (*A Midsummer Night's Dream*, V.i.14-7),

> And as imagination bodies forth
> The forms of things unknown, the poet's pen
> Turns them to shapes, and gives to aery nothing
> A local habitation and a name.

The Shakespearean Overplot

It is not Aristotle's fault when discussions of plot sound mechanical. The inspirational term he used, when he described it as the soul of tragedy, provided the Greek basis for our word *myth*—a word for whose current connotations the sky is the limit.[1] The Latin synonym, which has given us *fable,* seems constricting and moralistic by contrast. The Gallic equivalent, which is *intrigue,* conveys to us certain overtones of romance and of calculation. As for the Germanic expression, its English cognate is the businesslike *handling.* Our native monosyllable may well seem even more pedestrian, except that it sometimes introduces a sinister note. A plot originally meant a spot of some kind, and then (merging with *plat* and its associations of flatness) a patch of ground—like the one invaded

1. *Poetics,* iv, 14.

Delivered at a meeting of the Modern Language Association of America (Shakespeare Section) at New York on December 28, 1964; published in *Renaissance Drama,* VIII, ed. Samuel Schoenbaum (Evanston: Northwestern University Press, 1965).

by the Norwegians in *Hamlet.* Thence it came to mean the ground-plan for a building and, by abstraction, the plan or outline of a literary work. Subsequently it has denoted a scheme to be put into action, more and more pejoratively a scheme for nefarious action, roughly synonymous with the French *complot.* It is not for nothing that William Shakespeare was the contemporary of Guy Fawkes. We know that *plot* was a technical term for a scenario (or, more precisely, a list of scenes) posted backstage in the Elizabethan playhouse. Half a dozen such plots have survived from the repertory of the Henslowe-Alleyn companies.[2] In the producer's account-book we also read of a plot (in this case, a sketch for a tragedy) outlined by Ben Jonson and filled in by George Chapman.[3] It was doubtless through such journeywork that Anthony Munday gained the repute, according to Francis Meres, of "our best plotter." [4]

Shakespeare, as a concordance will demonstrate, draws upon most of these meanings and extends them characteristically. "This blessed plot," for John of Gaunt, is England; "this green plot," at the behest of Peter Quince, becomes a stage (*Richard II,* II.i.50; *A Midsummer Night's Dream,* III.i.3). "When we mean to build," says Lord Bardolph in the Second Part of *Henry IV,* "We first survey the plot, then draw the model," and his explicit speech goes on to underline the metaphorical transference from a plot of ground to a conspiracy (I.iii.41-2). Accordingly, it is not uncommon to speak of *laying* a plot. This machination, depending upon the context, could be either an in-

2. Reproduced in the second volume of W. W. Greg, *Dramatic Documents from the Elizabethan Playhouse* (Oxford, 1931).

3. *Henslowe's Diary,* ed. R. A. Foakes and R. T. Rickert (Cambridge, 1961), pp. 73, 100.

4. In *Elizabethan Critical Essays,* ed. G. Gregory Smith (Oxford, 1904), II, 320.

surrection or a practical joke. Hence, in the First Part of *Henry IV,* Hotspur calls the Percy revolt "a noble plot," while Gadshill tells a thievish accomplice: "thou layest the plot how" (I.iii.279; II.i.52). Either situation presupposes the agency of what Shakespeare, referrring to Aaron the Moor, designates as a "plotter" (*Titus Andronicus,* V.iii.325). Whether the agent is prompted by malice or mischief can spell the difference between a tragic villain and a comic funster. His victim, whether Othello or Parolles, is entitled to cry out with the latter: "Who cannot be crush'd with a plot?" (*All's Well That Ends Well,* IV.iii.325). Yet in *The Winter's Tale* Leontes suspects plots where there are none, and this is a moot point between the Tribunes and Coriolanus (*The Winter's Tale,* II.i.47; *Coriolanus,* III.i.38,41). Such characters may be the victims of circumstance or of their own natures, rather than of contrivance. In that event, it is the playwright who does the plotting; in fact it is always he who contrives those patterns which his *dramatis personae* attribute to fate or chance, if not to some human motive. Shakespeare, however, makes no literal mention of *plot* in the theatrical sense. His alternative, borrowed from the vocabulary of rhetoric, is *argument.*

Nonetheless we have frequent occasion to discuss his plots and, since they are complex, to disentangle the principal sequence of events from what is known—in eighteenth-century usage—as the underplot or—in more recent terminology—as the subplot. *Subplot,* being an etymological bastard, is probably to be preferred by Merriam-Webster stylists; but, since I am timidly feeling my way toward a neologism, I draw back at the prospect of *superplot,* which nothing east of Hollywood could live up to. That the underplot (and the word itself goes back to

Dryden) is not a gratuitous episode, but a thematic off-shoot of the main plot, has been a gradual realization of Shakespearean criticism. In the Japanese theater the farcical *kyogen* are not organically related to the solemn *Noh* plays with which they alternate. Zanies and *graciosos*, waggish servants who mimic their stylish masters, have indeed been a standard feature of European comedy. But it is English drama which, to the most elaborate degree, has been characterized by parallel construction, from the ritualized buffooneries of the Wakefield *Second Shepherds' Play* to the baroque derangements of *The Changeling*. And, while such lesser playwrights as Thomas Heywood exploited the license to patch odd pairs together, Shakespeare exerted his genius for harmonizing incongruities. The most suggestive treatment of this subject is William Empson's essay on "Double Plots." This, in turn, is the longest of seven diversified essays which Mr. Empson has consolidated by presenting them as variations on the pastoral theme. If his deft presentation gives seven ambiguous twists to the convention of pastoralism, he is not the man to be deterred by ambiguity. Yet his thesis gets in the way of his analysis by insisting that underplots should be pastoral.

So they are, in the callow dramaturgy of Robert Greene which Mr. Empson takes as his starting point. With Shakespeare it is much less easy to generalize. A more careful scrutiny of his plots would not stop at the assumption that these are merely double; more often than not they are triple, not to say multiple. Mr. Empson's observations are more cogent than his generalizations, and he is justifiably perplexed at applying the twofold formula to the First Part of *Henry IV*. "There are three worlds," he very clearly perceives, "each with its own hero; rebel camp, tavern, and court; chivalric idealism, natural gusto, the cautious politician." [5] To his misgiving that "this makes an unmanageable play," he himself suggests the answer that "the prince belongs to all three parties," consequently managing to meet each of them on their respective grounds. Thus Prince Hal effects that intermingling of kings and clowns which, while scandalizing the classicists, established a peculiarly Shakespearean decorum. If his central conflict with Hotspur forms the main plot and his raffish companionship with Falstaff the underplot, surely his strategic relationship with the title character at the most exalted level deserves to be discriminated and named. If the concept of the overplot did not already exist, it would not be difficult to invent, given its analogy with the underplot and the complementary function it could fill. I have found it helpful for understanding the morphology of pre-Shakespearean drama.[6] Consider *The Spanish Tragedy,* by no means the best of models, but perhaps the most influential of Elizabethan plays in its time. Here the story of revenge entangled with love is expressly framed by the choric role of the ghost, whose own vendetta foreshadows and goads on the other revenges.

This framework not only initiates the enveloping action but orients the plot toward a wider perspective, the war between Spain and Portugal wherein the ghost lost his life, so that Kyd's title has a collective significance. Few overplots are as formal as this, but most of them occupy a comparable position, looking backward and forward from the highest vantage-point over the broadest area,

5. William Empson, *Some Versions of Pastoral* (Norfolk, Connecticut, 1960), p. 41.
6. Harry Levin, *The Overreacher: A Study of Christopher Marlowe* (Cambridge, Massachusetts, 1952), pp. 67ff.

and reaffirming those principles of social and cosmic order which Ulysses enunciates in *Troilus and Cressida*. Insofar as the histories focus on kings, their major business takes place at the elevation of the overplot, while personal matters and lesser personages are brought into the foreground episodically. *Henry V*, an extreme example, maintains the heroic story-line of the epic, with excursions into both the romantic and the realistic. If the king is the animating plotter, he is likely to be a usurper, notoriously so in *Richard III*. When the royal protagonist is plotted against, like Henry VI, he yields the forestage to his rivals and deputies. Shakespeare's Roman plays can treat political themes with greater flexibility, precisely because their protagonists are private individuals. Although Julius Caesar's aspirations to sovereignty accord him a title role, it is Brutus who dominates the dramatic predicament. In his terms, the issue lies between a "personal cause" and "the general"—in other words, the main plot and the overplot—and that formulation holds true for *Coriolanus* and *Antony and Cleopatra* (*Julius Caesar*, II.i.11-2). Against the Alexandrian individualism of the lovers, Shakespeare counterpoises the claims of Roman responsibility; the scale of the sexual involvement is augmented by the imperial forces marshaled against it; the world itself, resounding verbally forty-four times through the play, heightens the stature of the hero (*Antony and Cleopatra*, V.i.17-9).

> The death of Antony
> Is not a single doom, in the name lay
> A moi'ty of the world.

Later playwrights, giving more weight to feminine roles and erotic motives, might regard the world as well lost. To that extent they slough off the overplot, which is the primary vehicle for the assertion of public duty and higher morality. Shakespeare's tragedies, derived as they are from quasi-historic material, start from and return to the commonweal, both in its foreign and its domestic aspects. Even when they are based on love-stories, which were generally considered more congenial to comedy, they never lose sight of the state. At the beginning, the middle, and the end of *Romeo and Juliet,* the Prince of Verona appears in order to remind the feuding families of their civic obligations. Othello's final reminder that he has "done the state some service" consummates an inner struggle which parallels the combats between the Venetians and the Turks (V.ii.339). Since *Hamlet* is the most fully elaborated of Shakespeare's works, we are not surprised to find its overplot so highly developed. The time-scheme is laid down by the goings and comings of the Ambassadors, Danish and English. The national crisis in Denmark is matched by the international tension of its relations with Norway and Norway's with Poland. Hamlet, as a revenger, has two counterparts: Laertes on the lower plane and Fortinbras on the higher. To omit the Norwegian Prince is to devalue the play by ignoring one of its largest dimensions. Yet Fortinbras was cut out and his closing speech reassigned to Horatio in a recent production at Stratford, Connecticut—a fittingly anticlimactic culmination to that annual record of short-sighted bungling and heavy-handed bumbling which has made the American Shakespeare Festival little more than a cultural embarrassment.

Small wonder, then, if we fail to discern the overplot. Can it be that our latter-day sense of existence, which discovers its chaotic mirror in the Theater of the Absurd, has no use for Shakespeare's valedictions with their reassurances of cosmos? Doubtless it is because the Elizabethans and Jacobeans were harassed by the uncertain succession to the throne that their tragedies are so preoccupied with problems of dynastic continuity. Since a dynasty is both a family and a regime, its internal conflicts may be envisaged as relating the main plot to the overplot. The division between Albany and Cornwall, alluded to in the first line of *King Lear* and again in the first scenes of the Second and Third Acts, is only resolved by the death of Cornwall in the Fourth and the Franco-British battle in the Fifth. More broadly, the "little world of man" is subjected to decay and cruelty in the macrocosm of outer nature (III.i.10). The condition of the body politic is supernaturally challenged when the apparition in *Hamlet* "bodes some strange eruption to our state" (I.i.69). Similarly, but more intensively, *Macbeth* is set in motion by supernatural machinery. Witches, omens, and oracles sketch a fatalistic background for the exercise of human will, and document the play's unique concern with eschatology, with damnation and hell. Macbeth's three opponents, linked to him by the question of succeeding progeny, are Macduff, the predestined avenger, Malcolm, the immediate heir to the crown, and Fleance, the ultimate link between the line of Banquo and the house of Stuart. The single scene in England, with its ironic cross-reference to the King's Evil, far from being tangential, constitutes the vital center of the overplot.

Insofar as the comedies deal with frankly fictitious subject-matter, and depend less upon the concerns of statecraft, they are less dependent on overplots. *The Merry Wives of Windsor* does without one altogether; that may help to explain why it seems comparatively thin; Falstaff can no longer be mock-heroic when he is demobilized from the field of heroics. On the other hand, *The Comedy of Errors,* possibly the most trifling piece in the canon, is reinforced by the suspense of Egeon's condemnation. Tragic elements play a minor part in comedy, with Shakespeare, just as comic elements do in tragedy. Menaces averted by happy endings tend to produce those Polonian hybrids which we have retrospectively agreed to classify as romances. An Italianate plot is no match for the British overplot of *Cymbeline,* especially when aided by a Welsh underplot. The antagonisms of *The Winter's Tale,* shifting from marital jealousy to parental dudgeon with the generations, move from Sicilia to Bohemia and back again for a tragicomic resolution. Here the geographical displacement makes room for a pastoral retreat, as it elsewhere does when courtiers withdraw into the forest. Typically, in *As You Like It,* the exiled Duke ends by returning to court along with the suitably mated lovers, relinquishing the Forest of Arden to its bucolic denizens. The structure of *The Tempest* is diagrammatic, not simply in its perfected unity, nor in its symbolic pattern of withdrawal and return, but in its three analogous conspiracies: Sebastian for the Kingdom of Naples, Antonio for the Dukedom of Milan, and Caliban for the rule of the island. Prospero, through his magical control of spirits, attains an overview which sees all and thwarts cross-purposes.

Comparably, in *Measure for Measure,* the Duke is a retiring *deus ex machina;* his unworthy regent, Angelo, is tested and discredited by being temporarily elevated to the overplot. *All's Well That Ends Well* allows its decisions to hinge on the King of France, as the god in a much more loosely plotted machine. Yet it is not supernal authority so much as men's wits—or, more commonly, women's—which intervene to counterplot against trickery. *The Merchant of Venice* conflates two traditional motifs, the Pound of Flesh and the Choice of Caskets, when Portia crosses over to Venice from Belmont and tempers legalism with love, as well as justice with mercy. There are times, however, when such countermeasures are less effective than mere contingencies. "Our indiscretion sometime serves us well," so Hamlet puts it, "When our deep plots do pall" (V.ii.8-9). In *Much Ado about Nothing* the witless constabulary blunders into the exposure of a wile which has deceived the more serious characters. "What your wisdoms could not discover," they are admonished, "these shallow fools have brought to light" (V.i.232-4). Folly, in the person of the fool, sheds more light than self-complacent wisdom; but greatness is not thrust upon the lowly, as Malvolio painfully learns in *Twelfth Night,* where he remains the lowest of four aspirants seeking Olivia's hand at four different levels of society and of the plot. The social and amorous hierarchy of *A Midsummer Night's Dream* is at least as extensive. Above the two interchangeable pairs of Athenian lovers stand two sets of presiding figures, Oberon and Titania mutually suspecting one another of interrelationships with Hippolyta and Theseus, while Bottom momentarily ascends from his nethermost status to bask in the favors of the Fairy Queen.

This chain of courtship reaches its sublimated height when Oberon pays his compliments to the "fair vestal," Queen Elizabeth (II.i.158). Royal command may well have created something of an additional overplot in the very pageantry of the initial performance. The play-within-the-play reflects those circumstances, while burlesquing the theme of lovers' frustrations. The myth it dramatized, Pyramus and Thisbe, is seriously paralleled by *Romeo and Juliet.* It is among the various mythological precedents evoked by the third happy couple of *The Merchant of Venice,* Jessica and Lorenzo in Portia's garden: "In such a night as this . . ." (V.i.1ff.). Shakespeare's characters learn to know themselves by projecting archetypes from Greco-Roman mythology or, with deeper resonance, from Judeo-Christian scripture. Richard II goes through his deposition scene as if he were reenacting a passion play. Cardinal Wolsey recognizes, at the opposite pole, that when the king's favorite falls, "he falls like Lucifer, / Never to hope again" (III.ii.371-2). All tragedy, of course, could be traced to that original fall; it was the overplot that adumbrated all subsequent plots. It had been Lucifer, rearising from Hell as Satan, who unrolled the mystery cycles. When Marlowe's Faustus inquires about devils, Mephistophilis informs him that they are

> Unhappy spirits that fell with Lucifer,
> Conspir'd against our God with Lucifer,
> And are forever damn'd with Lucifer.[7]

Just as the conjurations of Dr. Faustus are parodied by the antics of clowns, so his destiny is prefigured by that of the Eternal Adversary. And just as the relation of the underplot to the main plot is parodic, so the relation of the overplot to the main plot is figural—a glimpse exemplifying some grander design, an indication that the play at hand is but an interlude from a universal drama performed in the great *theatrum mundi.* Curiously enough, the same Marlovian cadence reechoes when the Percies conspire against Henry IV. Their bone of contention is Edmund Mortimer (probably a more legitimate claimant to the kingship than the more active contenders), whose absent claim becomes vocal as Hotspur fills the stage with his name (I.iii.219-22):

> He said he would not ransom Mortimer,
> Forbade my tongue to speak of Mortimer,

7. Christopher Marlowe, *The Tragical History of Doctor Faustus,* ed. F. S. Boas (London, 1932), p. 72 (I.iii.73-5).

But I will find him when he lies asleep,
And in his ear I'll hollow "Mortimer."

With the First Part of *Henry IV* we come back to our organizing principle, in the hope of having illustrated some of its possible uses, since that showpiece embodies the three Shakespearean genres within its structural equilibrium: the comedy of Falstaff as the underplot, the tragedy of Hotspur as the main plot, and the history of Henry IV as the overplot.

Evangelizing Shakespeare

Shakespeare has incited such throwing about of brains that, given the critical urge to say something new, overinterpretation is more likely to be the rule than the exception. His very richness and responsiveness, plus the problematic character of his medium, seem to offer a standing invitation to the kind of commentators who seek in him a mirror for their own obsessions. If these are not clearly demonstrable, so much the better; then the game can be played with hidden allusions, secret signals, or cryptograms; after all, the more occult the finding, the more intrinsically Rosicrucian. Historical scholarship has normally managed to draw some sort of line between such far-fetched lucubrations and its more objective endeavors. Anti-Stratfordianism, though there are still proponents of Bacon, Oxford, Marlowe, or others for the authorship of Shakespeare's works, has more to do with

---

This review-article, on *Shakespearean Tragedy: Its Art and Christian Premises* by R. W. Battenhouse, was first published in the *Journal of the History of Ideas*, XXXII, 2 (April–June, 1971).

abnormal psychology than with literary history. Yet the book that initiated this movement, *The Philosophy of the Plays of Shakespeare Unfolded* (1857), started as a venture into the history of ideas; it was only because Delia Bacon found so much serious expression of contemporaneous thought within the plays that she ended by attributing them to a philosopher rather than to a playwright.

Scholars, if not stage directors or dramatic critics, can "be quite sure that *King Lear* was not written in the spirit of, say, Beckett's *Endgame*," as Roy W. Battenhouse incontrovertibly puts it—in other words, that Jan Kott has ignored the intellectual context and has superimposed a modish absurdism in presenting his *Shakespeare Our Contemporary.* Wholly agreeing that Shakespeare cannot be fully understood except from the vantage-point of his period, we soon come to realize that Professor Battenhouse takes an extremely retrogressive view of that period. Thus his book does heavy polemical duty in the long and sharp controversy over the *Weltanschauung* of the Renaissance and the extent to which it differed from that of the Middle Ages. Shakespeare may well be a test case for posing this problem, since he gives us such concrete instances of men and women reacting to circumstances. But by the same token, precisely because he was a dramatist and not a systematic thinker, he speaks through many contradictory voices, none of them to be very closely identified with his own. And though the highest mode of his drama, tragedy, has an ethos fraught with philosophical implications, its basic norms were first developed and traditionally formulated under a pre-Christian dispensation.

Indeed it has been argued, by I. A. Richards among others, that the tragic outlook is incompatible with the eschatological tenets of orthodox Christianity, which looks forward to the prospect of a divine comedy, a happy ending in another world. The explicitly Christian conception, ably traced by Willard Farnham in *The Mediaeval Heritage of Elizabethan Tragedy,* was constricting and highly didactic, narrative rather than dramatic in form, emphasizing the falls of princes, the vicissitudes of fortune, and an unhumanistic contempt for the material world. That devout Anglican, T. S. Eliot, and that skeptical naturalist, George Santayana, in a stimulating interchange, reached some measure of agreement on "the absence of religion in Shakespeare." For A. C. Bradley, whose *Shakespearean Tragedy* was the great watershed between Romantic and modern criticism, secularism had been a precondition. During subsequent years, largely under the mystagogic influence of G. Wilson Knight, religious presuppositions and theological terms have increasingly figured in Shakespearean discussions. Professor Battenhouse's zealous effort may be said to mark the culmination of a trend. But meanwhile, in 1963, Roland Mushat Frye brought out an authoritative monograph, *Shakespeare and Christian Doctrine,* which should have been permitted to remain the last word on the subject.

After a thorough canvass, with due regard for the incidental role that religion was bound to play, this study nonetheless was able to conclude: "Shakespeare's works are pervasively secular, in that they make no encompassing appeal to theological categories and in that they are concerned with the dramatization (apart from distinctively Christian doctrines) of universally human situations within a temporal and this-worldly arena." Professor Battenhouse, refusing to accept so well-tempered a conclusion, taxes Professor Frye with having neglected the patristic and scholastic authorities. It is true that the latter's documentary background is primarily based on sixteenth-century theologians—notably Luther, Calvin, and, above all, Hooker's normative exposition of English faith. But if we are viewing Shakespeare in the light of his time, these are the contemporary formulations and influences. To argue for "a strong holdover of the older theology" might have some point when the writer influenced happens to be a learned hierophant like Donne or Milton; it can hardly make sense with a practical man of the theater. Such medievalists as D. W. Robertson, though their typological reinterpretations have not gone unquestioned, have obviously been operating on somewhat firmer ground than those who would reread the secular literature of the Renaissance in "a theological perspective."

Now Mr. Battenhouse is not to be numbered among those amateur "theologizers" whom Mr. Frye corrects. He has learning as well as zeal; he taught church history at the Episcopal Theological School before he became a professor of English literature at Indiana University; and he has edited a useful *Companion to the Study of Saint Augustine*. The trouble lies in his insistence on making Saint Augustine into an inseparable companion for the study of Shakespeare. Between the two there is no evidence whatsoever for any direct relationship. The most conscientious and comprehensive students of Shakespeare's reading, such as T. W. Baldwin and V. K. Whitaker, have not tried to establish specific links. Nor has Mr. Battenhouse shouldered this burden of proof; instead he has committed a *petitio principii*, taking for granted Shakespeare's "Christian premises" and assuming that not only Shakespeare himself but also the "Elizabethan auditors" were as steeped in Augustinianism as Mr. Battenhouse. His opening example, a "re-vision" of *The Rape of Lucrece*, "the tragedy in which Shakespeare has summed up his most subtle insights into evil," owes more to *The City of*

God than to Ovid or Livy. "An ultimate key to the logic of Hamlet's personal tragedy" is a passage from the *Confessions,* wherein the saint accuses his earlier self of "rottenness."

Similarly, "the reshaped meaning of Coriolanus" emerges from "an Augustinian perspective." Volumnia would seem to be the key-figure here—even though her famous plea, which is cited, follows North's Plutarch virtually word for word. Mr. Battenhouse bravely carries his holy war into the camp of the enemy when, *a fortiori,* he endeavors to Christianize the Roman plays. Shakespeare's feeling for historic distinctions was actually such that, while duly proscribing suicide for a Christian hero like Hamlet or Romeo, he justifies it by the Stoic ethics of Brutus and Cleopatra. Mr. Battenhouse, quite predictably, subordinates the Greek tragedians to his own peculiar notions of Christian tragedy; his curt reading of the *Antigone* might almost be called vindictive. Yet he goes out of his way to invoke the sanctions of Aristotle's *Poetics,* despite the fact that it was not translated nor widely available nor markedly influential in Elizabethan England. To be sure, his Aristotelian terminology has been "ontologized and Christianized": *hamartía* has become deadly sin. The treatment of each individual play tends to be a casuistic reckoning of the trespasses that condemn the protagonist. The spectacle is moralized into an evangelical tract. The word "art" stands in the subtitle not so much for dramatic craftsmanship as for theological supersubtlety.

Reading between the lines, at so hermeneutic a level, yields its quota of novel subtexts. Many of Shakespeare's own moralists, such as Friar Lawrence and Menenius Agrippa, turn out to be villains in disguise. Hamlet should have heeded the warnings against the Ghost, who is truly a spirit of darkness, coming not from Purgatory but from Hell to perpetrate mischief against a Claudius and a Gertrude unduly maligned. Not the least of Hamlet's numerous sins is his humanism, which expresses an addiction to a false pagan ideal. He might better have escaped from his dilemma by taking religious orders. A revealing, if unsympathetic, footnote compares him with the student radicals of today. As for Othello, his prototype is Judas—no matter if the Folio's "base Judean" came out as "base Indian" in the Quarto (V.ii.347). Attention naturally focuses on the death-speech, and Mr. Battenhouse devotes some of his most ingenious casuistry to the Turkish foe, whom he refers to as an "uncircumcized dog." Well, Saint Paul was willing to overlook the difference between circumcision and uncircumcision; but Shakespeare's actual phrase is "circumcised dog"; his point is not that Othello was a "Judaizer" but that he prided himself on being a Christian, even at the moment of realization that he must share the fate of the infidel.

Although the slip is a trivial one, it is so centrally related to the theme of the book that it makes the reader wary of the exegete—and not less so when the exegesis resorts to the method of biblical prefiguration. On the surface, it would seem that Shakespeare alludes less often to the Bible than to classical mythology. But explicit references can always be eked out by symbolic analogies. Noah's flood, of course, is the archetype of all deluges, including King Lear's storm. It is suggested that, when Edgar disguises himself as Tom o'Bedlam, the train of association carried the audience far beyond the madhouse of Saint Mary of Bethlehem to the original scene of Christ's nativity. Antony's gaudy nights are sinister parodies of the Last Supper, and Romeo's poisoned cup is "a kind of blind *figura* of the Christian Mass." Juliet's forty-two hours of drug-induced sleep constitute a "shadow-parallel to Christ's salvific forty hours in the region of the dead." Here one might observe that even numerology has its ground-rules; that, when the integers differ however slightly, no connection is left. Nor can much be made of forty-two as the number of scenes in *Antony and Cleopatra,* since they went unnumbered in the Folio and could scarcely be counted during performance.

The frisking lambs of pastoral convention can, by this Procrustean fixation, be apotheosized into symbols of Jesus; and the leeks in *Henry V* are explained by "warping the meaning" of the Book of Numbers, rather than by the presence of Fluellen and the produce of his native Wales. One wishes that Mr. Battenhouse had scrutinized the Shakespearean texts as painstakingly as he has applied his scriptural glosses (*e.g.,* an ear for iambic pentameter might have prevented the misquotations on pages 227 and 248). His descriptions of plot and character, whether through willful distortion or lapsing memory, are sometimes rather hard to recognize. Pompey, for example, is repeatedly characterized as a pirate—whereas Shakespeare presents him as an exceptionally disinterested figure amid the conflicting interests of *Antony and Cleopatra,* the last representative of the noble Roman republic, who deliberately rejects the act of piracy proposed to him in the tense scene on his galley. Again, the suggestion that the Player's evocation of Pyrrhus is a comment on Hamlet's Pyrrhic victory can be no more than a meaningless pun; for the battle-weary Pyrrhus, King of Epirus, must be dated nearly a thousand years after his Homeric pseudo-ancestor. Mr. Battenhouse seems to have been moved by the spirit of early Christian hostility against the Greeks and the Romans.

Fundamental questions of belief, diverse assumptions

regarding the nature of the cosmos, form a climate for all of Shakespeare's tragedies and set a standard by which his characters act. However, *King Lear* occupies a special and central position among them, because it so directly raises those questions and weighs those assumptions. Located in pre-Christian Britain, invoking deities with pagan names, it counterposes piety and skepticism, providential design and blind circumstance. A recent study by William R. Elton, *King Lear and the Gods,* analyzes these discrepant attitudes and traces the strands of opinion from which they derive. Though Mr. Battenhouse mentions this contribution in passing, he makes no attempt to meet its carefully reasoned and formidably documented argument for interpreting the play as "a syncretically pagan tragedy." With a proper respect for the complexity of the subject—not to say the mystery of things—Professor Elton hinges his interpretation upon the concept of an unrevealed god, *deus absconditus.* It is interesting to note that Lucien Goldmann has adumbrated a similar pattern in his book on Racine, Pascal, and the Jansenists, *Le Dieu caché.* Another book that bears upon the present inquiry, Theodore Spencer's *Shakespeare and the Nature of Man,* achieves an equipoise by balancing the survivals of medieval tradition against the emergent questionings of the Renaissance.

Tragedy resides in the tension and interplay between such opposing forces as faith and doubt or hope and despair. If divine justice were everywhere manifest, this would be the better world that men sigh for, and there would simply be no need for them to take a tragic stance. If they do so, it is because life consists of alternatives and ambiguities, and because death casts so absolute a shadow. Marlowe was the first playwright in English to sound those existential depths, and his voice still rings for

most of us with an angry and rebellious undertone—
though it should be recalled that Professor Battenhouse,
in his doctoral thesis, reshaped *Tamburlaine* into a model
of orthodoxy. But, to extend the disagreement no further, Marlowe's insights do seem extreme and one-sided
when contrasted with the maturer breadth of Shakespeare's balanced vision. Its unique quality has been to
embrace a whole spectrum of diverging opinions, to show
what Coleridge termed a "wonderful philosophical impartiality," to know that any human situation has at least
two sides. Single-minded dogmatism, since it brooks no
uncertainties, can feel sure which course is right and
which is wrong. Consequently, tragedy lapses into an austerely moralistic commentary on a dreary sequence of
avoidable mistakes; and Shakespeare's heroes, never rising to heroic stature, are reduced to a parcel of delin-
quents, truants, and heretics.

Shakespeare was indubitably a Christian, ethically and
culturally speaking, insofar as Christendom had shaped
his frame of reference. Yet, ontologically and psychologically, he lived through and responded to a widening of
collective experience which was to reach its ripest expression in his work. We need not forget that, like every Englishman of his generation, he had Roman Catholic
grandparents, or that his parents' generation had
watched Protestants and Catholics being burned for
heresy in shockingly brief succession. When both camps
had their martyrs and zealots, it was time for the alert
and sensitive spectator to be impressed by the very clashing of creeds, the reawakening of rivalry between beliefs
and disbeliefs. Literature, in particular, had been secu-
larized by the infiltration of the classics. Shakespeare
picked up Stoicism as well as stagecraft from Seneca, and
discovered his *vade mecum* in the *Essays* of Montaigne. As

Lucien Febvre showed, when he studied the religion of Rabelais in *Le Problème de l'incroyance au XVIe siècle,* latter-day atheism or Voltairean rationalism was not germane to the age. It is not a question of irreligion but of free-ranging speculation. It is not important whether Shakespeare was himself a skeptic or an agnostic; what matters is his full awareness of uncanonical currents, his dynamic sense of living in an open universe. Hence the Renaissance is inaccessible to the scholar who has closed his mind.

II
COMMENTARIES

Form and Formality
in *Romeo and Juliet*

"Fain would I dwell on form," says Juliet from her window to Romeo in the moonlit orchard below (II.ii.88-9),

> Fain would I dwell on form, fain, fain deny
> What I have spoke; but farewell compliment!

Romeo has just violated convention, dramatic and otherwise, by overhearing what Juliet intended to be a soliloquy. Her cousin, Tybalt, had already committed a similar breach of social and theatrical decorum in the scene at the Capulets' feast, where he had also recognized Romeo's voice to be that of a Montague. There, when the lovers first met, the dialogue of their meeting had been formalized into a sonnet, acting out the conceit of his lips as pilgrims, her hand as a shrine, and his kiss as a culminating piece of stage-business, with an encore after an additional quatrain: "You kiss by th' book" (I.v.110). Neither had known the identity of the other; and each, upon

---

Delivered at a meeting of the Modern Language Association (English Section I) at New York on December 28, 1958; published in the *Shakespeare Quarterly*, IX, 1 (Winter, 1960).

finding it out, responded with an ominous exclamation coupling love and death (118, 138). The formality of their encounter was framed by the ceremonious character of the scene, with its dancers, its masquers, and—except for Tybalt's stifled outburst—its air of old-fashioned hospitality. "We'll measure them a measure," Benvolio had proposed; but Romeo, unwilling to join the dance, had resolved to be an onlooker and carry a torch (I.iv.10). That torch may have burned symbolically, but not for Juliet; indeed, as we are inclined to forget with Romeo, he attended the feast in order to see the dazzling but soon eclipsed Rosaline. Rosaline's prior effect upon him is all that we ever learn about her; yet it has been enough to make Romeo, when he was presented to us, a virtual stereotype of the romantic lover. As such, he has protested a good deal too much in his preliminary speeches, utilizing the conventional phrases and standardized images of Elizabethan eroticism, bandying generalizations, paradoxes, and sestets with Benvolio, and taking a quasi-religious vow which his introduction to Juliet would ironically break (I.ii.88). Afterward this role is reduced to absurdity by the humorous man, Mercutio, in a mock-conjuration evoking Venus and Cupid and the inevitable jingle of "love" and "dove" (ii.i.10). The scene that follows is actually a continuation, marked in neither the folios nor the quartos, and linked with what has gone before by a somewhat eroded rhyme.

> 'Tis in vain
> To seek him here that means not to be found,

Benvolio concludes in the absence of Romeo (41-2).Whereupon the latter, on the other side of the wall, chimes in, aside (II.ii.1):

> He jests at scars that never felt a wound.

Thus we stay behind, with Romeo, when the masquers depart. Juliet, appearing at the window, does not hear his descriptive invocation. Her first utterance is the very sigh that Mercutio burlesqued in the foregoing scene: "Ay me!" (II.ii.25). Then, believing herself to be alone and masked by the darkness, she speaks her mind in sincerity and simplicity. She calls into question not merely Romeo's name but—by implication—all names, forms, conventions, sophistications, and arbitrary dictates of society, as opposed to the appeal of instinct directly conveyed in the odor of a rose. When Romeo takes her at her word and answers, she is startled and even alarmed for his sake; but she does not revert to courtly language.

> I would not for the world they saw thee here,

she tells him (74), and her monosyllabic directness inspires the matching cadence of his response (76):

> And but thou love me, let them find me here.

She pays incidental tribute to the proprieties with her passing suggestion that, had he not overheard her, she would have dwelt on form, pretended to be more distant, and played the not impossible part of the captious beloved. But farewell compliment! Romeo's love for Juliet will have an immediacy which cuts straight through the verbal embellishment that has obscured his infatuation with Rosaline. That shadowy creature, having served her Dulcinea-like purpose, may well be forgotten. On the other hand, Romeo has his more tangible foil in the person of the County Paris, who is cast in that ungrateful part which the Italians call *il terzo incomodo,* the inconvenient third party, the unwelcome member of an amorous triangle. As the official suitor of Juliet, his speeches are always formal, and often sound stilted or priggish by contrast with Romeo's. Long after Romeo has abandoned his sonneteering, Paris will pronounce a sestet at Juliet's tomb (V.iii.12-6). During their only colloquy, which occurs in Friar Lawrence's cell, Juliet takes on the sophisticated tone of Paris, denying his claims and disclaiming his compliments in brisk stichomythy. As soon as he leaves, she turns to the Friar, and again—as so often in intimate moments—her lines fall into monosyllables (IV.i.44-5):

> O, shut the door, and when thou hast done so,
> Come weep with me, past hope, past cure, past help!

Since the suit of Paris is the main subject of her conversations with her parents, she can hardly be sincere with them. Even before she met Romeo, her consent was hedged in prim and mannered phraseology (I.iii.97):

> I'll look to like, if looking liking move.

And after her involvement she becomes adept in the strategems of mental reservation, giving her mother equivocal rejoinders and rousing her father's anger by chopping logic (III.v.68-203). Despite the intervention of the Nurse on her behalf, her one straightforward plea is disregarded. Significantly Lady Capulet, broaching the theme of Paris in stiffly appropriate couplets, has compared his face to a volume (I.iii.87-90): [1]

> This precious book of love, this unbound lover,
> To beautify him, only lacks a cover.
> The fish lives in the sea, and 'tis much pride
> For fair without the fair within to hide.

That bookish comparison, by emphasizing the letter at the expense of the spirit, helps to lend Paris an aspect of

1. On the long and rich history of this trope, see the sixteenth chapter of E. R. Curtius, *European Literature and the Latin Middle Ages,* tr. W. R. Trask (New York, 1953).

unreality; to the Nurse, more ingenuously, he is "a man of wax" (76). Later Juliet will echo Lady Capulet's metaphor, transferring it from Paris to Romeo (III.ii.83-4):

> Was ever book containing such vile matter
> So fairly bound?

Here, on having learned that Romeo has just slain Tybalt, she is undergoing a crisis of doubt, a typically Shakespearean recognition of the difference between appearance and reality. The fair without may not cover a fair within, after all. Her unjustified accusations, leading up to her rhetorical question, form a sequence of oxymoronic epithets: "Beautiful tyrant! fiend angelical! . . . honorable villain!" (75-9). W. H. Auden, commenting on these lines, cannot believe they would come from a heroine who had been exclaiming shortly before: "Gallop apace, you fiery-footed steeds . . ." [2] Yet Shakespeare has been perfectly consistent in suiting changes of style to changes of mood. When Juliet feels at one with Romeo, her intonations are genuine; when she feels at odds with him, they should be unconvincing. The attraction of love is played off against the revulsion from books, and coupled with the closely related themes of youth and haste, in one of Romeo's long-drawn-out leavetakings (II.ii.156-7):

> Love goes toward love as schoolboys from their books,
> But love from love, toward school with heavy looks.

The school for these young lovers will be tragic experience. When Romeo, assuming that Juliet is dead and contemplating his own death, recognizes the corpse of Paris, he will extend the image to cover them both (V.iii.81-2):

2. In the paper-bound Laurel Shakespeare, ed. Francis Fergusson (New York, 1958), p. 26.

> O give me thy hand,
> One writ with me in sour misfortune's book!

It was this recoil from bookishness, together with the farewell to compliment, that animated *Love's Labor's Lost,* where literary artifice was so ingeniously deployed against itself, and Berowne was taught—by an actual heroine named Rosaline—that the best books were women's eyes. Some of Shakespeare's other early comedies came even closer to adumbrating certain features of *Romeo and Juliet:* notably, *The Two Gentlemen of Verona,* with its locale, its window scene, its friar and rope, its betrothal and banishment, its emphasis upon the vagaries of love. Shakespeare's sonnets and erotic poems had won for him the reputation of an English Ovid. *Romeo and Juliet,* the most elaborate product of his so-called lyrical period, was his first successful experiment in tragedy.[3] Because of that very success, it is hard for us to realize the full extent of its novelty, though scholarship has been reminding us of how it must have struck contemporaries.[4] They would have been surprised, and possibly shocked, at seeing lovers taken so seriously. Legend, it had been heretofore taken for granted, was the proper matter for serious drama; romance was the stuff of the comic stage. Romantic tragedy—*"an excellent conceited Tragedie of Romeo and Juliet,"* to cite the title-page of the First Quarto—was one of those contradictions in terms which Shakespeare seems to have delighted in resolving. His innovation might be described as transcending the usages of romantic comedy, which are therefore very much in evidence, particu-

3. H. B. Charlton, in his British Academy lecture for 1939, *"Romeo and Juliet" as an Experimental Tragedy,* has considered the experiment in the light of Renaissance critical theory.

4. Especially F. M. Dickey, *Not Wisely But Too Well: Shakespeare's Love Tragedies* (San Marino, California, 1957), pp. 63–88.

larly at the beginning. Subsequently, the leading characters acquire together a deeper dimension of feeling by
expressly repudiating the artificial language they have
talked and the superficial code they have lived by. Their
formula might be that of Sidney's anti-Petrarchan sonnet:

> Foole said My muse to mee, looke in thy heart and write.[5]

An index of this development is the incidence of rhyme,
heavily concentrated in the First Act, and its gradual re-
placement by a blank verse which is realistic or didactic
with other speakers and unprecedentedly limpid and passionate with the lovers. "Love has no need of euphony,"
the eminent Russian translator of the play, Boris Pasternak, has commented. "Truth, not sound, dwells in its
heart." [6]

Comedy set the pattern of courtship, as formally embodied in a dance. The other genre of Shakespeare's earlier stagecraft, history, set the pattern of conflict, as formally embodied in a duel. *Romeo and Juliet* might also be
characterized as an anti-revenge play, in which hostile
emotions are finally pacified by the interplay of kindlier
ones. Romeo sums it up in his prophetic oxymorons
(I.i.175-7):

> Here's much to do with hate, but more with love.
> Why then, O brawling love! O loving hate!
> O any thing, of nothing first create!

And Paris, true to type, waxes grandiose in lamenting
Juliet (IV.v.58):

> O love, O life! not life, but love in death!

5. Sir Philip Sidney, *Astrophel and Stella*, ed. Albert Feuillerat (Cambridge, 1922), p. 243.
6. Boris Pasternak, "Translating Shakespeare," tr. Manya Harari, *The Twentieth Century*, CLXIV, 979 (September, 1958), 217.

Here, if we catch the echo from Hieronimo's lament in *The Spanish Tragedy,*

> O life! no life, but lively form of death,

we may well note that the use of antithesis, which is purely decorative with Kyd, is functional with Shakespeare. The contrarieties of his plot are reinforced on the plane of imagery by omnipresent reminders of light and darkness, youth and age, and many other antitheses subsumed by the all-embracing one of Eros and Thanatos, the *leitmotif* of the *Liebestod,* the myth of the tryst in the tomb.[7] This attraction of ultimate opposites—which is succinctly implicit in the Elizabethan ambiguity of the verb *to die* (also used for experiencing an orgasm)—is generalized when the Friar rhymes "womb" with "tomb," and particularized when Romeo hails the latter place as "thou womb of death" (II.iii.9, 10; V.iii.45). Hence the "extremities" of the situation, as the prologue to the Second Act announces, are tempered "with extreme sweet" (14). Those extremes begin to meet as soon as the play's initial prologue, in a sonnet disarmingly smooth, has set forth the feud between the two households, "Where civil blood makes civil hands unclean" (4). Elegant verse yields to vulgar prose, and to an immediate riot, as the servants precipitate a renewal—for the third time—of their masters' quarrel. The brawl of Act I is renewed again in the *contretemps* of Act III and completed by the swordplay of Act V. Between the street-scenes, with their clashing welter of citizens and officers, we shuttle through a series of interiors, in a flurry of domestic arrangements and family relationships. The house of the Capulets is the logical center of action, and Juliet's chamber its central sanc-

---

7. Caroline Spurgeon, *Shakespeare's Imagery and What It Tells Us* (New York, 1936), pp. 310–6.

tum. Consequently, the sphere of privacy encloses Acts II and IV, in contradistinction to the public issues raised by the alternating episodes. The temporal alternation of the play, in its accelerating continuity, is aptly recapitulated by the impatient rhythm of Capulet's speech (III.v.176-8):

> Day, night, work, play,
> Alone, in company, still my care hath been
> To have her match'd.

The alignment of the *dramatis personae* is as symmetrical as the antagonism they personify. It is not without relevance that the names of the feuding families, like the Christian names of the hero and heroine, are metrically interchangeable (though "Juliet" is more frequently a trochee than an amphimacer). Tybalt the Capulet is pitted against Benvolio the Montague in the first street-fight, which brings out—with parallel stage-directions—the heads of both houses restrained by respective wives. Both the hero and heroine are paired with others, Rosaline and Paris, and admonished by elderly confidants, the Friar and the Nurse. Escalus, as Prince of Verona, occupies a superior and neutral position; yet, in the interchange of blood for blood, he loses "a brace of kinsmen," Paris and Mercutio (V.iii.295). Three times he must quell and sentence the rioters before he can pronounce the final sestet, restoring order to the city-state through the lovers' sacrifice. He effects the resolution by summoning the patriarchal enemies, from their opposite sides, to be reconciled. "Capulet! Montague!" he sternly arraigns them, and the polysyllables are brought home by monosyllabics (291-3): [8]

> See what a scourge is laid upon your hate,
> That heaven finds means to kill your joys with love.

8. *Heaven* is regularly a monosyllable with Shakespeare.

The two-sided equipoise of the dramatic structure is well matched by the dynamic symmetry of the antithetical style. One of its peculiarities, which surprisingly seems to have escaped the attention of commentators, is a habit of stressing a word by repeating it within a line, a figure which may be classified in rhetoric as a kind of *ploce*. I have cited a few examples incidentally; let me now underline the device by pointing out a few more. Thus Montague and Capulet are accused of forcing their parties (I.i.94-5)

> To wield old partisans, in hands as old,
> Cank'red with peace, to part your cank'red hate.

This double instance, along with the wordplay on "cank'red," suggests the embattled atmosphere of partisanship through the halberds; and it is further emphasized in Benvolio's account of the fray (114):

> Came more and more, and fought on part and part.

The key-words are not only doubled but affectionately intertwined, when Romeo confides to the Friar (II.iii.59):

> As mine on hers, so hers is set on mine.

Again, he conveys the idea of reciprocity by declaring that Juliet returns "grace for grace and love for love" (86). The Friar's warning hints at poetic justice (and note the shifting accentuation of the key-word) (II.vi.9):

> These violent delights have violent ends.

Similarly Mercutio, challenged by Tybalt, turns "point to point," and the Nurse finds Juliet—in *antimetabole*— "Blubb'ring and weeping, weeping and blubb'ring" (III.i.160; iii.87). Statistics would prove illusory, because some repetitions are simply idiomatic, grammatical, or—in the case of old Capulet or the Nurse—colloquial.

But it is significant that the play contains well over a hundred such lines, the largest number being in the First Act with scarcely any left over for the Fifth.

The significance of this tendency toward reduplication, both stylistic and structural, can perhaps be best understood in the light of Bergson's well-known theory of the comic: the imposition of geometrical form upon the living data of formless consciousness. The stylization of love, the constant pairing and counterbalancing, the *quid pro quo* of Capulet and Montague, seem mechanical and unnatural. Nature has other proponents besides the lovers, especially Mercutio, their fellow victim, who bequeathes his curse to both their houses. His is likewise an ironic end, since he has been as much a satirist of "the new form" and Tybalt's punctilio in duelling "by the book of arithmetic" as of "the numbers that Petrarch flow'd in" and Romeo's affectations of gallantry (II.iv.34, 38; III.i.102). Mercutio's interpretation of dreams, running counter to Romeo's premonitions, is naturalistic, not to say Freudian; Queen Mab operates through fantasies of wish-fulfillment, bringing love to lovers, fees to lawyers and tithe-pigs to parsons; the moral is that desires can be mischievous. In his repartee with Romeo, Mercutio looks forward to their fencing with Tybalt; furthermore he charges the air with bawdy suggestions that—in spite of the limitations of Shakespeare's theater, its lack of actresses and absence of close-ups—love may have something to do with sex, if not with lust, with the physical complementarity of male and female.[9] He is abetted, in that respect, by the malapropistic garrulity of the Nurse,

9. Coleridge's persistent defense of Shakespeare against the charge of gross language does more credit to that critic's high-mindedness than to his discernment. The concentrated ribaldry of the gallants in the street (II.iv) is deliberately contrasted with the previous exchange between the lovers in the orchard.

Angelica, who is naturally bound to Juliet through having
been her wet-nurse, and who has lost the infant daughter
that might have been Juliet's age. Nonetheless, her
crotchety hesitations are contrasted with Juliet's youthful
ardors when the Nurse acts as go-between for Romeo.
His counselor, Friar Lawrence, makes a measured entrance with his sententious couplets on the uses and
abuses of natural properties, the medicinal and poisonous
effects of plants (II.iii.25-6):

> For this, being smelt, with that part cheers each part,
> Being tasted, stays all senses with the heart.

His watchword is "Wisely and slow," yet he contributes to
the grief at the sepulcher by ignoring his own advice,
"They stumble that run fast" (94).[10] When Romeo up-
braids him monosyllabically,

> Thou canst not speak of that thou dost not feel,

it is the age-old dilemma that separates the generations:
Si jeunesse savait . . . , si vieillesse pouvait (III.iii.64). Banished to Mantua, Romeo has illicit recourse to the Apoth-
ecary, whose shop—envisaged with Flemish precision—
unhappily replaces the Friar's cell, and whose poison is
the sinister counterpart of Lawrence's potion.

Against this insistence upon polarity, at every level, the
mutuality of the lovers stands out, the one organic relation amid an overplus of stylized expressions and attitudes. The naturalness of their diction is artfully gained,
as we have noticed, through a running critique of ar-
tificiality. In drawing a curtain over the consummation of
their love, Shakespeare heralds it with a prothalamium

---

10. This is the leading theme of the play, in the interpretation of Brents Stirling, *Unity in Shakespearian Tragedy: The Interplay of Themes and Characters* (New
York, 1956), pp. 10–25.

and follows it with an epithalamium. Juliet's "Gallop apace, you fiery-footed steeds," reversing the Ovidian *lente currite, noctis equi,* is spoken "alone" but in breathless anticipation of a companion (III.ii.1). After she has besought the day to end, the sequel to her solo is the duet in which she begs the night to continue. In the ensuing *débat* of the nightingale and the lark, a refinement upon the antiphonal song of the owl and the cuckoo in *Love's La- bor's Lost,* Romeo more realistically discerns "the herald of the morn" (III.v.6). When Juliet reluctantly agrees, "More light and light it grows," he completes the paradox with a doubly reduplicating line (35, 36):

> More light and light, more dark and dark our woe!

The precariousness of their union, formulated arithmeti- cally by the Friar as "two in one" (II.vi.37), is brought out by the terrible loneliness of Juliet's monologue upon tak- ing the potion (IV.iii.19):

> My dismal scene I needs must act alone.

Her utter singleness, as an only child, is stressed by her father and mourned by her mother (v.46):

> But one, poor one, one poor and loving child.

Tragedy tends to isolate where comedy brings together, to reveal the uniqueness of individuals rather than what they have in common with others. Asking for Romeo's profession of love, Juliet anticipates: "I know thou wilt say, 'Ay' " (II.ii.90). That monosyllable of glad assent was the first she ever spoke, as we know from the Nurse's childish anecdote (I.iii.44). Later, asking the Nurse whether Romeo has been killed, Juliet pauses self-con- sciously over the pun between "Ay" and "I" or "eye" (III.ii.45-51):

> Say thou but ay,
> And that bare vowel I shall poison more
> Than the death-darting eye of cockatrice.
> I am not I, if there be such an ay,
> Or those eyes shut, that makes thee answer ay.
> If he be slain, say ay, or if not, no.
> Brief sounds determine my weal or woe.

Her identification with him is negated by death, conceived as a shut or poisoning eye, which throws the pair back upon their single selves. Each of them dies alone— or, at all events, in the belief that the other lies dead, and without the benefit of a recognition-scene. Juliet, of course, is still alive; but she has already voiced her death-speech in the potion scene. With the dagger, her last words, though richly symbolic, are brief and monosyllabic (V.iii.170):

> This is thy sheath; there rust, and let me die.

The sense of vicissitude is reenacted through various gestures of staging; Romeo and Juliet experience their exaltation *"aloft"* on the upper stage; his descent via the rope is, as she fears, toward the tomb (III.v.56).[11] The antonymous adverbs *up* and *down* figure, with increasing prominence, among the brief sounds that determine Juliet's woe (*e.g.*, V.ii.208-9). The overriding pattern through which she and Romeo have been trying to break—call it Fortune, the stars, or what you will—ends by closing in and breaking them; their private world disappears, and we are left in the social ambience again. Capulet's house has been bustling with preparations for a wedding, the happy ending of comedy. The news of Juliet's death is not yet tragic because it is premature; but it

11. One of the most pertinent discussions of staging is that of Richard Hosley, "The Use of the Upper Stage in *Romeo and Juliet*," *Shakespeare Quarterly*, V, 4 (Autumn, 1954), 371-9.

introduces a peripety which, in reverse, will become the starting point for *Hamlet*.

> All things that we ordained festival
> Turn from their office to black funeral,

the old man cries, and his litany of contraries is not less poignant because he has been so fond of playing the genial host (IV.v.84-90):

> Our instruments to melancholy bells,
> Our wedding cheer to a sad burial feast;
> Our solemn hymns to sullen dirges change;
> Our bridal flowers serve for a buried corse;
> And all things change them to the contrary.

His lamentation, in which he is joined by his wife, the Nurse, and Paris, reasserts the formalities by means of what is virtually an operatic quartet. Thereupon the music becomes explicit, when they leave the stage to the Musicians, who have walked on with the County Paris. Normally these three might play during the *entr'acte,* but Shakespeare has woven them into the dialogue terminating the Fourth Act.[12] Though their art has the power of soothing the passions and thereby redressing grief, as the comic servant Peter reminds them with a quotation from Richard Edwards' lyric *In Commendacion of Musicke,* he persists in his query: "Why 'silver sound'?" (129). Their answers are those of mere hirelings, who can indifferently change their tune from a merry dump to a doleful one, so long as they are paid with coin of the realm. Yet

12. Professor F. T. Bowers reminds me that inter-act music was probably not a regular feature of public performance when *Romeo and Juliet* was first performed. Some early evidence for it has been gathered by T. S. Graves in "The Act-Time in Elizabethan Theatres," *Studies in Philology,* XII, 3 (July, 1915), 120–4—notably contemporary sound cues, written into a copy of the Second Quarto and cited by Malone. But if—as seems likely—such practices were exceptional, then Shakespeare was innovating all the farther.

Peter's riddle touches a deeper chord of correspondence, the interconnection between discord and harmony, between impulse and discipline. "Consort," which can denote a concert or a companionship, can become the fighting word that motivates the unharmonious pricksong of the duellists (III.i.49). The "sweet division" of the lark sounds harsh and out of tune to Juliet, since it proclaims that the lovers must be divided (v.29). Why "silver sound"? Because Romeo, in the orchard, has sworn by the moon (II.ii.108)

> That tips with silver all these fruit-tree tops.

Because Shakespeare, transposing sights and sounds into words, has made us imagine (165-6)

> How silver-sweet sound lovers' tongues by night,
> Like softest music to attending ears!

Falling into musical parlance more or less inevitably, I have ventured to speak of the nightingale-lark interchange as an epithalamium, since it takes place so soon after the bridal pair has been united. It might even more appropriately have been termed an *aubade,* in that it more closely resembles the dawn-songs of the Troubadours, warning the lover to take his reluctant departure from his beloved's bed. That this intimate genre is not peculiar to Provençal culture alone has been monumentally demonstrated in a recent compilation, edited by A. T. Hatto and published under the auspices of UNESCO, which traces and compares examples drawn from some fifty different languages.[13] Thus the expression of sentiments by lovers parting at dawn may be said, in anthropological terms, to be universal. "Love is an admitted emotion"—so declares

---

13. A. T. Hatto (ed.), *Eos: An Enquiry into the Theme of Lovers' Meetings and Partings at Dawn in Poetry* (The Hague, 1965).

an eminent professor of anthropology, Margaret Mead, in a book which bears the all-embracing title *Male and Female*. Yet her subtitle, *A Study of the Sexes in a Changing World,* seems to particularize the implied universal.

> Love is an admitted emotion felt by people who can be visualized as like ourselves, wearing clothes, driving cars, competing with rivals, fighting back depression when rejected, climbing to dizzy heights when accepted by the loved one. Even when the story of *Romeo and Juliet* is read carefully, Romeo and Juliet are seen as very like young Americans, with the feud between the Montagues and the Capulets as just part of the plot. After all, no one knows how Romeo and Juliet did feel. Shakespeare knew very little more than we as he, an English dramatist, wrote about them for a seventeenth-century audience. A knowledge of the past may inform our tongues with lovely words, but they are recognized as including sentiments that are foreign to modern life, where fidelity even after death is regarded as a suspect emotion, hard on one's friends and family, and probably deserving the attentions of a psychiatrist more than those of a poet.[14]

Professor Mead, for an anthropologist, seems curiously incurious about such Italian folkways as the vendetta of blood-feud, which—when perpetrated by the Mafia—still breaks out from time to time among us. Shakespeare, for an undeniably English dramatist, has taken considerable pains to understand and explain an endemic situation to—as only a little knowledge of the past should remind us—his sixteenth-century audience. Young American readers may or may not be aware of the Capulets and the Montagues, but they have probably heard about the Hatfields and the McCoys feuding in the hills of Kentucky or Tennessee. If perchance they have not, they must have seen or heard about the film based on Leonard Bern-

14. Margaret Mead, *Male and Female: A Study of the Sexes in a Changing World* (New York, 1955), p. 37.

stein's jazz operetta, *West Side Story*, a fascinating cross-cultural experiment, closely adapting the mores and motives of Shakespeare's romantic tragedy to the precincts of street fights and juvenile delinquency, and of devotion and bravery as well, among the young Puerto Ricans in upper Manhattan. If the expression of youthful sentiments can be transposed so far, Shakespeare was warranted in his transposition from England to Italy; and coming-of-age may be no less rapturous in Verona than it is in, let us say, Samoa. May I go farther and suggest that, if the problem is to communicate some awareness of that rapture, your poet is likely to prove more helpful in the long run than your psychiatrist?

Falstaff Uncolted

The role of the horse in Elizabethan drama, it would seem, was one of those matters which were left to the imagination of the spectator. There is a certain amount of evidence that smaller animals, like Launce's dog, took an occasional part in theatrical performances.[1] Hobby-horses were probably not altogether forgotten, in spite of Moth's—and Hamlet's—lament.[2] And Philip Henslowe's property-lists even include a suggestive reference to "j great horse with his leages."[3] But the posting of messengers, the assembling of mounted troops, the swift equestrian movement from place to place and scene to scene—these characteristic incidents could not be represented on the stage; they invariably happen behind the

1. Louis B. Wright, "Animal Actors on the English Stage before 1642," *PMLA* (September, 1927), XLIII, 3, 656–9.
2. E. K. Chambers, *The Elizabethan Stage* (Oxford, 1923), I, 372.
3. *Henslowe's Diary*, ed. R. A. Foakes and R. T. Rickert (Cambridge, 1961), p. 320.

Published in *Modern Language Notes*, LXI, 5 (May, 1946).

scenes and are relayed to the audience by the usual means. Pushing the problem toward negative conclusions, W. J. Lawrence instanced at least a dozen plays in which the playwright takes pains to account for the absence of horses, when their presence would naturally be required by dramatic realism.[4] The best-known instance occurs in *Macbeth* (III.iii), where Banquo and Fleance leave their mounts offstage and walk into the murderer's ambush.[5] Lawrence's point receives *a fortiori* support from the subsequent studies of G. F. Reynolds, who concludes that real horses are "conspicuously avoided" in the otherwise spectacular repertory of the Red Bull playhouse.[6] Professor Reynolds points to an analogous situation in *A Woman Killed with Kindness* (V.iii), where Mistress Frankford, accompanied by her coachman, makes a pedestrian entrance and exit, while her coach is presumably waiting in the wings. In vain we search for a clear example of an actor riding horseback onstage.[7] On the other hand, we find so many characters walking on with the announcement that they have just dismounted, or walking off with the de-

---

4. W. J. Lawrence, *Pre-Restoration Stage Studies* (Cambridge, Massachusetts, 1927), pp. 270–6.

5. The assumption that Macbeth made his first entrance by "riding" onstage, originally suggested by the problematic account of Simon Forman and recently revived, has definitively been set at rest by Leah Scragg in "Macbeth on Horseback," *Shakespeare Survey*, 26 (Cambridge, 1973), pp. 84–6.

6. G. F. Reynolds, *The Staging of Elizabethan Plays at the Red Bull Theater, 1605–1625* (New York, 1940), p. 87.

7. Kyd's *Solyman and Perseda*, I.iii, is not really an exception, since the "courser" of the braggart soldier Basilisco is specified in the stage directions as a mule. The exception that proves the rule is the pre-Shakespearean First Part of *Richard II*, with its business called for by the stage-direction: "(Enter a spruce Courtier on Horseback)." This is characterized as a "stunt" by the modern editor, who goes on to comment: "I have no idea whether there can have been anything less than a real horse." See A. P. Rossiter (ed.), *Woodstock: A Moral History* (London, 1946), pp. 129, 223.

clared intention of mounting a steed, that we are justified in recognizing the observance of a convention.

In this, as in so many other conventions, Shakespeare is surprisingly consistent. Thus, in *Titus Andronicus* (II.iii.56, 75, 76), he is careful to explain that the queen and huntress Tamora has been "unfurnish'd," "sequest'red," and "dismounted," while the atmosphere of hunting is produced by sound effects. While the noise of battle is conventionally signalized by an alarum-bell, the deployment of armies may be reduced to a few excursions of armed supernumeraries; but occasionally, as in the Second Part of *Henry VI* (V.ii.8), there is some suggestion that the cavalry was expected and failed to show up: "What, all afoot?" The unhorsing of Troilus, the presentation of his horse to Cressida, and the continuation of his struggle with Diomedes on foot are integrated by the mock-heroic plot of *Troilus and Cressida* (V.v.1-2; vi.6-7), though only the latter episode is directly presented. Whatever is lacking on the stage and in the business can be supplied, according to Elizabethan practice, by drawing upon the expressive resources of the language. Shakespeare's imagery is so pervaded with terms of horsemanship, and his descriptive passages are such a vivid substitute for the actual appearance of horses, that we seldom miss the animals themselves.[8] Petruchio's nag cuts a striking figure in *The Taming of the Shrew* (III.ii.49-64), not because he actually appears, but because Biondello describes him. In *Antony and Cleopatra* (I.v.20-4), Enobar-

8. See Caroline F. E. Spurgeon, *Shakespeare's Imagery and What It Tells Us* (New York, 1936), pp. 108, 109. If this work tends to connect Shakespeare's writing rather too intimately with his conjectured biography, the opposite tendency is implicit in Carleton Brown's learned article, "Shakespeare and the Horse," *The Library* (April, 1912), Third Series, X, 3, 152–80, which assumes that Shakespeare was dependent on classical and medieval sources for his depiction of that strange beast.

bus' description of Cleopatra on her barge has its counterpart in her own description of Antony on horseback.
Perhaps this device is most poignantly employed in *Richard II* (V.v.76-94) when a former groom tells the deposed
sovereign how Bolingbroke rode to his coronation on
Richard's favorite steed, roan Barbary.[9] Defending the
conventions of the theater against the attacks of such realists as Ben Jonson, the prologue to *Henry V* makes an
explicit bid for the imaginative cooperation of the audience (26-9): [10]

> Think, when we talk of horses, that you see them
> Printing their proud hoofs i' th' receiving earth;
> For 'tis your thoughts that now must deck our kings,
> Carry them here and there . . .

If the Elizabethan drama had been as strictly conven-
tionalized as—let us say—the Chinese, no apologies
would have been necessary. But the growing demands of
realism made the dramatists peculiarly conscious of the
differences between everyday life and theatrical usage.[11]
The increasing self-consciousness of their medium is
amply attested by parodies, burlesques, and choruses. A

---

9. Though "neighing coursers" are mentioned by the younger Mowbray, retrospectively describing the tournament at Coventry in *2 Henry IV* (IV.i.119),
these are conspicuous by their absence from Shakespeare's direct presentation
of the scene (*Richard II,* I.iii). Perhaps it should be added, as a comment upon
our changing sense of convention, that John Barton introduced hobby-horses
into his recent Stratford production of that play (and that horses are currently
being mimed by actors in Peter Shaffer's *Equus*). Tournaments are side-
stepped by being held offstage in *The Two Noble Kinsmen* (V.iii) and between the
scenes in *Pericles* (II.ii,iii).

10. Jonson's principal attack, his prologue to the revised version of *Every Man
in His Humour,* was probably written some years later than *Henry V;* but it
echoes the earlier strictures of Sidney and others, as has been shown by J. E.
Spingarn (ed.), *Critical Essays of the Seventeenth Century* (Oxford, 1908), I, xii–xv.

11. On the interplay between realism and convention, see the reply to William
Archer by T. S. Eliot, *Selected Essays* (New York, 1932), pp. 91–9.

convention was not tacitly accepted and rigidly enforced; it was continually rationalized and played upon. Because feminine roles were taken by boys, it has often been noted, the heroine acquired the habit of disguising herself in masculine attire, and this ambiguity became the dominant theme of such plays as Lyly's *Galathea,* Shakespeare's *Twelfth Night,* and Jonson's *Epicene.* Similarly, the very lack of horses becomes a kind of *leitmotif.* If they were unavailable, for purposes of drawing a chariot across the stage, then Tamburlaine's famous chariot drawn by kings becomes a particularly ingenious piece of stagecraft. Again, in *Dr. Faustus,* Marlowe's hero prefers walking to riding; his illusory horse, ridden into a pond, turns out to be a bottle (or bundle) of hay; and the Horse-courser re-enters, "all wet," to describe that *dénouement.* [12] Would it be far-fetched to discern an ironic recurrence of this theme, another parallel between plot and comic underplot, in Faustus' last appeal to the Ovidian horses of the night? [13] Certainly these considerations lend a note of fatalistic irony to the iterated cry of *Richard III* (V.iv.7, 13): "A horse, a horse! my kingdom for a horse!" And what proves to be a final tragic twist, in Richard's case, is a running comic gag for Falstaff. That the fat knight should be constantly dismounted, that "this horseback-breaker" should never be seen on horseback, that his crew of would-be highwaymen should perforce become "foot land-rakers," in Gadshill's phrase—this is not the least of the contradictions that make up his char-

---

12. C. F. Tucker Brooke (ed.), *The Works of Christopher Marlowe,* (Oxford, 1910), ll. 1112-4, 1149–62.

13. We may note in passing, since it heightens the contrast between Shakespeare's imagery and Marlowe's, that Juliet evokes the horses of the day. Whereas Faustus wants the night lengthened, she wants the day shortened (*Romeo and Juliet,* III.ii.1): "Gallop apace, you fiery-footed steeds . . ."

acter (*1 Henry IV*, II.iv.242; II.i. 79). Viewed in this light, the Prince's words acquire a new emphasis: Falstaff "lards the lean earth as he *walks* along" (II.ii.109).[14]

A casual glance at a concordance confirms the impression that horses figure more prominently in the First Part of *Henry IV* than in any other Shakespearean play. On the historical level they are associated with Hotspur, whose adopted name suggests his chivalric significance. In his absent-minded colloquy with his wife, he keeps reverting to his roan horse (II.iii); this obsession is parodied by Prince Hal in the following scene (II.iv.101-11); and Falstaff, a few moments later, pays his respects to the horsemanship of the Douglas (343-56). At the climax, when the Prince reforms, dons armor, and challenges his rival, his emergence is the subject of a glowing equestrian portrait by Sir Richard Vernon (IV.i.104-10). But the two Harries are not destined to meet "hot horse to horse" (122-3); the horses are "journey-bated" on one side and outnumbered on the other (IV.iii.25-9); and the heroes, as always, fight it out on the ground in hand-to-hand combat. Meanwhile the high-mettled ideals of chivalry have been overtaken by a more pedestrian conception of honor, and it is Falstaff who drags Hotspur's body away. The Prince and Poins have set the pace of the comic underplot by hiding Falstaff's horse behind a hedge (II.ii.70-1).[15] His subsequent discomforts, as he plods along the highway, stands at the foot of Gadshill, and fretfully waits for the dismounted travelers to walk down, form a sequence of

14. Here the pedestrian motif is associated with the numerous metaphors of cookery that hover about Falstaff's person. Cf. Spurgeon, *op. cit.,* p. 122.

15. In the earlier play, *The Famous Victories of Henry V,* ed. J. S. Farmer (Tudor Facsimile Texts, 1913, A3), the travelers identify the horses of the Prince and Sir John Oldcastle. In Shakespeare's play (I.ii.198, 199), the Prince and Poins agree to hide their own horses in a wood.

jests on the inexhaustible topics of his cumbrous bulk and his debatable courage.[16] Words like "foot" and "afoot" come in for a good deal of byplay (12, 36, 47); the highwayman's cry of "Stand!" is given a painful new meaning (48-9). When the Prince indignantly refuses to play the ostler and restore Falstaff's horse, Falstaff complains that he has been cheated, or "colted," and the Prince's retort sums up the situation: "Thou liest, thou art not colted, thou art uncolted" (37-9). Challenged for his incomprehensible lies in the tavern scene (II.iv.225), or meditating remorsefully on the morning after (III.iii.11), Falstaff likens himself to a horse, "a brewer's horse." The battle of Shrewsbury repeats the practical joke of Gadshill on a grand scale by providing him with "a charge of foot" (III.iii.186). He accepts with tragicomic resignation: "I would it had been of horse" (187).

The sequel begins with a rush of messengers, posting the roads with contradictory reports. It is not surprising to hear that Falstaff, on his return to London in the Second Part of *Henry IV* (I.ii.50-3), has sent Bardolph to Smithfield to buy him a horse. The equine humors continue as he quibbles with Mistress Quickly about riding the mare (II.i.79), and as Poins conjectures that Doll Tearsheet must be "some road" (II.ii.166). The entrance of Pistol, that inveterate playgoer, brings a garbled echo from Marlowe: Tamburlaine's pampered jades of Asia are now imagined, a decade after they first crossed the stage, trotting along dejectedly beside "packhorses" and

16. J. Dover Wilson, *The Fortunes of Falstaff* (New York, 1944), pp. 93–4, makes this acute and sympathetic comment: "The appeal to our laughter is made in the name of his helplessness, bodily and spiritual. We are asked to contemplate him staggering along life's way, with his broken wind, although eight yards of its uneven ground is to him what a pilgrimage of threescore and ten miles would be to anyone else; and which villain among us is stony-hearted enough to turn a deaf ear, sheer blarney as we know it all to be?"

"Galloway nags" (II.iv.163, 191). When the alarum strikes up again, Falstaff takes to the road, continuing his adventures with the infantry. This time, in Justice Shallow's orchard, they march and drill before our eyes (III.ii.257-71). When Pistol brings the news of the King's death and the Prince's accession, Falstaff rides all night to get from Gloucestershire to Westminster (V.iii.13), and there encounters his greatest anticlimax. To complete his humiliation, in *The Merry Wives of Windsor* (IV.v.69-70), he is triply uncolted: his horses are pawned to mine host of the Garter, who in turn is cheated by "three German devils, three Doctor Faustuses." Nemesis has decreed, it seems, that knighthood should go horseless. It is not merely Shakespeare's resourcefulness in reconciling us to this fate, throughout his Falstaffian trilogy, that stays with us, however; it is not only his ability to create a mock-hero who combines the qualities of Rosinante with those of Don Quixote and Sancho Panza. It is his success in achieving, within the limitations of drama, all the range and mobility of picaresque fiction. The same rough magic that could conjure up a battlefield, a dizzying cliff, or another part of the forest can turn the stage into a highroad: the hedges, the orchards, the tavern at Sutton Colfield, the red-nosed innkeeper of Daventry, poor Robin Ostler who died when the price of oats rose, the sounds and sights and smells of a Rochester innyard. The prospect from Gadshill looks in one direction toward Chaucer's pilgrims, and in the other toward the coaching days of Dickens.

The figure of a horseless knight is, of course, a self-contradictory recognition that knighthood no longer is in flower, that the days of chivalry—of the *chevaleresque*—are over, that the cavalry has been outmanoeuvered by the artillery. This would be the message of Cervantes just a few years afterward, whose anti-hero would be unseated again and again. Shakespeare brings the implication home, and salutes the murderous invention that made knightly prowess obsolete, in Falstaff's cynical character-ization of his regiment as "food for powder" (IV.ii.66). These ragged foot-soldiers, conscripts unable to buy themselves off, are consequently marked to be victims of gunpowder at Shrewsbury. Though it is characteristically tinged with a gastronomical metaphor, Falstaff's phrase is a sinister one, which has had an interesting history of its own. It was literally translated as *Futter für Pulver* in the standard German version of A. W. Schlegel. That in turn evoked a freer but less ambiguous echo in the term *Kan-onenfutter,* which seems to have first been used in print by the Polish cosmopolite Adam Gurovsky, writing about still another country, Belgium, in 1845.[17] It has been Gurovsky's grimly ironic locution which was retranslated into English as "cannon-fodder," the familiar compound designating expendable troops whenever the pros and contras of warfare are discussed. Falstaff's absolute an-tithesis, Henry Percy, the truly quixotic Hotspur, fighting for a losing cause with obsolescent weapons, is fated to die on the battlefield, exclaiming with tragic irony,

> No, Percy, thou art dust,
> And food for—

Here he breaks off, and it is his victorious opponent, Prince Hal, who completes the culinary death-speech with a macabre tribute (V.iv.85-7):

17. This curious character, hardly remembered today, is worth at least a foot-note by himself. Count Gurovsky was a political exile and radical journalist who, after turbulent years in Russia, Germany, and France, emigrated to the United States, where he lectured on Roman law at Harvard, wrote a first-hand book about the Civil War, and ended as a translator in the State Department. In Washington he was known as "President Lincoln's mad Pole."

> For worms, brave Percy. Fare thee well,
> great heart!

In the French version of *Henry IV* by François-Victor Hugo (son of the poet), Falstaff's Germanized phrase has its close equivalent: *chair à canon*. This is the expression that springs to the compassionate lips of Tolstoy's Prince Andrei, when he views the splashing and shivering bodies of his Russian soldiers in *War and Peace*. War and peace indeed! Shakespeare has here compressed these eternally conflicting values into an explosive word or two which have humanely reechoed across the world's battle-lines.

The Underplot of
Twelfth Night

The kind of comedy that was practiced by Shakespeare has repeatedly challenged definition. Though his last comedies have been retrospectively classified as romances, most of their components are equally characteristic of his earlier ones: love, adventure, coincidence, recognition, and occasional pathos. The problem is not simplified by the circumstance that his greatest comic character, Falstaff, was far more impressive in two histories than he is in *The Merry Wives of Windsor*. Traditional definitions of the comic somehow fail to hit the Shakespearean mark, perhaps because they tend to emphasize the spectatorial attitude of ridicule. Shakespeare's attitude is more participatory; its emphasis falls upon playfulness, man at play, the esthetic principle that Johan Huizinga has so brilliantly illuminated in his historico-cultural study, *Homo Ludens*. Whereas we may laugh at Ben Jonson's characters, we generally laugh with Shakespeare's; indeed, if we

---

Contributed to *De Shakespeare à T. S. Eliot: Mélanges offerts à Henri Fluchère*, ed. M. J. Durry, Robert Ellrodt, and M. T. Jones-Davies (Paris: Librairie Marcel Didier, 1975).

begin by laughing at Falstaff or the clowns, we end by laughing with them at ourselves; semantically speaking, they are therefore not ridiculous but ludicrous. The critical approach that best succeeds in catching this spirit, it would seem to me, is that of C. L. Barber in *Shakespeare's Festive Comedy*. That the same approach can be applied to Plautus, as Erich Segal has convincingly demonstrated in his book *Roman Laughter*, suggests that "the Saturnalian pattern" may well be universal. *Twelfth Night* very appropriately marks the culmination of Professor Barber's argument. Since the play is so rich and the argument so fertile, I am tempted to add a few notes here, encouraged by his gracious recollection that our personal dialogue on comedy has extended over many years.

Any speculation about *Twelfth Night* might start with its alternative title, which has no counterpart among the other plays in the First Folio. The subtitle *What You Will* echoes the common and casual phrase that Olivia uses at one point in addressing Malvolio (I.v.109); it would later be used as a title by John Marston; and the German version is simply entitled *Was ihn wollt*. It is not equivalent to *As You Like It,* Bernard Shaw would argue; the latter means "this is the sort of play you would like"; the former means "it doesn't really matter what you call this play." To designate it by the seasonal dating would have touched off some associations, especially since *Twelfth Night* signalized the grand finale to the Christmas entertainment at Queen Elizabeth's court, and sometimes featured a performance by Shakespeare's company. But the English term seems relatively vague, when contrasted with the overtones of the French and Italian translations. *La Nuit des Rois* almost seems to promise a visitation of the Magi; Shakespeare anticlimatically gives us, instead, the iconological joke about "We Three" and a clownish snatch of song from Sir Toby, "Three merry men be we" (II.iii.17, 76-7). *La Notte dell'Epifania* may also hold theological—or at least, in Joycean terms, psychological—connotations. Shakespeare merely seems concerned to promise his audience a pleasant surprise by evoking a winter holiday, even as he did with the opposite season in *A Midsummer Night's Dream*. Festivals are the matrices of drama, after all, and that "holiday humor" in which the transvested Rosalind invites Orlando to rehearse his wooing sets the prevalent mood for Shakespearean comedy (*As You Like It,* IV.i.69).

Some of Shakespeare's other comedies have titles so broadly general that they could be interchanged without much loss of meaning: *The Comedy of Errors, Much Ado About Nothing, All's Well That Ends Well. Twelfth Night,* which has figured more prominently in the repertory than most of the others, has frequently been cited by concrete reference to its most memorable characterization. Thus Charles I entitled it "Malvolio" in his inscribed copy of the Second Folio, and a court production for James I was entered into the records under that name. As it happens, five of the other parts in the play are actually longer than Malvolio's: in order of length, Sir Toby's, Viola's, Olivia's, Feste's, and even Sir Andrew's. Yet stage history has gradually made it clear that, with slightly less than ten per cent of the lines, this has come to be regarded as the stellar role. The other roles I have listed offer varied opportunities to actors and actresses, and Viola's embodies the special attraction of the hoydenish heroine in tights. That advantage is somewhat lessened by the complication of having to be passed off as identical with her unexpected twin brother Sebastian. Hence the plot "wants credibility," as Dr. Johnson put it, though our incredulity is all but disarmed by the Pirandellian comment of Fabian: "If this were play'd upon a stage now, I could condemn it as an improbable fiction" (III.iv.127-8). Henry Irving, Herbert Beerbohm Tree, and many other stars have absurdly twinkled in the part of Malvolio. There may be a latent significance in the fact that the leading actor of the Restoration, Thomas Betterton, played the adversary role of Sir Toby Belch.

The impression registered in the diary of John Manningham, who had attended a performance at the Middle Temple in 1602, is particularly significant:

> At our feast wee had a play called "Twelue Night, or What You Will", much like the Commedy of Errores, or Menechmi in Plautus, but most like and neere to that in Italian called *Inganni*. A good practise in it to make the Steward beleeve his Lady widdowe was in love with him, by counterfeyting a letter as from his Lady in generall termes, telling him what shee liked best in him, and prescribing his gesture in smiling, his aparaile, &c., and then when he came to practise making him beleeue they tooke him to be mad.

It is true that Shakespeare's adaptation from Plautus had likewise dealt with a pair of twins divided by shipwreck and reunited after the *contretemps* of mistaken identity. Manningham might also have mentioned *The Two Gentlemen of Verona,* where the heroine disguises herself as a page so that she may serve the man she loves. And Manningham's Italian cross-reference has led the source-hunters to various plays and *novelle* which are quite analogous to the main plot. But the episode he singles out for praise does not figure in any of them. Malvolio, with no established source behind him, must be reckoned as one of Shakespeare's originals. Efforts to discern an actual prototype in the court gossip about Sir William Knollys, who was Comptroller to Her Majesty's Household, have carried little conviction. Nor is there much topical impli-

cation in Maria's qualified epithet, "a kind of puritan,"
which she herself immediately rejects in favor of "time-
pleaser" and "affectioned ass" (II.iii.140, 148). There is
not very much in common between Jonson's Ananias or
Zeal-of-the-Land Busy and this Italianate upstart who
aspires to "be proud" and "read politic authors"
(II.v.161). He is undoubtedly puritanical in the psychological sense; as Professor Barber perceptively comments,
"he is like a Puritan because he is hostile to holiday."
William Archer considered him more of a Philistine than
a Puritan, more to be approached as a sequence of "comic
effects" than as "a consistent, closely-observed type," and
therefore somewhat opaquely presented as a personality.
"He has no sense of humour," so Archer summed it up,
"—that is the head and front of his offending."

In a formal as well as a functional manner, he is thus
an intruder into the play. Shakespeare's plot, as its forerunners had shown, could have got along without him.
Olivia already had two suitors to be rejected, plus the
masculine twin who was ready to replace his sister as the
object of Olivia's choice. The lovesick Duke Orsino, after
the fiasco of his vicarious courtship, could submit no less
quickly and rather more gracefully than she to this sudden change of partners. The odd-man-out, Sir Andrew,
might have weakly borne the full onus of the underplot,
insofar as it burlesques the main plot and has its *agon* in
the reluctant duel. Music sets the keynote at the beginning, at the conclusion, and throughout. Illyria would almost seem to be the idyllic setting for an operetta. Yet,
despite the roistering snorts of melody and the high-kick-
ing capers of the roisterers, the cadence often has a dying
fall. "O mistress mine" is balanced against "Come away,
death," and the singer Feste—whom G. L. Kittredge
called "the merriest of Shakespeare's fools"—shares his

concluding refrain with the tragic Fool of *King Lear:* "For the rain it raineth every day" (II.iii.39ff; iv.51ff.; V.i.392; cf. *King Lear,* III.ii.77). Even in the sunniest of Shakespeare's comedies, there are shadows now and then, and it is worth remembering that *Twelfth Night* was probably conceived in the same year as *Hamlet.* The aura of melancholy emanates from Olivia's household, but it extends to Orsino's palace because of his unwelcome suit. Widow-like, the veiled Olivia mourns her dead brother; Viola, the go-between, though she depicts herself as the mourning figure of "Patience on a monument," cherishes justified hopes for her own brother lost at sea (II.iv.114).

Together, these adventurous siblings are destined to dispel the shade that has overcast the Illyrian horizon. Olivia's house of mourning should have been, and will again become, a house of mirth—to reverse the language of Ecclesiastes. Toward that end her kinsman, Sir Toby Belch, and his gregarious crew of what Malvolio will term "the lighter people" have been doing their damnedest to turn the kitchen into a tavern and to obliterate the differences between night and day (V.i.339). Over their eructations the hard-drinking Sir Toby fitly presides as a sort of miniature Falstaff, the local agent of revelry and misrule. "Th'art a scholar," he tells his eager gull Sir Andrew Aguecheek, the carpet knight whose linguistic accomplishments are as limited as his skills at fencing and dancing, "Let us therefore eat and drink" (II.iii.13–4). Sir Andrew's surname bespeaks his pallid face and quivering figure; all his claims to wit and gallantry and bravado only exist in order to be put down. When Feste asks "Would you have a love-song, or a song of good life?" and Toby responds, "A love-song, a love-song," Andrew gives himself away by blurting out, "Ay, ay, I care not for good life" (35-8). Akin to Justice Shallow and Master

Slender, he is the ancestor of those witless foplings who will strive so vainly to cut a caper in Restoration comedy. And yet this ninny is not without his touch of Shakespearean poignance. When his mentor Toby—who is, if nothing else, a genuine *bon vivant*—complacently avows himself to be adored by Maria, Andrew sighs, "I was adored once too" (181). Behind that sigh lies some namby-pamby case-history, about which we are relieved to hear no more.

Maria, the classic soubrette, is the most effectual of the plotters against Malvolio, and her recompense for forging the letter is marriage with Sir Toby. This provides a comic parallel for the two romantic betrothals, and it is announced by Fabian in the absence of the less-than-joyful couple, Toby having been discomfited along with Andrew by Sebastian. Since Andrew has essentially been a figure of fun, not a funster, he is gradually supplanted among the merrymakers by Fabian. It is Fabian who faces Olivia in the final disentanglement, backed by the festive exultations of the fool. Feste's maxim—"Better a witty fool than a foolish wit"—underlines the implicit contrast between himself and Andrew (I.v.36). One of the jester's assumed *personae* is that of the Vice, the principal mischief-maker in the old-fashioned morality plays (IV.ii.124). As "an allow'd fool," he has the privilege of raillery, which we hear that Olivia's father "took much delight in" (I.v.94; II.iv.12). Her father's death, which cannot have happened very long before, has presumably added to her brother's in deepening the gloom of the abode where she now finds herself mistress. Shakespeare has gone out of his way to darken the background of the conventional situation among the lovers, possibly reflecting the widespread preoccupation with the theme of melancholia during the early years of the seventeenth century. If so, his ultimate concern was to lift the clouds, to brighten the effect of the picture as a whole by the deft use of *chiaroscuro*, to heighten the triumph of the comic spirit by presenting it under attack. And, of course, with the rise of Puritanism, it was increasingly subject to attackers.

Such considerations may help to explain why Shakespeare went even farther by introducing the character of Malvolio—a superimposition so marked that one of the commentators, F. G. Fleay, has argued that the two plots are separable and may have been composed at different times. That seems too mechanical an inference, since Shakespeare has taken pains to unify them; since Olivia is "addicted to a melancholy," it follows that she should employ a majordomo who is "sad and civil," as she says, "And suits well for a servant with my fortunes" (II.v.202; III.iv.5-6). Though she tolerates Feste, her first impulse is to dismiss him from her company. His response is both a catechism and a syllogism, demonstrating that she should not mourn because her brother is better off in heaven and proving the fool's dialectical point that his interlocutor must be still more foolish than he: "Take away the fool, gentlemen" (I.v.71-2). She is mildly cheered by the nimbleness of the repartee; but Malvolio is distinctly not amused; and his hostile and humorless reaction is our introduction to him. Gleefully and ironically recalling this exchange, Feste will reveal the natural antipathy that was bound to operate between himself and Malvolio: " 'Madam, why laugh you at such a barren rascal? An you smile not, he's gagg'd.' And thus the whirligig of time brings in his revenges" (V.i.374-7). Malvolio and Feste are brought together and kept at odds by a certain complementarity, like that between the melancholy Jaques and the festive Touchstone in *As You Like It* or the clowns and

the "humorous men" of Jonson and Marston. The pretensions of the Alazon are thus laid open to the exposures of the Eiron.

The issue is sharply drawn by Sir Toby's entrance
speech: "What a plague means my niece to take the death
of her brother thus? I am sure care's an enemy to life"
(I.iii.1–2). As a master of the revels, he and his fellow
revelers embody the forces of life, on the one hand. On
the other, the interloping Malvolio represents the force
of care, which has usurped a temporary control over
once-carefree Illyria. It is not for nothing that his name
signifies "ill-wisher." He is the perennial spoilsport, fighting an aggressive rearguard action against a crapulous
playboy and his Bacchanalian cohorts. As Olivia's steward, Malvolio's functions are more than ceremonial; he
can not only cut off the daily bounties of existence; he
can threaten, and he does, to expel the incumbent devo-
tees of good living. After Toby's rhetorical question on
behalf of cakes and ale, seconded by Feste's plea for
ginger, their prodigal levity takes the offensive against his
false dignity. By a convention which is not less amusing
because it is artificial, the practical jokers overhear—and
react to—the soliloquy expressing Malvolio's fantasies and
delusions of grandeur: "To be Count Malvolio! . ."
(II.v.35). It brings home the self-love and the ambition to
regulate the lives of others that they have resented all
along. And it plays into the trap that Maria has baited,
the letter that he is obliging enough to read aloud. To act
out its malevolent instructions is to betray his solemn and
pompous nature. Not only must this non-laugher—this
agelast, as Meredith would classify him—doff his somber
black for yellow stockings and cross-garters, but he must
force his atrabilious features into an unremitting smile.

The romance of the main plot is ordered, or disordered, by the workings of chance: Viola has been saved "perchance," and so may Sebastian be (I.ii.6, 7). The satire of the underplot is managed by human contrivance, which motivates the duel and fabricates the letter. Malvolio ascribes his prospective elevation to a wise providence ("it is Jove's doing"), but we know that it is a hoax on the part of Maria and her tosspot companions (III.iv.74-5). He is thereby prompted to strut through his grand scene of *hubris*, all the more ironic in its deliberate reduction of self-importance to silliness. Instead of having greatness thrust upon him, he is thereupon thrust down into a dark room, where he is bound and treated like a madman—like the Ephesian Antipholus in *The Comedy of Errors*, whose questioners look for symptoms of derangement in his answers. Malvolio's most pertinacious visitor and inquisitor is Feste, who has thrown himself into the *persona* of the neighboring curate Sir Topas. When the prisoner complains that the house is dark as hell, the pseudo-curate replies in Feste's vein of Rabelaisian nonsense: "Why, it hath bay windows transparent as barricadoes, and the clerestories toward the south north are as lustrous as ebony; and yet complainest thou of obstruction" (IV.ii.36-9). At the height of his vainglory, Malvolio has admitted that his sartorial alteration had caused "some obstruction in the blood"; but this was nothing, if the result pleased Olivia; and to her inquiry about the state of his health he has answered, "Not black in my mind, though yellow in my legs" (III.iv.21, 26-7). The trouble was that so black a mind could never have become accustomed to bright colors.

It is therefore fitting that he be plunged into literal darkness, although Feste's paradoxes seem to suggest that brightness may have something to do with the eye of the beholder. Maria had begun by requesting Sir Toby to "confine" himself "within the modest limits of order," and he had blustered back with a pun: "Confine? I'll confine myself no finer than I am" (I.iii.8-11). When we see Malvolio confined, we may be weak enough to feel sorry for him; Charles Lamb, with Romantic perversity, has even worked up "a kind of tragic interest"; and some of those leading actors who have appeared in the part have made the most of that potentiality. However, though Shakespeare's laughingstocks have a way of enlisting our sympathies, though we may be torn by Prince Hal's repudiation of Falstaff, though Shylock and Jaques may take with them some measure of respect when they make their solitary departures, we should be glad to get rid of Malvolio. Poetic justice prevails in comedy if not in tragedy, and it requires that he be finally "baffled" (V.i.369). Olivia can charitably speak, as his patron, of his having been "notoriously abused" (379). But his parting vow of revenge has been neutralized by Fabian's wish that "sportful malice"—a combination of the ludicrous and the ridiculous—"May rather pluck on laughter than revenge" (365-6). Nor, having witnessed his threat of expulsion to Sir Toby and his crew, should we repine at seeing this gloomy interloper expelled. As a sycophant, a social climber, and an officious snob, he well deserves to be put back in his place—or, as Jonson would have it, in his humor, for Malvolio seems to have a Jonsonian rather than a Shakespearean temperament.

What we have been watching is a reenactment of a timeless ritual, whose theatrical manifestation takes the obvious form of the villain foiled, and whose deeper roots in folklore go back to the scapegoat cast into the outer darkness. The business of baiting him is not a sadistic gesture but a cathartic impulse of *Schadenfreude:* an affirmation of Life against Care, if we allow Sir Toby to lay down the terms of our allegory. We could point to an illustration so rich in detail and so panoramic in design that it might prove distracting, if it were not so sharply focused on the conflict before us, Pieter Breughel's *Battle between Carnival and Lent.* There the jolly corpulent personification of *Mardi Gras,* astride a cask of wine and armed with a spit impaling a roasted pig, jousts against a grim penitential hag carted by a monk and a nun, and flourishing a paddle replete with two herrings. Beggars and buffoons and many others, the highly variegated proponents of revelry and of self-mortification, intermingle in the teeming crowd. Which of the antagonists will gain the upper hand? Each of them, in due season. J. G. Frazer has instanced many analogues for the observance, both in the Burial of the Carnival and in the mock-sacrifice of Jack o' Lent. Shakespeare loaded his dice on the side of carnival, in that hungover hanger-on, Sir Toby, as against the lenten Malvolio, that prince of wet-blankets. But Shakespeare was writing a comedy—and, what is more, a comedy written in defense of the comic spirit. He could commit himself, in this case, to the wisdom of folly and to the ultimate foolishness of the conventional wisdom. But, in his dramaturgy, he was moving onward to care, to death, to mourning, and toward tragedy.

Othello
and the Motive-Hunters

Coleridge is justly famed for posing problems that brook no clear-cut solution, and this may well be one of them. He never set a hare for more critics to chase, or did more to sponsor the casuistic approach to Shakespeare's characters, than when he made his alliterative comment on Iago's first soliloquy: "the motive-hunting of motiveless malignity—how awful!" To be sure, it was Iago who brought the pack down on himself, from the moment he uttered his last defiance (V.ii.303-4):

> Demand me nothing; what you know, you know.
> From this time forth I never will speak word.

Criticism was bound to accept that challenge and to fill in that silence with words, words which have racked Iago as exhaustively as those cunning tortures to which he is condemned by Lodovico. Yet it cannot be said that Iago has

---

Delivered at a meeting of the Modern Language Association (English Section I) at Washington on December 27, 1962; published in the *Centennial Review,* VIII, 1 (Winter, 1964).

had no chance to speak for himself; he has spoken, line for line, more volubly than anyone else in the play. Though he completely deceives Othello and Cassio, still he is partly sincere with Roderigo and Emilia, and there would be no point to all his soliloquizing if he were deceiving himself. It is not for nothing that he swears by Janus; for his intimate face is quite different from, and much more complex than, his mask of sincerity. The admissions he makes to himself, of course, are not lacking but overabounding in motives. Wherefore the super-subtle commentators have been stimulated to look far beyond them, just as the abundance regarding Shakespeare's matter-of-fact biography has incited the anti-Stratfordians to seek a mythical author. Motive, whether it be provocation or pretext, has become as much of a sticking-point for *Othello* as delay is in the discussion of *Hamlet*.

Now the opportunist who has missed his opportunity, the tough-minded soldier of fortune whose fortunes have turned against him and who has therefore turned malcontent, ready to put into action all the uninhibited resources of his embittered cynicism—we recognize him in plays by Marston and Webster and others, indeed in many competitive situations of life. When someone aspires so desperately to second place and is relegated to third, rightly or wrongly that rejection can become a ranking grievance against the incumbents of second and first place. There is surely a kernel of truth in Emilia's surmise:

> I will be hang'd if some eternal villain,
> Some busy and insinuating rogue,
> Some cogging, cozening slave, to get some office,
> Have not devis'd this slander. I'll be hang'd else.

Otherwise there would be no irony in Iago's hypocritical response (IV.ii,130-4):

> Fie, there is no such man; it is impossible.

His lie about Cassio and Desdemona is deeply grounded in his own vindictive suspicion of Emilia—wife for wife—with both Othello and Cassio. One name comes to his lips as readily as the other, for he is totally promiscuous in his suspicions. That there are no grounds for them whatsoever is a salient fact about his mind. In his consistent low-mindedness, he is just as suspicious of everybody as the high-minded Othello is unsuspecting. None of the *dramatis personae* could be low-minded enough to see through Iago, though a rough sketch of his character might have been adumbrated by Cornwall in *King Lear,* where it signally fails to apply to Kent (II,ii.95-103):

> This is some fellow
> Who, having been prais'd for bluntness, doth affect
> A saucy roughness, and constrains the garb
> Quite from his nature. He cannot flatter, he,
> An honest mind and plain, he must speak truth! . . .
> These kind of knaves I know, which in this plainness
> Harbor more craft and more corrupter ends
> Than twenty silly-ducking observants. . . .

Hypocrites of the drama are usually, like Angelo or Tartuffe, pretenders to virtue who succumb to vice, attempt to brazen it out, and are ultimately exposed. Iago seems unique among them because, by his own confession from the outset, he is presented as a liar who enjoys especially good repute as a truth-teller, a professional plain-speaker. The frankness of his soliloquies is a kind of hypocrisy in reverse, imposing its vicious assumptions upon the virtuous. When he begins by confiding to Roderigo his hatred for the Moor and his resentment for not having been promoted, we are alerted to his basic dishonesty. Thereafter Shakespeare keeps reiterating the epithet *honest,* ringing the changes for William Empson to gloss, in order to make Othello's trust more convincing under the somewhat doubtful circumstances. The first of the numerous parts that Iago will play, the notorious Elizabethan role of coney-catcher with Roderigo as gull, presents to us in paradigm his notion of the relationship between man and man: the simple and crass alternative of cozening or being cozened. As for woman, even if she be honest, in the peculiarly feminine sense of chaste, she may be suspected of being dishonest, and the suspicion is just as bad as the certainty. For Iago, like Shakespeare's other villains, reckons by the world's opinion rather than by moral actuality. In his official post of Ancient, ensign, flag-bearer, as he so appropriately puts it, he "must show out a flag and sign of love" (I.i.156). Yet, as Emilia will suspect when she likens his jealousy to Othello's, his wit is turned "the seamy side without" (IV.ii.146).

So he judges others, by a hard-boiled awareness of his own potentialities for knavery. If their lives possess a daily beauty which makes his look ugly by contrast—and here again he must be thinking in terms of appearances, and of the higher status that Cassio now enjoys—then he can taint them with the contamination of his ugliness, as he proceeds to do by bringing about Cassio's disgrace and—"my peculiar end"—Othello's tragedy (I.i.60). Though he does not set forth so explicit a credo as the baritone does in Boito's libretto to Verdi's *Otello,* he would doubtless have subscribed to the statement:

> *Son scellerato*
> *Perchè son uomo.*

He is a rogue because he is a man; such, at least, is Iago's view of human nature. If he seems blacker than Shakespeare's other villains, it is because the scope of his operations is so thoroughly negative, so much less ambitious than theirs. On the Machiavellian principle that, if you do enough damage, you are not a common criminal but a great tyrant, kingdoms are at stake for Macbeth, for Richard III, and even for Edmund the Bastard. It is fairly obvious that Iago, though he incidentally gets his promotion, was not prompted by the profit-motive. But there were many other motives for one who embodied what he calls "our country disposition" (III.iii.201). Given the way the Elizabethans conceived the Italian temperament, they could have swallowed tragedies about more hideous revenges for smaller slights.

Hazlitt, who enjoys less prestige among students of Shakespeare because he gave sensible answers to some of the questions that Coleridge raised, makes a suggestive counterstatement here: "[Shakespeare] knew that the love of power, which is another name for the love of mischief, is natural to man." Hence Iago, far from searching a nonexistent conscience, is zestfully indulging in "diseased intellectual activity." One of Hazlitt's illustrations, boys killing flies for sport, harks back to *King Lear;* it might also look forward to William Golding's *Lord of the Flies.* To be fair to Coleridge, we should note that he qualifies his characterization of Iago as fiendish: "a being next to devil and not quite devil." But there have been other commentators to press the point much farther, and to limn him with the flashing *chiaroscuro* of a Mephistopheles or a Satan. Such archetypal speculations are warranted, if only by Othello's term *demi-devil* or by his belated attempt to discern a cloven foot; and it has proved illuminating to reconsider Iago in relation to the Vice of the moralities, as Bernard Spivack has done in his solid study, *Shakespeare and the Allegory of Evil*. Veritably Iago is a Tempter; he may be the Eternal Adversary, or Evil Incarnate as Salvini believed, insofar as Othello is Everyman; and those associations help to account for Iago's universal aura and resonance.

Yet if his animus cannot be accounted for except on an allegorical plane, then he remains a personification rather than an individual, and the play is not literally coherent; it does not fully materialize; it abstracts itself into a *psychomachia*. Alternatively, following Stoll and Schücking, we might cut the Gordian knot by conceding that Shakespeare was simply accepting the old convention of folklore, the *motif* of the Calumniator Credited. But to adopt that makeshift solution would also be to admit a serious flaw in Shakespeare's dramatic coherence. Some pertinacious scholars have sought light from the psychological treatises of the Renaissance; but contemporaneous theories of the passions seem absurdly crude, when contrasted with Shakespeare's subtle demonstrations. To label Othello choleric, or Iago melancholic, scarcely helps us to distinguish Othello from Hotspur or Iago from Hamlet. Modern psychologizing, with its prying conjectures as to the latent impulses and the offstage experiences of the characters, takes us farther and farther away from the play. Dr. Ernest Jones propounded the psychoanalytic hypothesis that Iago was animated by homosexuality, and—as Marvin Rosenberg has shown in his informative stage-history, *The Masks of Othello*—Sir Laurence Olivier found that interpretation virtually impossible to act out.

"What annoyed Iago more than anything, however, was that even Othello's intimate heart affairs, his love for

Desdemona and her abduction, were concealed from him, Iago, and confided to Cassio." This confidence was concealed from the rest of us too, until it was revealed to mankind—not by A. C. Bradley but by Konstantin Stanislavsky, whose production notes read like a nineteenth-century novel. That is precisely the way the armchair critics have read Shakespeare, from Morgann's essay on Falstaff until L. C. Knights's essay on Bradley. Their viewpoint has been essentially novelistic, and Iago constituted their greatest enigma because he resisted that mode of realization. The world they lived in seemed reasonable enough, if not wholly rational. Malice could be observed at work in it, but always with an understandable purpose; villains were hardly necessary when passions spun the plot. It remained for our problematic century to rediscover what Shakespeare knew as well as Pascal or Freud: that the heart may have reasons, obscurely subconscious; that one man might come to hate another not because he was injured but because he had inflicted an injury; that superior rank or bodily strength could be neutralized by a difference in pigmentation; that pointless malignity could itself be a motive. After all, we have witnessed fictional heroes of our time committing an *acte gratuit* in Gide's *Vatican Swindle* or an all but unmotivated crime in Camus' *Stranger*.

Motivation would seem to have been a special concern of the nineteenth century. The English word itself, as it is registered in the *Oxford English Dictionary,* does not seem to have been employed before 1873. I suspect that it had a previous record in German philosophy and psychology, and that the principal intermediary was Gustav Freytag's influential handbook, *The Technique of the Drama.* There *motivieren* or *motivate* becomes a technical term of playwriting, though a clear distinction is maintained between the directness of Shakespeare and the introspection of Schiller. The word *motive,* on the other hand, has a long English history and is often employed by Shakespeare himself: sometimes in its original physical meaning, a moving force, and sometimes metaphorically, psychologically. I suspect that Shakespeare's German lexicographer, Alexander Schmidt, has overdrawn this distinction; that an Elizabethan ear would have been more conscious of the metaphor, would have conceived the matter less abstractly, than we. Significantly the *Oxford Dictionary* indicates that, whereas the earlier verbal phrase was *act on a motive,* later usage shifted to *act from a motive*—in other words, a shift from outer stimulus to inner prompting.[1]

Shakespeare's outlook was by no means subjective, in spite of T. S. Eliot's criticism of *Hamlet* for failing to express some private problem which consequently will never be understood. Eliot joined the motive-hunters when, in his essay on Senecanism in Shakespeare, he described Othello's final monologue as an effort to cheer himself up. If that were Shakespeare's intention, one might agree that the effort was unsuccessful; cosmic cheerfulness somehow does not break in. But Eliot had an ulterior motive, as he usually has in his criticism: here it is an invidious comparison between the Stoic and the Thomistic worldviews. He was well aware of how much was meant in Elizabethan tragedy by the manner of one's death, the posture of dying, the image bequeathed to posterity. Yet here he chose to interpret convention in a naively personal fashion—much as certain other interpre-

1. Since this paper was first published, I have endeavored to trace the term and concept *motif* in the *Dictionary of the History of Ideas,* ed. Philip Wiener (New York, 1973), III, 235–44.

ters, confusing the medium with the characterization, find Othello histrionic because he has such a bravura part in the Shakespearean repertory, or rhetorical because his speech is so magniloquent. He himself claims it is rude, as did the eloquent Hotspur, and that his tales are unvarnished. Nonetheless they must be told because they cannot be acted out on the stage. Magniloquence must represent the magnitude of his actions, the scope of his far-flung adventures. Poetry must take the place, must convey the effect, of soldierly prowess.

Othello's tales are already twice-told at the Council Scene, when he speaks of the spells by which he has won Desdemona, and strikes the high note he recaptures at the midpoint of the play with his stirring farewell to the battlefield and the "Pride, pomp, and circumstance of glorious war!" (III.iii.354). Iago, whose sardonic and spicy prose runs to the very opposite extreme, has burlesqued Othello's diction in the opening scene, when he spoke of "bumbast circumstance/ Horribly stuff'd with epithites of war" (I.i.13-4). Properly speaking, Othello's style is epic, whereas—as has been suggested by Edwin Booth among others—Iago plays the comedian. As such, not merely does he contrive the plot; he serves as its stage-manager and its chorus; and, what is more fundamental, he inhabits that all-suspecting comic world where every man is a knave at heart and every woman a potential whore, where both sexes forfeit their respective pretensions to honesty. Hence the atmosphere of epos is grossly reduced to the lowest level of comedy in the scene where Iago proves his case by persuading Othello to spy upon Cassio and Bianca and, above all, in that chilling reduction of values to prices known as the Brothel Scene.

One implication of that harrowing scene is how ill at ease Othello feels in the company of women. Only with

Desdemona has he lately come to feel secure, and now that haven is under assault (IV.ii.57-8):

> . . . there, where I have garner'd up my heart,
> Where either I must live or bear no life.

It must be all or nothing, depending on whom to believe; if Iago is honest, Desdemona is not; and Othello is—paradoxically—too magnanimous to doubt the story that reaches him first and gains support from both contrivance and chance, the stage-managed interview and the stray handkerchief. Like those other great soldiers, Macbeth and Coriolanus, Othello is at a loss when he is out of his element. Prodigious in battle, he is powerless before intrigue. With his occupation gone, the man of action can merely be acted upon. His bravery, his dignity, his monolithic simplicity can be no match for the protean malevolence of the multi-faceted Iago. Othello's has been perforce a man-to-man existence, built upon the mutual dependence of a general and his subalterns, and credulity is the defect of his quality. He is not jealous by native disposition, any more than Macbeth is a criminal type or Hamlet a vacillating neurotic. This can be seen by comparing Othello's emotions with those of Leontes or Master Ford. Iago's poison works through a transference of his own jealousy to Othello. The irony is that the hero takes his worst enemy for a confidant and ends by making his best beloved his victim.

Shakespeare's source-book, the novella by Giraldi Cintio, makes a good deal more than Shakespeare does of the Ensign's thwarted desire for the heroine. Cintio, however, makes very little of the Moorishness of the Moor, except for warning young maidens never to disobey their parents by running off and marrying strangers. It is Shakespeare who deliberately charges the air with ethnic antagonism, and it is Iago who becomes the mouthpiece of racial prejudice. It is he who announces the marriage at the beginning, begriming it with foul-mouthed epithets and foul-minded images. Throughout he loses no occasion to dwell on the "foul disproportions" of the match (III.iii.233). In the days when foul and fair had seemed as clear to Shakespeare as black and white, he had created Aaron the Moor in *Titus Andronicus,* a villain modeled on Marlowe's Jew of Malta, Barabas, or his Moorish accomplice, Ithamore. Though Portia received the Prince of Morocco politely in *The Merchant of Venice,* she was glad to see his suit fail because she disliked his tawny countenance. But, at the point where Shakespeare could discern consummate villainy masking itself with a reputation for honesty, he was morally prepared to extend his increasingly sympathetic insight to the dark-skinned races.

Actors and critics, Coleridge among them, have tried to minimize the negroid aspect of Othello's appearance, making him out to be Ethiopian, Abyssinian, Saracen—anything but an authentic blackamoor. Yet anyone who remembers Paul Robeson's performance is likely to be unimpressed by the voice and stature and presence of white actors playing Othello. Ben Jonson's *Masque of Blackness,* performed before the Stuart court at the request of the Queen two months after the presentation of *Othello* there, attests that colored people were looked upon with some degree of friendly curiosity at the time. Physiognomic preconceptions, to be sure, were vague, and Shakespeare used that vagueness to create a strong ambivalence: on the one hand, exotic grandeur, nobility of person; on the other, thick lips, sooty bosom. Marked as a foreigner, the noble Moor cuts a conspicuous figure in Venice, a half-assimilated outsider and yet—unlike his despised fellow townsman, Shylock—no infidel; for this particular Moor has been Christianized, and is careful to remind the Senators that he goes to confession. It is ominous when Iago declares that Othello would renounce his baptism at the caprice of Desdemona, and it is ironic when he calls the roistering brawlers to order by asking, "Are we turn'd Turks . . . ?" (II.iii.170).

Brabantio, his unwilling father-in-law, for whom the connection is a misalliance because it is a miscegenation, compares his own loss of a daughter with what Venice would lose if the Turks were permitted to conquer Cyprus. This analogy proves to be a back-handed acknowledgment of Othello's importance to the republic, since Brabantio's particular grief is soon swept aside by the general care, and the Venetian Senate entrusts Othello with the command of Cyprus. After the Italianate prologue of Act I, we are swept across the enchaféd flood to that island setting near the gorgeous East: a European garrison at a Levantine outpost, a background where we are never allowed to forget the centuries of interracial tension, crusades and piracies, mercantile rivalries, Islam against Christendom. Here, in this ambiguous context, Othello gropes and stumbles toward his journey's end, and the very seamark of his isolation and his estrangement. By his own bloody hands, he finally realizes, he has justified the most bigoted predictions; he has been led, by his fears and Iago's ruses, to put himself on the outside again; and his lone weapon is overwhelmingly surrounded by the bright swords of the Venetian insiders, who have taken over his authority. His actual trial was the Council Scene; and now, with the grim justice of *Alice in Wonderland,* he ends by committing the crime for which he has been punished.

Coming full cycle, then, in his death-speech we hear

him regaining his martial voice. We watch him assuming monumental stature even as he resumes his occupation and recalls his services to the state. Momentarily he seems to be reunited with his ideal of Christian honor, but actually he is alienated forever. Whether he likens himself to the base Judean—possibly Judas—as in the Folio text, or to a base Indian (the Quarto reading), he is the dark interloper who has rashly thrown away a pearl of the purest whiteness. Meanwhile he weeps tears which, not irrelevantly, resemble the aromatic drippings from Arabian trees. Reverting to the vein of those traveler's tales which had so charmed Desdemona, "Of moving accidents by flood and field," he rounds out his ultimate story (I.iii.135). Eliot viewed this as a last-moment endeavor to escape from reality. On the contrary, the final gesture brings the whole situation home with a uniquely vengeful impact. Even as Othello acts out his remembrance of leading the Venetians against the Turks, he seems to change places with the grappling enemy. Suddenly the heroic defender of Venice turns into his Turkish assailant: a cringing dog, malignant, turbaned, circumcised. In seizing his own throat and smiting down himself, Othello ends where he began, a benighted stranger cast into outer darkness.

Eliot, in one of his portentous *obiter dicta,* averred that he had yet to see a cogent refutation of Thomas Rymer's strictures against *Othello.* After that intimidating caveat, any such attempt would seem to be the sheerest bravado. In any case, it is rather too late in the game to try. The fact that no one has risen to Shakespeare's defense—or did Eliot mean to imply that there have been some ineffectual defenses?—might indicate no more than that Rymer's attack did no substantial damage. Without presuming either to refute it or to apologize for *Othello,* I should like to conclude with one or two suggestions on behalf of Desdemona, since she was Rymer's main target just as Iago was Coleridge's and Othello himself is Eliot's. Rymer, at all events, was born too soon to be a motive-hunter, as we—I venture to argue—have been born too late. He was concerned not with the secret springs of behavior but with the outward conformities, with a neo-classical decorum which he construed dogmatically not by a system of ethics but by a code of etiquette. Thus Iago offended him by not behaving as a good soldier correctly should on the stage. Desdemona's conduct was light and unfilial, to say the least; in taking the paternal side against her, it should be added that Rymer has been joined by certain other commentators, and notably by the patriarchal John Quincy Adams.

Rymer's anti-Negro sneers at Othello, and at the Venetians for inviting him into their homes and appointing him to a high military post, make the Restoration critic sound to us for all the world like the demagogic governor of a southern state. Yet they have the incidental value of attesting that hostile near-contemporaries could recognize and react to the warmth of Shakespeare's compassionate interest in the position of a black man. Rymer's method of reducing the play to absurdity was to summarize the plot with heavy-handed facetiousness, much as Voltaire would do when he campaigned against *Hamlet.* By dwelling upon its homeliest details, with a zeal for exposing vulgarity which in the long run incriminated himself, Rymer sought to reduce *Othello* to what he termed "a bloody farce." The modern term *domestic drama* would come nearer the mark, and would hint at what was so disturbing to a rigid neo-classicist. That tragedy could hinge upon a commonplace article of domestic utility, so humble an object as a handkerchief, outraged both his personal sense of propriety and all his canons of probability. Jocosely he suggested that *Othello* be retitled *The Tragedy of the Handkerchief*. Archly he proposed a moral: "This may be a warning to all good wives, that they look well to their linen." We should be thankful that Rymer did not compose a commentary on the legend of Saint Veronica.

It should be conceded, for better or worse, that housewifery has a real thematic significance for the play. It is discussed at some length in the banter between Iago and Desdemona, while they are awaiting Othello's arrival at Cyprus. In a sharp series of improvised couplets, with characteristic misogyny, Iago sketches cynical vignettes of woman's role. Desdemona requests a more favorable portrait, and Iago obliges up to a point, building up through a climactic sequence of feminine virtues:

> She was a wight (if ever such wights were)—

When Desdemona eagerly asks, "To do what?," he clinches the verses triumphantly (II.i.158-60):

> To suckle fools and chronicle small beer.

Paragon of the virtues though she be, it will be her anticlimactic and anti-feministic lot to have babies and keep household accounts. But alas! such is not to be Desdemona's lot. Not without reason Iago plays upon the polarity of the word *housewife* and its raffish derivative, *hussy*. The courtesan Bianca—and, given the interplay between blacks and whites, her name may have some purport—is introduced as "a huswife who by selling her desires/ Buys herself bread and clothes" (IV.i.94-5). There is a significant interchange, involving another equivocal key-word, when Emilia calls Bianca a strumpet and the latter flares back (V.i.122-3):

> I am no strumpet, but of life as honest
> As you that thus abuse me.

Desdemona and Bianca, with Emilia midway between them, stand at the polar extremes of womanhood. That the handkerchief should pass from the one to the other, by way of the go-between, is no mere contingency but a sign and a portent—a dumb-show, as it were, of purity bewhored and love confounded with lust.

The original charge against Othello, it will be remembered, was that he had bewitched Desdemona. The truly sinister witchcraft, as it ironically turns out, is the spell cast on Othello by Iago's wit. This theme of sorcery, which is so richly interwoven through the language of the drama, has been traced in rewarding detail by Robert Heilman's *Magic in the Web.* Its concrete embodiment is the handkerchief, which is therefore as meaningful a stage-property as could be imagined. Like Nerissa's ring, it is a love-token; more than that, it becomes a talisman of life and death. It is hallowed with superstitious awe by Othello's strange tale of the Gypsy charmer and the heirloom from his mysterious past. Shakespeare invests it with romantic mystery as a magic symbol of Othello's passion and a mystic omen of Desdemona's murder, since it will provide the ocular proof that seals Iago's calumny. The stark word *handkerchief* is enunciated no less than twenty-four times, and its vehement iterance by Othello punctuates the most suspenseful dialogue of the play, as who should say upon what trivial hazards our happiness depends. Bianca intends, for Cassio, to *take the work out,* to copy the pattern. But Shakespeare's point is that—though venal loves, like hers for him, can easily be replaced or duplicated—the genuine love of a woman and a man cannot be copied. It is unique and irreplaceable.

When Othello warns Desdemona that the loss of the handkerchief would threaten perdition, the warning reverberates to his earlier avowal (III.iii.90-2):

> Perdition catch my soul
> But I do love thee! and when I love thee not,
> Chaos is come again.

Chaos does come again; damnation overtakes him; his world is brought down in ruins by the wave of a handkerchief, the neat trick of a wily conjuror abetted by circumstance. Cunning has done its best, and luck its worst. And since the crucial evidence is false, since Desdemona herself is innocent, in the end it is not Iago but Othello who does the motive-hunting (V.ii.1):

> It is the cause, it is the cause, my soul.

But Desdemona has rightly denied it (III.iv.158):

> Alas the day, I never gave him cause.

And Cassio will deny it on his part (V.ii.299):

> Dear general, I never gave you cause.

The catastrophe is needless, then, if not motiveless. The lovers are not star-crossed; the protagonist is neither hounded by fates nor predestinated by oracles; the retrospective design bears the signature, not of necessity, but of chance; we listen in vain for the ring of inevitability. Can *Othello* still be considered a tragedy, in the grander meaning of the form? Should it not be qualified as a domestic drama—if not, to please Bernard Shaw, as "pure melodrama"? Or, if we prefer more flexible categories, ought we not to consider that Bradley regarded it as the most romantic of Shakespeare's tragedies? Victor Hugo, in a famous manifesto, defined the Romantic drama as an admixture of the sublime and the grotesque, and illustrated that definition by the old fairy-tale of Beauty and the Beast. A richer illustration would be a picture of Desdemona listening to Othello. It would be highlighted by the recurring imagery of lights and shades. It would harbor the attraction, along with the underlying repulsion, of opposites. There would be implications of bestiality: dogs, goats and monkeys, the beast with two backs. But these would be counterpoised by touches of wonder, which link Desdemona with the heroines of Shakespeare's later romances. Bacon, in his essay "Of Beauty," stressed the element of "strangeness in the proportion." Pater, echoing Bacon, characterized romance as strangeness conjoined with beauty.

Bradley had his hesitations about admitting *Othello* to that canon of major Shakespearean tragedy which, following the lead of Coleridge's lectures, his book did so much to establish. There are good grounds for arguing that the play might more appropriately be flanked by *Romeo and Juliet* on one side and by *Antony and Cleopatra* on the other. Certainly it does not attain the scale of the other three works treated in *Shakespearean Tragedy*. More particularly, it lacks the terror of *King Lear,* where nature is brought to the verge of her confine, or of *Hamlet* and *Macbeth,* where man is brought face to face with supernatural forces. *Othello* bears the brunt of society rather than nature, and perhaps it compensates with pity for what it misses in terror. Hence Wordsworth deemed it "the most pathetic of human compositions." This did not endear it less to the sympathies of its audiences; Rymer attacked it because it seems to have been, during the seventeenth century, the most popular tragedy on the English stage; and there are many anecdotes of spectators becoming so enthralled in the action that they have sought to intervene between the Moor and his bride. The basis of their mutual understanding, so long as it lasts, is compassion, pathos, pity. When Othello first told Desdemona his tales, she sighed (I.iii.160-1),

> She swore, in faith 'twas strange, 'twas passing strange;
> 'Twas pitiful, 'twas wondrous pitiful.

And he went on to sum up his case for the Senators (I.iii.167-8):

> She lov'd me for the dangers I had pass'd,
> And I lov'd her that she did pity them.

The conclusion that the tragedy was not inevitable, that the tragic misunderstanding could have been avoided, that so much evil is mere malice and so much folly sheer credulity, and that the essential dignity of man is at the mercy of both malice and credulity—"But yet the pity of it, Iago! O Iago, the pity of it, Iago!" (IV.i.195-6).

The Heights and the Depths:
A Scene from *King Lear*

Speaking of depths and heights, I hope that my title has not provoked a wider curiosity than can be sharply focused by my subtitle. I shall not be talking about the periods of Shakespeare's development, or looking for his autobiography in his dramaturgy, or assuming—with Edward Dowden and others—that he wrote his tragedies out of some private grief and later, when he felt mellower, turned back to comedies. The moods and changes that continue to interest us today are not those which we attribute to the artist in person, but those which we experience through his art. Its characteristic transitions from splendor to torment, from *O altitudo* to *de profundis,* seem to accord with a basic principle of tragic vicissitude. What I propose to discuss, in some contextual detail, is one extremely specific illustration of that principle, a text often cited but seldom reexamined, probably because our modes of stagecraft have strategically changed.

Delivered at the Summer School of The Shakespeare Memorial Theatre, Stratford-upon-Avon, September 1, 1958; published in *More Talking about Shakespeare,* ed. John Garrett (London: Longmans, Green and Co., 1959).

"Gain Shakespeare's effects by Shakespeare's means when you can." Such was the sound advice of Harley Granville-Barker for the modern interpretation of Shakespeare. However, there are times when the theatrical interpreter cannot use Shakespearean means, even though the academic interpreter may know how a certain Shakespearean effect was accomplished. We cannot cast a boy as Cleopatra, though Shakespeare did; very few actresses are up to the part in our time, even after a long and respectable career in the theater. Shakespeare would never have been able to spread his drama of *Antony and Cleopatra* through forty-two scenes, crossing and recrossing the Mediterranean, had he been forced to compress it within a proscenium, relying upon a succession of backdrops or perhaps a revolving stage. Working within an adaptable but permanent structure—mainly a forestage flanked by adequate exits or entrances, backed by some sort of curtained area and an upper balcony, and surrounded by spectators on three sides and at three levels—Shakespeare achieved unlimited effects by limited means.

These were primarily verbal. To one with his gift for turning words into pictures, the absence of scenery was a stimulus to the pictorial imagination. Hence Shakespeare did his own scene-painting, verbally. As Robert Atkins has said, reminiscing about the Old Vic, "we owe many of Shakespeare's finest descriptive passages to the absence of painted canvas." "This castle hath a pleasant seat," says Duncan, praising the air; and Banquo goes on to enlarge our mental picture of Glamis Castle with his lyrical speech about the temple-haunting martlet, the pendent bed, and the heaven's breath (I.vi.1). This delicate imagery has the quality of repose in painting, or so Sir Joshua Reynolds has commented. Repose? The comment is unconsciously ironic, for it is here that the gentle Duncan will all too soon be taking his last repose; before morning that heavenly courtyard will be all the drunken porter fancies, when he envisages it as a gateway to hell; and we shall have been transported, as it were, from the heights to the depths.

Shakespeare used no programs, and does not seem to have put much faith in locality-boards.

> Alack, the night comes on, and the bleak winds
> Do sorely ruffle,

says Gloucester, thereby setting the time and place at the end of the Second Act of *King Lear* (II.iv.300-2),

> for many miles about
> There's scarce a bush.

And with a clatter of doors being closed and shutters banged, the clanging of gates and other sound-effects which are actually verbal, the stage is set—that vastest and barest of stages—for the storm scenes of Act III, which alternate between the indoors and the open air, and gain the effect of wind and rain by means of the old King's efforts to outscorn them. Granville-Barker's preface to *King Lear* is a professional rebuttal of A. C. Bradley's influential and paradoxical argument that, though it may be Shakespeare's greatest achievement, it is too huge for the stage. This, in turn, was a philosophical rationalization of Charles Lamb's opinion that performance was unbearable. Now Lamb was more of a theater-goer than Bradley, but he could only have witnessed the play in productions which were cruelly cut and badly adulterated. He therefore concluded that the spectacle of an old man, tottering about in a storm with a stick, could only be painful or disgusting.

Other critics have recoiled more strongly from that terrifying scene where Gloucester's eyes are put out *coram populo,* not behind scenes as in *Oedipus Rex,* but in full view of the audience and in complete violation of classical decorum. It is a deliberate and definitive breach, a more flagrant gesture of indecorum than the Elizabethan inter-mixture of hornpipes with funerals, or the abasement of kings to the level of clowns in the companionship of Lear and his Fool. Yet even that horrendous act has a certain propriety as a literal climax to a whole train of metaphors involving eyesight and suggesting moral perception, the lack of which is so fatal for Gloucester and Lear. None so blind as those who have eyes and see not. Their eyes may be open, but—like those of Lady Macbeth in her sleep-walking scene—their sense is shut. This visual metaphor is generalized into *hubris,* the pride that goes before a tragic fall, with the self-denunciation of Antony (III.xiii.111-5):

> But when we in our viciousness grow hard
> (O misery on't!) the wise gods seel our eyes,
> In our own filth drop our clear judgments, make us
> Adore our errors, laugh at's while we strut
> To our confusion.

When we become too intimately involved in the tragic experience, we tend to feel pain and disgust as Lamb did, rather than pity and fear. *Catharsis,* if it clears the mind through those classic emotions, does so by placing the ob-ject at an esthetic distance from the spectator. He must, of course, apprehend it through sympathy, empathy, or some sort of identification with it. But he also achieves a sense of perspective through his detachment from it. Re-cent dramatic theory would stress this latter stage, which Bertolt Brecht terms estrangement (*Verfremdung*), as the most important aspect of the emotional process. But long ago Lucretius evoked the intellectual pleasure of looking out on troubled waters when one was safe ashore, of looking down on the violent conflicts of men from the heights of philosophy. Tragedy presents such knowledge, not in philosophic abstraction but in concrete ex-emplification. Thus, though it cries to us out of the depths, it offers us a way of temporarily detaching our-selves from the human predicament, and rising above those situations in which it has vicariously involved us.

The example for which I should like to claim your par-ticular attention is neither the pitiful involvement of Lear in the storm nor the terrible blinding of Gloucester. It is a subsequent and incidental episode, the sixth scene of the Fourth Act, a curiously didactic scene best known for its purple passage describing Dover Cliff. How near we re-ally come to Dover Cliff is a moot question, as I shall try to show in my attempt to recover a unique effect which could only have been attained through Shakespearean means. Elsewhere in drama it has certain precedents and analogies, but none of them comes very close to the mat-ter at hand. In the *Plutus* of Aristophanes, the others threaten to throw the blind god over a precipice, and the threat is averted when he reveals his name. The suicidal plunge in Tasso's *Aminta* is a mock-death which leads to a happy ending. In the repertory of Japanese Kabuki, the dance-drama *Shakkyo* concerns an old lion who pushes a young one off a cliff as a kind of test: by climbing back, the cub proves his manhood—or rather, his lionhood.

That would seem to be the normal relationship be-tween the two generations, father and son. Shakespeare reverses it, when Edmund accuses Edgar of maintaining that "the father should be as ward to the son" (I.ii.73). The accusation will come true ironically, when the disguised Edgar leads the blinded Gloucester. "In this play," Dame Edith Sitwell has aptly observed, "we see the upheaval of all Nature, the reversal of all histories."

Tragedy always seems to hinge upon a reversal, or peripety. Here a peripety is the starting-point, when the King reverses his traditional role by stepping down from the throne. As the tragedy broadens, moving out of the realm of history into the sphere of nature, it sets off a series of further reversals. The antagonism between crabbed age and flaming youth, always a latent tension in Shakespeare's plays, breaks into overt conflict in *King Lear*. It was implicit in classical comedy, to be sure, and terribly explicit in the dire prophecy of Matthew: "And brother shall deliver up brother to death, and the father his child: and children shall rise up against parents, and cause them to be put to death."

This abrogation of the' most fundamental commitments, straining family ties beyond endurance and turning simple affections into complex hatreds, is still a major source of power in literature. Filial ingratitude is an obsessive theme with Proust, just as parricide is with Dostoevsky. Like the sons of Old Man Karamazov, Edgar and Edmund incarnate the good and evil of their father's character. Science, natural philosophy, "the wisdom of nature can reason it thus and thus, yet nature finds itself scourg'd by the sequent effects," the superstitious Gloucester laments at the outset, anxious to blame his fate upon the stars (I.ii.104-6). The worst of the many symptoms of upheaval that he enumerates is "the bond cracked between son and father." In Gloucester's own case, it is "son against father," though he suspects the wrong son as it turns out. In the King's case, it is "father against child," and Gloucester underlines the parallel (108-12). Shakespeare never made bolder use of the double plot than when he matched the dynastic struggle of the main plot with its domestic counterpart, the Gloucester underplot. To take a *donnée* so exceptional, to hit

upon so unheard-of a set of circumstances and double
them, was to call the entire moral order into question, as
A. W. Schlegel pointed out.

The story in outline harks back, far beyond the old
play that Shakespeare adapted, through chronicle and
legend, to the mounds of British prehistory and the fens
of Druidical myth. But Shakespeare, shrewd folklorist
that he was, found the same archetype at work in the
most fashionable book of romantic fiction among his contemporaries, Sir Philip Sidney's *Arcadia*. Two heroes of
that romance, in the course of their princely adventures,
had encountered the blind King of Paphlagonia begging
his dutiful son to lead him to headlong death from the
top of a rock because, as he put it, "I cannot fall worse
than I am." From the doleful speeches of father and son,
it emerged that a bastard son and brother had betrayed
them both through his "unnaturall dealings"—a protesting phrase which Gloucester echoes at the moment when
the two plots first come together in the play. The interpolated narrative ends in a battle and a reinstatement,
with the blind King dying joyfully and the rightful heir
forgiving his perfidious half-brother.

Sidney devotes a single chapter to this minor encounter; yet he tells us it is "worthy to be remembered for the
un-used examples therein, as well of true natural good-
nes, as of wretched ungratefulness." Edgar and Edmund,
then, are exemplary figures, models of filial conduct, for
better and worse. The worse of the two has an obvious
dramatic advantage. It is always easier to play an effectual
villain than a young man of simple-minded good will.
Some of Milton's critics have sympathized more with his
Satan than with his Son of God. Yet the title-page of the
First Quarto leaves no doubt as to who, after Lear himself, is the male protagonist: who is, so to speak, the *jeune*

premier. It reads in part: *"With the unfortunate life of Edgar, sonne and heire to the Earle of Gloster, and his sullen and assumed humor of Tom of Bedlam."* Instead of remaining just a nice young man, rather pallid and timid, Edgar is allowed to rival Shakespeare's dynamic villains by assuming a dangerous and colorful role.

Edmund has played his part from the beginning, though he already looks toward a *dénouement* of some sort when he summons Edgar from hiding: "Pat! he comes like the catastrophe of the old comedy" (I.ii.134). Even while Edmund is soliloquizing, he is rehearsing his initial interview with his half-brother, and the notes he sings— *mi contra fa*—significantly form the forbidden interval known as *diabolus in musica*. His own "cue," as it happens, will become Edgar's: "a sigh like Tom 'o Bedlam" (135-6). But Edgar, at this point, is no less credulous than their father. With Gloucester he falls into Edmund's trap, is suspected of parricidal intentions, and proscribed as an outlaw. In his fugitive soliloquy, he determines (II.iii.7-9)

> To take the basest and most poorest shape
> That ever penury, in contempt of man,
> Brought near to beast.

He will disguise himself, paradoxically, by taking off his clothes and exposing himself to the elements. "With presented nakedness," when we next see him, he will be attempting to (11-2)

> outface
> The winds and persecutions of the sky.

And Edgar seems to anticipate the storm, even as Lear seems to conjure it up with his imprecations of blast and fog.

As Edgar goes on to describe the role of Poor Tom, we can understand why it made him so popular on the Elizabethan stage. But, though it is quasi-comic, we can scarcely regard it as comic relief; rather, with its vagrant grotesquerie, it intensifies the tragic pathos. Those Bedlam beggars were harmless madmen released from their lunatic asylum, the notorious Hospital of St. Mary's of Bethlehem at London. Wandering aimlessly about the countryside, with their teeth chattering from exposure and their bare flesh lacerated by self-torture, they besought the stranger's alms with their prayers or curses. Edgar not only dresses, or undresses, the part; he fills it in with apt charms and exorcisms and brilliant bits of histrionic improvisation. He even seems to have worked up the names of devils from a current theological pamphlet: Turleygod, Flibbertigibbet, Frateretto (the last a likely name for a diabolical brother). Not the least of many ironies is that this innocent youth must pretend to be the victim of demonic possession, haunted by the foul fiend in many shapes—albeit these demons, on naturalistic inspection, are merely vermin.

Dramatic tradition gave Tom of Bedlam a forerunner in the person of Diccon the Bedlam, the Vice or mischiefmaker in the crude old Cambridge comedy of *Gammer Gurton's Needle*. Edgar too will play the Vice in his later manipulations, when he intervenes on behalf of Gloucester. Meanwhile he acts as an object-lesson for Lear. The extent of Lear's reversal may be grasped by contrasting the First Scene of Act I with the last in Act II. In the former the bidding goes up, as Goneril and Regan bid for the kingdom with their large speeches of love. In the latter the haggling goes down, as the daughters cut down the retinue of their father. A hundred, fifty, five-and-twenty knights. "Ten? or five?" "What need one?" (ii.iv. 261, 263). By that time we are ready to move on with Lear from the court, the world of superfluity, to the heath, the world of necessity—from the heights toward the depths. His retort in farewell is the first of his speeches on need and its opposite, luxury, especially luxurious clothing and the difference it makes between the sophisticated courtier and the basest beggar, between man's life and beast's (264-70).

When Lear has exposed himself to the pinch of necessity, when he has felt the storm and first expressed a new insight into the houseless lives of naked wretches, it is then that the ragged Edgar appears as the personification of abject poverty and misery. "Is man no more than this?" the King demands, striving to emulate Tom by removing his own regal garments. "Unaccommodated man"—the naked wretch in the state of nature—"is no more but such a poor, bare, forked animal as thou art" (III.iv.102-3, 106-8). Commentators have told us how richly the prose of this passage is interlarded with primitivistic speculations from Montaigne, whom Shakespeare knew so well through Florio's translation, and who had inspired so much of Hamlet's self-questioning. Lear has his own version of Hamlet's exclamation, "What a piece of work is a man!" (*Hamlet,* II.ii.303-4) Unaccommodate him, banish him from the commodities of the court, take away the trappings of civilization, complete his exposure to the elements. What is there left to differentiate him from all the other animals, by whose sharpened fangs we feel increasingly surrounded? Will he be naturally good, as Rousseau would argue? Or is he inherently evil, as Hobbes would have it, a wolf to his fellow man?

The Machiavellian bastard, Gloucester's natural son Edmund, dedicates himself to the goddess Nature, as he ruthlessly envisions her; while, through his cruel machinations, Edgar is placed in such a false position that their father calls his legitimate son an "unnatural villain"

(I.ii.76). On the other hand, Edgar stands closer to nature; Lear hails him as a natural philosopher, who should be able to answer his questions concerning "the cause of thunder" and the other mysteries of the cosmos (III.iv.155). This affinity, based on the fact that Edgar is Lear's godson, is confirmed by their respective plights, as Edgar will keenly realize: "He childed as I fathered!" (III.iv.110). As the pair enter the hovel together, Edgar's snatches of balladry and fairy-tale transform it into a legendary dark tower, where a young squire is undergoing a ritual of knightly initiation while nameless giants objurgate: "Fie, foh, and fum" (III.iv.183). Edgar is more a spectator than a feature of the spectacle in the ensuing scene, summing it up in the sententious understatement that "grief hath mates" or misery loves company (III.vi.107).

This is the hallucinatory arraignment, where his own half-hearted pretense meets Lear's actual madness, accompanied by the half-witted folly of the natural fool with his one pathetic joke: the rain rains every day for those who are excluded from the sunshine of royal favor. The only person present who can speak sanely, Kent in his servant guise of Caius, counsels patience. Edgar is so moved at times that his tears interfere with his impersonation, "mar" his "counterfeiting" (61). Gloucester, whom Edgar has welcomed as a squinting fiend, reenters to terminate the scene by ordering that the King be conveyed on a litter to Dover. Thereafter, in his master's absence, he becomes the scapegoat. What follows is the scene of his sacrifice, upon which there is no temptation to dwell, except for pointing out that this reversal—despite its extreme brutality—is humanely mitigated by a recognition. Peripety, according to Aristotle, is most effective when it coincides with such a recognition, *anagnórisis*.

When Cornwall inquires, "Where is thy lustre now?," Gloucester responds, "All dark and comfortless" (III.vii.83-4). Then, when the malicious Regan apprises him of Edmund's villainy, he suddenly recognizes that Edgar is innocent. Thus, at the very moment of blinding, Gloucester sees how blind he has been all along. "I stumbled when I saw," he will live to say (IV.i.19). Now, in the absence of eyesight, he will be guided by a kind of ethical illumination. One of the servants, an old man, suggests that the "roguish madness" of "the Bedlam" would qualify him to be Gloucester's guide (III.vii.103-4). Their conjunction is brought about in the First Scene of the Fourth Act. Kent has previously consoled himself with the thought that he could fall no lower than the stocks, and that any turn of Fortune's wheel would mean a rise in the world for him (II.ii.173). Similarly, Edgar *solus* now views himself as "The lowest and most dejected thing of fortune," whose condition any change would improve (IV.i.3). But alas, he speaks too soon. The sight of his bleeding father is worse than anything he has met so far.

"The worst is not," Edgar thereupon reflects, "So long as we can say, 'This is the worst'" (27-8). This may be regarded as Shakespeare's variation on the tragic theme of Sophocles, "Call no man happy until he is dead," or the cry from the depths when Job curses the light and gropes in the dark. Gloucester, in spite of his infirmity, half-recognizes Edgar as that thing between a madman and a beggar which made him "think a man a worm," but also made him think of his son (33). And it is at this significant juncture that Gloucester voices his pessimistic view of the human condition (36-7):

> As flies to wanton boys, are we to th' gods;
> They kill us for their sport.

The worldview that opens up is as hopeless as Hardy's, governed by nothing more serene or secure than crass casualty and blind chance. It seems proper to Gloucester that a madman should lead a blind man, so long as he knows the way to Dover Cliff. "From that place," he declares with grim succinctness, "I shall no leading need" (77-8). In his desperation, faced with what seems to be the pointless hostility of the universe, what can he do but dispatch his own "nighted life" (IV.v.13)? That is the last resort of Stoicism; and Shakespeare, in his Roman plays, consistently treats suicide as an honorable mode of death. In his tragedies with a Christian background, the attitude is shaded with disapproval, and he appeals to God's canon against self-slaughter.

King Lear is supposed to take place in prehistoric Britain, and to be roughly contemporaneous with the ancient Kings of Judea. Shakespeare has taken pains to have his characters invoke the gods in the plural and swear by conspicuously pagan divinities. But Edgar, that Good Samaritan with his faith, humility, and charity, seems to be *anima naturaliter christiana*. Curiously enough, in the original legend, where Lear regains his crown and Cordelia is dethroned again after his death, she ends by committing suicide in prison. It is her ghost which arises to retell the family history and point the moral in the standard Elizabethan collection of poetic case-histories, falls of princes or sad stories of the deaths of kings, the *Mirror for Magistrates*. There the usual reversal, the change of fortune from prosperity to adversity, from the heights to the depths, is presented as a warning to those who are highly placed, lest they be precipitated

> From greatest haps, that worldly wightes atchieue:
> To more distresse then any wretche aliue.

So Cordelia's monologue concludes. Comparably the first play performed before Queen Elizabeth, *Gorboduc,* one of whose collaborators was co-author of the *Mirror for Magistrates,* warned the queenly magistrate against the division of her realm and even foreshadowed *King Lear* in introducing a dissension between rival Dukes of Cornwall and Albany.

Downfall was the formula for tragedy that Shakespeare inherited and elaborated, not only in plot and characterization but in language and staging as well. The dying fall is its traditional posture. Its vicissitudes, such as the ups and downs of Richard II's reign, lend their thematic pattern to his tragedy, wherein his fall is a come-down literally as well as figuratively. Aloft, on the upper stage, the imagined walls of Flint Castle, Richard compares himself to Phaëton; descending to the lower stage, he condescends to pun about the "base court" (III.iii.180). Descent is even more desperate in *King John,* where Prince Arthur is killed in escaping from the Castle of Angiers. Elevation as the basis of a godlike overview is dramatized at those moments when Prospero is "*on the top,*" apparently looking down from the musicians' gallery (*Tempest,* III.iii.17). Antony, coming down from his vantage-point after the battle or hoisted up to Cleopatra's Monument in death, acts out the movement of his destiny. The danger of high places, the tragic vertigo, is vividly brought home in Horatio's fear lest Hamlet topple off some dreadful summit "That beetles o'er his base into the sea" (*Hamlet,* I.iv.71). And that is all we need to know in order to establish the certainty that Shakespeare never visited Denmark, which is as conspicuous for its summits as Bohemia is for its seacoasts.

But we must turn back to Dover. "Wherefore to

Dover?" Three times Gloucester is asked this question by his torturers (III.vii.52, 53, 55). Lear was there, of course; and Lear was there because the French army was there, though the King of France had discreetly withdrawn so that his rescue party would not be mistaken for a foreign invasion. There the gleaming white cliffs, greeting the traveler on his return from the continent, mark a perpetual bourn. "Within these breakwaters English is spoken," writes W. H. Auden,

> without
> Is the immense improbable atlas.

Nature in Lear, he has been chastened to learn, "is on the very verge/ Of his confine" (II.iv.147-8). Just as the tempest in his mind, in the "little world of man" or microcosm, is a reverberation of the macrocosm, the disturbance of outer nature; so now Gloucester, led by Edgar, has reached the "extreme verge," the edge of the precipice (III.i.10; IV.vi.26). It is like the thin line between life and death, between the known and the unknown, that lies before Tolstoy's heroes in *War and Peace*.

Here Edgar, the assumed madman, addresses his charge, the blind man—and remember that we are just as blind as Gloucester. Theatrical convention prescribes that we accept whatever is said on the subject of immediate place as the setting. We may grow slightly suspicious, when Gloucester fails to notice the slant of the ground or the sound of the sea; and we join him in remarking an alteration of tone, since Poor Tom has shifted to blank verse and soon embarks on his topographical passage (11-2).

> How fearful
> And dizzy 'tis, to cast one's eyes so low!

His downward glance proceeds to the halfway point, where it encounters the samphire-gatherer at his precarious business of picking the herb of Saint-Pierre from the rocks. Thence to the beach, where the fishermen look like mice, the birds like insects, the ships like their boats, and the buoys are invisible. Everything suffers a diminution in scale. "I'll look no more," vows Edgar at the end of fifteen lines,

> Lest my brain turn, and the deficient sight

—a relevant phrase, "deficient sight," which universalizes the blindness of Gloucester while commenting on the trepidation of heights (23-5)—

> I'll look no more,
> Lest my brain turn, and the deficient sight
> Topple down headlong.

This may strike the average reader or hearer with a distant, dizzying, vertiginous impact; Addison remarked that it could hardly be read without producing giddiness; but Dr. Johnson refused to be impressed. A precipice in the mind, he argued, should be "one great and dreadful image of irresistible destruction." Here we were too readily diverted by "the observation of particulars." Clearly, Johnson's criterion was the neo-classical grudge against concreteness that prompted him to inveigh against numbering the streaks of the tulip. In Boswell's account, he went even farther, when he discussed Edgar's speech with Garrick and others: "It should be all precipice—all vacuum. The crows impede your fall." It was the same Miltonic taste that emended Macbeth's "blanket of the dark" to "blank height." Yet Lessing found Shakespeare's description superior to Milton's lines where the angels scan the "vast immeasurable abyss" of chaos. In *Paradise Lost* the declension is out of scale, Lessing asserted; the distance traversed is too vast to be fathomable in human dimensions. To jump to the beach from a cliff as high as ten masts is breathtaking danger, whereas a limitless precipitation through the void is mere astronomy. That vista may be even less thrilling today, as traffic increases in outer space.

The sense of immediacy and the sense of remoteness, the sensation of being up here one moment and down there a few seconds later, together with all the other sensations heightened by the hazards of the plunge, these feelings are concentrated into our identification with Gloucester and our prospective detachment from him. He is presumably standing at the brink as he lets go Edgar's hand, rewarding him and bidding him farewell. Whereupon Edgar, in a cryptic aside, gives us our first hint that the situation is not precisely what Gloucester believes it to be (33-4):

> Why I do trifle thus with his despair
> Is done to cure it.

From this announcement, at least, it is clear that Edgar has a stratagem for saving Gloucester; but, on a non-representational stage, it would still be difficult to foresee how the rescue might be effected. On a proscenium stage, the whole situation would be impossible; for, depending upon realistic scenery, we should be fully aware whether Gloucester was or was not at the top of a hill. The best that nineteenth-century staging could do was to cut the passage heavily, letting Edgar catch Gloucester as he lurches forward into a faint, and quickly shifting to the next phase of the scene with the entrance of Lear. Meanwhile the audience would not be undergoing any throes of suspense, since the scenic arrangements would have indicated that Gloucester was perfectly safe. On occasions, the Dover Cliffs have been painted on the backdrop; it was to be inferred that Edgar had taken Gloucester directly to the beach, where he should not have had any trouble in hearing the waves.

"He falls," according to the Quarto stage-direction, which editors have embellished but not improved. Most of them add *"forward";* some add *"and swoons."* He falls, at all events, but not far. Not so far as from the upper stage, I should guess, inasmuch as Romeo needed a rope and—lacking one—Prince Arthur lost his life. There may be a single step or a simple platform; or, again, the business may be enough—enough for Edgar to play his trick upon Gloucester and to lay bare the trick that Shakespeare has played upon ourselves, his audience. Gloucester, having gone through the motions of an ineffectual jump, lies on the ground; Edgar, assuming another character, now rushes up to revive him; and both are changed men. In complementary verses, breathless with polysyllabics, Edgar describes how Gloucester has fallen perpendicularly from a vast altitude and somehow survived: "Thy life's a miracle" (55). Vainly, but not without irony, he exhorts him: "Look up a-height" (58). And in contrast to all the *hubris,* the giddy exaltation of looking down from the heights, we seem to have plunged into the depths and to have touched bottom; we can fall no lower.

This is the nadir; the worst is over; we seem to be looking up; and the situation is framed by larger perspectives. "As I stood here below, methought . . . ," begins Edgar, as if he were recounting a dream, a bad dream which ends with Tom of Bedlam turning into a fiend and flying away (69). Edgar's portrayal of his departing self is an exorcism, leaving innocence no longer possessed by guilt.

Just as Gloucester utters his cry of despair—comparing the gods to boys and ourselves to flies—on his first encounter with mad Tom, so with Tom's departure Edgar voices his answering affirmation (73-4):

> Think that the clearest gods, who make them honors
> Of men's impossibilities, have preserved thee.

Providence must be at work, after all; and if we discern the workings of cosmic design in our personal destinies, then no man has a right to take his life; he must bear the slings and arrows of fortune, however outrageous they seem. To the Stoic argument for suicide Edgar would oppose the Christian attitude, in words which reverberate from the Gospel of Luke: "The things which are impossible with men are possible with God."

Since our eyes have been opened, we are bound to bear witness that Edgar himself has been fully responsible for the stratagem he now attributes to divine intervention. His intentions were kindly, where Edmund's have been malign; but he has deceived their father quite as much with his imaginary fall as Edmund earlier did with his forged letter. "Let's see," said Gloucester, snatching at that device, "Come, if it be nothing, I shall not need spectacles" (I.ii.34-5). He saw; he stumbled; and, now that he is sightless, he is rescued by the victim of the letter. Edgar has proved to be as good a stage-manager as Edmund, and in a better cause. Yet, unless his presence in the vicinity is the result of stage-management on the part of the gods—unless it is providential, that is to say, rather than coincidental—we must admit that his miracle is more truly a pious fraud; and we must conclude that the gods help those who help themselves, or else those who are so fortunate as to be helped by their fellow men.

Man stands on his own feet in *King Lear*. There is no

supernatural soliciting; there are no ghosts or witches or oracles; and the only demons are those which Edgar imagines while enacting his demonic role. Man takes his questionings directly to nature. Perhaps the ultimate meaning of Gloucester's fall is its symbolic gesture of expiation, reenacting his own original sin, as well as the fall of man and his consequent progression toward self-knowledge. Other agonists have undergone it under widely differing conditions: Herman Melville narrates it, in his *White-Jacket,* as a fall from the yard-arm of a ship at sea. Because he could not bear his great affliction without cursing the gods, Gloucester has attempted to shake it off "patiently" (IV.vi.36). But Edgar's moral, which completes the exercise, redefines patience as the ability to bear one's sufferings, to face and endure them in calm of mind: "Bear free and patient thoughts" (80).

Patience has been the greatest need of the King. He has resolved to be "the pattern of all patience"; whereupon he has run the gamut of passions, from rage through hysteria to delirium and finally lunacy (III.ii.37). It is as an escaping lunatic, grotesquely decked with weeds, that he is confronted by Edgar and Gloucester at this strategic moment of the play; and it may well be the shock of this reunion that has obscured the significance of their foregoing scene. From the interchange it would appear that, if Lear stands for reason in madness, Gloucester may stand for vision in blindness. When Lear asks if he sees how the world goes, Gloucester replies: "I see it feelingly" (IV.vi.142). His groping pun is heavily fraught with shame and remorse for the figure he has earlier cut: "the superfluous and lust-dieted man, . . . that will not see/ Because he does not feel" (IV.i.67-9). This parallels the insight that Lear has acquired on the heath: "to feel what wretches feel" (III.iv.34). Gloucester has immediately recognized Lear's voice; Lear rounds out the recognition-scene by naming Gloucester and preaching, "Thou must be patient" (IV.vi.178).

Lear is unquestionably the *persona patiens,* as Coleridge insisted; he is the agonizing figure of this passion play where all the characters suffer. Having committed his rash action, he suffers for it on and on, until he is justified in regarding himself as "a man/ More sinn'd against than sinning" (III.ii.59-60). Edmund is the main agent, in Coleridge's estimation; certainly, he is most active in pulling the strings at the outset. "The younger rises when the old doth fall" (III.iii.25). But the defeated opportunist concedes that, with its last revolution, his wheel has come full circle. Edgar, his polar rival, is passive at first; he suffers, then he acts; and it is his suffering that prepares him for action. When Gloucester thanks and blesses him for his anonymous aid, he characterizes himself as (IV.vi.221-3)

> A most poor man, made tame to fortune's blows,
> Who, by the art of known and feeling sorrows,
> Am pregnant to good pity.

As such, he is the right instrument for conveying a sense of fellow-feeling, both to Lear in the hovel on the heath and to Gloucester at Dover Cliff.

It is a cruel world where the honest Kent must go incognito, and where the once-naive Edgar has to run through a protean repertory of roles. After the disappearance of Tom of Bedlam, he is more simply a neutral benefactor, the Good Samaritan. But when he protects Gloucester from Oswald's attack and is called "bold peasant" by the courtier, he adapts himself to that appellation by replying in a rustic dialect (231). He disposes of Oswald, thereby saving the life that Gloucester would have thrown away. But he cannot disclose his identity before he has made his appearance as a nameless champion; and even this last masquerade is preceded by another one, that of the messenger delivering the challenge. However, the battle must precede the tournament. *"Drum afar off"* has terminated the Cliff Scene. The drumming grows louder when the French forces, flying Cordelia's colors, march to meet the British. While the engagement is taking place offstage, we await the outcome with Gloucester under a tree.

Hard upon the heels of retreating soldiers, Edgar reports the defeat and capture of Lear and Cordelia, and Gloucester reverts to his former mood of self-pity. Why should he let himself be led any farther? "A man may rot even here" (V.ii.8). But, just as growth yields to decay, so decay fosters growth, in the biological cycle. What is important, fulfillment, is a matter of timing. Man must reconcile himself to the fact that nature will take its course. Edgar, picking up Gloucester's negative image, transposes it into the most positive statement of the play (V.ii.9-11):

> Men must endure
> Their going hence, even as their coming hither,
> Ripeness is all.

Edgar's aphorism can be traced back to Montaigne's essay, "That to philosophize is to learn how to die." Such was the end of knowledge for the tragic playwright, as well as for the skeptical philosopher. It is rather more than a coincidence that the same sentiment is expressed, though not imaged, at the same point in *Hamlet:* "The readiness is all" (V.ii.222). The manner of one's death and the moment of it were ultimate concerns to the Elizabethans.

By averting the suicide and nursing his father's miseries, Edgar has saved him from despair. Could he but live to see his son in his touch, Gloucester has feelingly vowed, "I'd say I had eyes again" (IV.i.24). We do not witness the recognition-scene wherein this yearning is fulfilled at last. But in the final scene, when the explanations come out, Edgar relates the circumstances of Gloucester's happy death, "Twixt two extremes of passion, joy and grief" (V.iii.199). These mixed emotions match the smiles and tears with which Cordelia has received the news of her father: "Sunshine and rain at once" (IV.iii.18). Edmund, sincerely moved by his brother's report, resolves to do some good; but retrospective narration prolongs the delay, and his one humane impulse is thwarted; the reprieve of Cordelia comes too late. When the brothers fought and were reconciled, Edgar pronounced upon his brother and father in apocryphal terms (V.iii.171-2):

> The gods are just, and of our pleasant vices
> Make instruments to plague us.

Edmund's existence is at once the consequence of, and the retribution for, Gloucester's sin (173-4).

> The dark and vicious place where thee he got
> Cost him his eyes.

Where the inequities of this world have made Gloucester and Lear more and more doubtful as to the justice of heaven, Edgar is whole-heartedly its exponent. Albany, too, can point to the death of Cornwall, fatally wounded in the very act of torturing Gloucester, as an indication that the guilty are punished here below. But so are the innocent. So is Cordelia; and this, more than anything else, I suspect, is why critics have flinched at the notion of performing the play. There is a grim sort of poetic justice in the scene where the King refuses to accept her death; and his own demise, just afterward, is a deliverance for him. But audiences have frequently shared his and Gloucester's unwillingness to bear an unhappy ending patiently; the chronicle-history ended happily; while the adaptation of Nahum Tate, which all but replaced Shakespeare's tragedy for a hundred and fifty years, managed to marry off Cordelia to Edgar, who thanks the King with these concluding lines:

> Thy bright example shall convince the World
> (Whatever Storms of Fortune are decreed)
> That Truth and Vertue shall at last succeed.

Shakespeare's Edgar repeats to the dying Lear his optimistic counsel to Gloucester: "Look up, my lord" (V.iii.313). But he cannot contrive another miracle. The problem of evil is unresolved at the conclusion, though the prevailing catastrophe is accepted. It is, as Kent says, a presentiment of doomsday, "the promis'd end" (264). Edgar, rather than Albany, speaks the final speech in the Folio. Well might he proclaim a farewell to dissembling and a renewal of sincerity. It is high time to

> Speak what we feel, not what we ought to say.

And, in his terminal couplet, our deficient sight is contrasted with the insight painfully achieved through old age (325-7):

> The oldest hath borne most: we that are young,
> Shall never see so much, nor live so long.

We leave him looking across the straits, listening to the cadence of human misery in the ebb and flow of the tides, and catching that eternal note of sadness which Sophocles heard long ago and which Matthew Arnold caught in the heavy-hearted measures of "Dover Beach." As with Oedipus, blind and dying at Colonus, so with Gloucester at Dover. In each case, the passion of a patriarch has met with compassion on the part of a filial survivor, be it Edgar or Antigone. But it is Goethe who puts his finger on the archetype in that relationship:

Ein alter Mann ist stets ein König Lear.

May I translate freely, in order to keep the rhyme?

> An aged man is always like King Lear.
> Effort and struggle long have passed him by;
> And love and leadership are pledged elsewhere;
> And youth must work out its own destiny.
> Come on, old fellow, come along with me.

An Introduction to
Coriolanus

This play, which must have seen its first performance in
1608 or thereabouts, may be the last of Shakespeare's
tragedies as we define them today. Criticism has tended
to range it beside his greatest for its power, its amplitude,
and its craftsmanship. But it has never been so popular as
the others; and that is by no means surprising, since it so
expressly calls into question the equivocal values of popularity. On an elementary human basis, Shakespeare's appeal has always been exerted through his characters, and
through the bonds of sympathy that ally them with the
spectator or the reader. From the outset of *Coriolanus,*
however, such an identification is harshly repelled; and
modern ideology, which disposes us to sympathize less
readily with the hero than with the viewpoint of his antagonists, has slanted and colored our understanding of
both. Yet recent history, by grimly reviving the very
issues that Shakespeare dramatized, has greatly increased

This introduction was written for the Pelican Edition (Baltimore: Penguin
Books, 1957).

the importance and the impressiveness of his dramatization. *Coriolanus* has been found, on revival, to be more fraught with significance for our time than any other drama in the Shakespearean repertory. Max Reinhardt's production in Germany was turbulently prophetic. French crowds rioted when, in the years between the wars, it was performed at the Comédie Française.

Shakespeare's audiences, on occasion, could be quite as explosive. His England must often have seemed to be rifted internally, as well as externally menaced. Even while he was writing *Coriolanus,* outcries over the scarcity of grain were daily reaching London from the Midlands. A Stuart monarch, recently enthroned, claimed more authority and wielded less than his Tudor predecessors had done. Strong-willed men could make spectacular bids for power; Sir Walter Raleigh was being held in the Tower of London on charges of conspiracy; the Earl of Essex had incited Londoners to fight in the streets a few years before; and for that insurrection *Richard II* had been utilized as propaganda. Such, of course, had not been Shakespeare's purpose. His mounting sequence of histories had made England's coming-of-age coincide with his own, and had subsumed—along with the English past—the most triumphant decade of the first Elizabeth's reign. Therefore his chronicle plays had been somewhat controlled by considerations of patriotism, royal prerogative, and the relative familiarity of the facts. Seeking a freer field of political observation, shifting his concern from the ruler's rights and duties to those of the citizen, Shakespeare was inevitably led to a point where more distant roads converge: the archetype of city-states, the keystone of western traditions, Rome.

At the beginning of his tragic period—the opening years of the seventeenth century—he essayed this republican theme in *Julius Caesar.* He resumed it with an even grander sequel, *Antony and Cleopatra,* but not until after completing his exhaustive explorations of personality in *Hamlet, Othello, King Lear,* and *Macbeth.* Thus *Coriolanus* rounds out a trilogy, though it stands somewhat apart from the other two Roman plays, possibly nearer to *Antony and Cleopatra* in scope and to *Julius Caesar* in subject. All three, taken together, constitute a great debate on ethics, in which the statement of private interests is balanced against the counterstatement of public responsibilities. *Julius Caesar* lays the dialectical groundwork by showing a group of individuals in conflict over the state. *Antony and Cleopatra* shows its individualistic hero and heroine rejecting their obligations to their respective states and behaving as if they were laws unto themselves. *Coriolanus* explores the extreme situation of the individual who pits himself against the state. Here Julius Caesar might have proved a monumental counterpart; but Shakespeare's portrait was brief and enigmatic, registering the impact of Caesarism on others, notably on the conscience of Marcus Brutus; and Brutus, acting "in a general honest thought / And common good to all," presented the obverse of the Roman coin whereon Coriolanus is stamped incisively (V.v.71-2).

The historical Caius Martius Coriolanus, figuring in the earliest annals of the Republic, had won his victory at Corioli in 49 B.C. He may indeed have been a half-legendary embodiment of patrician resistance to the increasing demands of the plebeians and especially their newly appointed spokesmen, the Tribunes. Hence, instead of being elected to the consulate, he was banished, and went over to the enemy as the hero does in the play. In the end, as the historian Mommsen sums it up, "he expiated his first treason by a second, and both by death." Poetic justice was better served than either side. Shakespeare drew his version of these episodes from Plutarch's *Lives,* the source that inspired him most, that treasury of ancient biography which comprises a series of comparative studies in heroic citizenship. Plutarch, the Greek moralist, saw Coriolanus as an outstanding example of the peculiarly Roman conception of virtue: *virtus,* which is translated "valiantness." The vice that attended and finally defeated this salient quality was "willfulness." Plutarch's contrasting parallel is the career of Alcibiades, whose ingratiating suppleness—like Antony's—throws the intransigent arrogance of Coriolanus into bold relief. That the latter was brought up by his widowed mother, and was chiefly animated by the desire to please her, Plutarch is at pains to emphasize.

Shakespeare follows Plutarch so very closely that he often echoes the phraseology of the magnificent Elizabethan translation by Sir Thomas North. Volumnia's plea to her son in Act V, eloquently massive as it is, is scarcely more than a metrical adaptation of North's prose. On the other hand, her appeal to him in Act III is Shakespeare's interpolation; he has reserved his right to modify and augment his material in the interest of psychological motivation and dramatic equilibrium; and those two interventions of Volumnia, in each case changing the mind of Coriolanus, are the turning-points of the plot. Rhetoric, the art of persuasion, determined not only the style but also the structure of *Julius Caesar:* Cassius persuades Brutus, Brutus persuades the people, Mark Antony persuades them otherwise. *Coriolanus* is not less Roman in its recourse to public speech; and speech-making triumphs ironically over war-mongering; but now the forensic mode is that of dissuasion. The candidate actually dissuades the people from voting for him; the general at

length is dissuaded from pursuing his revenge. His vein
is negation: curses, threats, and invectives from first to
last. Once he rallies his men; many times he scolds them.
When he girds at the gods, his rant sounds more like the
misanthropic Timon than the iconoclastic Tamburlaine.
Yet how narrowly it misses the tone of Hotspur!

Coriolanus to the contrary, the word is not "mildly"
(III.ii.142). The language of the play reverberates with
the dissonance of its subject-matter and the thunder-like
percussion of its protagonist. The words are so tensely involved in the situation that they do not lend themselves
much to purple passages or quotations out of context.
Reflecting a stylistic transition, they seem to combine the
serried diction of Shakespeare's middle period with the
flowing rhythm of his later plays. The speeches
frequently begin and break off in the middle of a line;
but the cadence of the blank verse persists through occasional setbacks; and sometimes the overlapping pen-
tameters are more evident to the ear than on the page.
This has been a problem for editors, many of whom have
regarded the difficulties of the text as invitations to
change it. Yet it must be assumed that the unique redac-
tion of *Coriolanus,* which has come down to us through
the Folios, is more or less authoritative; at all events, it is
our sole authority; much of the refractoriness is inherent
in the style and subject-matter. The original stage directions, which are usually explicit, convey a suggestion of
pageantry commanding the full resources of the resplen-
dent Globe Playhouse. And from a contemporary sketch
of *Titus Andronicus,* we know that the Elizabethans could
approximate Roman dress.

Though the scenes march by in swift continuity, moving from camp to camp and faction to faction, the acts
are sharply divided, as if to stress the division among the

characters. Act I presents the hero in his proper field of action, the battlefield, where heroism can be demonstrated in its simplest terms as valiantness. Act II brings him reluctantly home to his triumph, and even more grudgingly into the electoral campaign. This goes against him in Act III and leads, after another disastrous attempt at propitiation, to the decree of banishment. Act IV pursues the exiled Coriolanus traversing the distance between Rome and Antium, and betraying himself and his fellow Romans to the Volscian general, Aufidius. Act V witnesses his capitulation and consummates his tragedy: military commitment, resisting civic pressure, yields to domestic. Throughout these vicissitudes he sustains his predominating role, the central figure when he is on stage, the topic of discussion when he is not. His monolithic character is measured by no single foil of comparable stature—least of all by his rival, Aufidius, who has failed to square accounts with him honorably, and vowed to do so through dishonorable means if necessary—but by his dynamic relations with all the others, on the diverging levels of family, city, and enemy.

The one is accordingly weighed against the many; and the tendency toward monodrama is counterpoised by an unusual number of choric roles—citizens, officers, soldiers, servants, other ranks of society. The scales tip during the roadside interview between a Roman and a Volscian, with its implication that Coriolanus is taking the same road to espionage and betrayal. As for the populace, the Tribunes can hardly speak for it because it is so vocal on its own behalf; the mistake of Coriolanus is to believe that its "voices" are merely votes. Generalization soon breaks down into Hob and Dick, and the types are individualized, loudly insisting upon their individuality. There are some ugly mob-scenes and one violent outbreak of street-fighting, but mother-wit is the characteristic weapon. The humorous mediator, Menenius Agrippa, can handle this pithy prose idiom. The crowd in turn can rise to the pitch of blank verse, while their shrewd heckling enlivens his tale of the belly and the members. The First Citizen, great toe though he may be, accepts the question-begging metaphor that identifies the organ of digestion with the deliberation of the Senate. But, logically enough, he presses the claims of the other parts, including the soldierly arm. The parable will apply to the choleric hero as much as to the angry mob.

In a subsequent argument, when Coriolanus is compared to a disease, Menenius retorts that he is rather a diseased limb which can be cured. By this time many sores and wounds have been metaphorically and literally probed, thereby revealing other aspects of the body politic. The age-old fable expounded by Menenius, appeasing the uproar of the introductory scene, has served to establish an ideal of social order—the concept of commonweal, *res publica*—more honored in the breach than the observance. It has also concretely grounded the imagery of the play in the matter at hand, the dearth of corn, the fundamental problem of nourishment. The struggling classes seek to feed on each other; Menenius is a self-confessed epicure; the poor justify themselves by hungry proverbs; and Coriolanus finds himself in their desperate position when he appears at the feast of Aufidius. In close association with these images of food, battle is described as if it were harvest, with the swords of destruction figuratively turning into the ploughshares of fertility. Another associated train of thought runs to animals, always an inspiration for name-calling. The hero is introduced as a dog to the people, who are curs to him then and crucially later. The prevailing code is dog-eat-dog.

Menenius points the moral succinctly when he demands: "On both sides more respect" (III.i.180). Since both sides indulge in such embittered polemics, interpretation has varied between the extremes of left and right, now underlining the dangers of dictatorship and now the weaknesses of democracy, according to the political adherence of the interpreters. Nothing could better attest what Coleridge, in this connection, called "the wonderful philosophic impartiality in Shakespeare's politics." His portrayal of the multitude, whose sedition he arms with a grievance, is anti-demagogic rather than anti-democratic. The demagogues are the Tribunes, portrayed in unequivocal cynicism, dissuading the plebs from the suffrage they have already pledged to Coriolanus. Coriolanus, on his side, is no friend of the people; and it is to the credit of his integrity that he cannot act a part he does not feel. He earns, with an authoritarian vengeance, the title that Ibsen would bestow in irony upon his humanitarian Dr. Stockmann—*An Enemy of the People*. All men are enemies, rivals if not foes, to Coriolanus. His aggressive temperament could never be happy until it had lurched all other swords of the garland. His fight against the world is not for booty nor praise nor office, but for acknowledged superiority; he does not want to dominate but to excel; and he cannot bear the thought of subordination.

We need not look far afield for the school that nurtured that spirit of single-minded competitiveness. The Roman matron, the masculine dowager, the statuesque Volumnia, is both father and mother to her son; and she has taught him aristocratic scorn along with martial courage. His wife, the gracious Virgilia, in contrast is sheer feminity; and her main attribute, like Cordelia's, is silence. His young son chases butterflies with congenital resolution; subsequently Coriolanus commands a Volscian army as eager as boys chasing butterflies. No man can withstand him and only one woman can plead with him. In yielding to her, in feeling this ultimate modicum of feminine tenderness, the strong man becomes again—as it were—a child. Thence the sting in the last taunt of Aufidius. Under the epithet "traitor" Coriolanus has slightly flinched. But "boy"! "Thou boy of tears!" (V.vi.100) In significant contradistinction, we are reminded continually that the Tribunes are elderly men. Leadership, as Volumnia's boy had learned it in the wars, was largely an individual matter of athletic prowess, having little to do with the sort of maturity that peaceful civilian government requires. Perhaps the trouble, as analyzed by Aufidius, lay in a soldier's inability to move "from th' casque to th' cushion" (IV.vii.43). The virtues of war may well be the vices of peace; the man on horseback, dismounted, a sorry creature.

T. S. Eliot's modernized *Coriolan* consists of two poems: "Triumphal March" and "Difficulties of a Statesman." These headings suggest the dilemma of Shakespeare's protagonist. His is not an internal struggle; so far as his two short soliloquies indicate, the treason causes him less mental anguish than the election; and, what is even worse, at Antium he employs the flatteries he has despised at Rome. Rather it is the external manifestation of his colossal pride that exalts him, all but deifies him, and renders the slippery turns of fortune more precipitous than the Tarpeian Rock. "Rome or I! One or the other must fall!" Such is the climax, verbalized by Wagner, to Beethoven's orchestration of this theme. "The note of banishment," the note that James Joyce kept hearing in Shakespeare's plays, is never more plangently sounded than in the parting denunciation of Coriolanus to the Romans: "I banish you!" (III.iii.123). Never was man more alienated than he, as the gates of Rome close behind him and he is forced to seek "a world elsewhere" (135). The scene reverses his initial triumph, when the gates of Corioles shut him in alone of all the attacking Romans. The ironic pattern is completed, on his return to the hostile town, by his fatal words to its citizens. And note the emphatic position of the first personal pronoun (V.vi.113-6):

> If you have writ your annals true, 'tis there
> That, like an eagle in a dove-cote, I
> Flutter'd your Volscians in Corioles.
> Alone I did it.

Othello, at a similar moment, had the satisfaction of recalling his services to the state. Caius Martius— Coriolanus no longer—can only glory in his isolation. The word "alone" is repeated more than in any other Shakespearean work; and, from the welter of similes, the most memorable is "a lonely dragon" (IV.i.30). We end by realizing the ambiguity of the foreign name this Roman has proudly flaunted. How can he expect it to be anything but a target of hatred for the orphans and widows and comrades-in-arms of men he has killed? After the combat in which he gained it, he had generously tried to befriend a certain Volscian, and had characteristically forgotten the poor man's name—a touch which Shakespeare added to Plutarch's anecdote. Shakespeare's insight, detailed as it is, confirms an observation cited from Plato by Plutarch: that such overriding egoism can only terminate in "desolation." This must be that desolation of solitude which the American imagination has paralleled in the career of another tragic captain, Melville's Ahab.

Shakespeare's Misanthrope

We do not need Herman Melville to warn us that *Timon of Athens* is an ambush for critics. Yet, in his nondescript edition of Shakespeare now at Harvard University, it is one of the plays most heavily marked. Marginal annotations are rare but pithy. Thus, when Timon urges the Bandits to plunder the shops of Athens, two of them are almost dissuaded from banditry. The third, an opportunist, tells his colleagues that it would be better to reform when less plunder is available: "There is no time so miserable but a man may be true" (IV.iii.456-7). This has been didactically paraphrased by the anonymous editor: "There is no hour in a man's life so wretched, but he always has it in his power to become *true*, i.e. honest." And Melville, in the margin, has glossed the comment, after crossing it out: "Peace, peace! Thou ass of a commentator!" His own feelings come to the surface when

Delivered at the fifteenth international conference of The Shakespeare Institute at Stratford-upon-Avon, August 26–September 1, 1972; published in *Shakespeare Survey*, 26 (Cambridge: Cambridge University Press, 1973).

Timon drives his false friends out of the banquet hall, and Melville comments with Yankee succinctness: "Served 'em right." In his other reading he would frequently return to his misanthropic touchstone. Where La Bruyère wrote skeptically about friendship, Melville commented: "True, Shakespeare goes further: None die but somebody spurns them into the grave." Melville's misquotation is even more absolute than the words of Shakespeare's Apemantus: "Who dies that bears not one spurn to their graves / Of their friends' gift?" (I.ii.141-2).

Timon of Athens provided a moral backdrop for Melville's *Confidence-Man,* as *Hamlet* had for *Pierre* and *King Lear* for *Moby-Dick.* His literary career bogged down at the stage that his biographers would call Timonism, and *The Confidence-Man*—with its masquerade of Emersonian ideals and Hawthornesque doubts, its dialectic between a self-deluding optimism and an ever-deepening mistrust— was the last work of fiction he published. But from first to last he worshipped at the Shakespearean pantheon, and ranked Timon with Lear and Hamlet as a spokesman for those bitter truths to which he felt the American public was deaf. Shakespeare's more professional interpreters, except for the emphatic Wilson Knight, have been less inclined to inflate the evaluation so subjectively. Some of the others, such as Una Ellis-Fermor, Willard Farnham, and Terence Spencer, have used classical precedent and textual scrutiny to frame the play in critical perspective. A substantial consensus, locating it somewhere in the sequence through Shakespeare's later tragedies to his romances, would regard it as an unpolished draft, probably set aside before it reached actual performance. This assumption might allow us a glimpse into the playwright's workshop, accounting for the rough spots and the obvious inconsistencies. Yet there are brilliantly finished scenes and powerful speeches: the diatribe on universal thievery, for example, from which Vladimir Nabokov stole his title *Pale Fire*.

Why then, we shall find ourselves asking, should the tragedy have been shelved? We can discern its limits as a tragedy by recalling Edmond Malone's observation: "Of all the works of Shakespeare, *Timon of Athens* possesses most the character of a satire." Now *satura* is traditionally a mixed mode, closer perhaps to the comic than to the tragic, and not always combining successfully with drama. Ben Jonson failed in his trilogy of so-called "comical satires," though *Volpone* would fully live up to that designation. Its effectiveness can be measured by comparing the savage indignation of Timon's speech on gold (IV.iii.381-92) with the controlled irony of Volpone's opening hymn to his treasure. Shakespeare's principal source is the *Timon* of Lucian, who is there and elsewhere the arch-satirist of gold. Lucian's Timon is presented as a poor laborer who, after the gods restore his lost riches, beats off the parasitical types that besiege him again. The Lucianic dialogue has dramatic elements, but it shows no development of character or conflict. It has no beginning, nothing more than a backward glance at former fortunes, and no ending, simply a hostile stance toward all other men. This is the figure that crystallized in popular mythology, the "critic Timon" mentioned in *Love's Labor's Lost,* the archetypal "Timonist" of Elizabethan allusion. The misanthrope's role was as clearly laid out for him as the pandar's was for Pandarus in *Troilus and Cressida*.

Hence he could self-consciously announce: "I am Misanthropos, and hate mankind" (IV.iii.54). But that is scarcely more than the application of a label, and it is inadequately dramatized when Lucian's Timon stones his interlocutors—let alone when Shakespeare's Timon bribes his visitors to go away. In "Some Thoughts on Playwriting" Thornton Wilder remarks: "The exposition of the nature of misanthropy . . . in Shakespeare's *Timon of Athens* has never been a success." [1] Solitude, after all, is antisocial by definition, and anchorites can express their distaste for society by undramatically avoiding it. Molière's *Misanthrope,* on the other hand, takes place in a highly social setting. To be sure, its hero is constantly contemplating a retirement to some desert island: *"Trop de perversité règne au siècle où nous sommes, / Et je veux me tirer du commerce des hommes."* Yet it takes the mundanity of the court to bring out the misanthropy of Alceste; his intransigent sincerity has its foil in the worldly hypocrisy of the courtiers; and we end by wondering which has been the more sharply satirized. *Timon of Athens,* by contrast, moves in the direction of a monodrama which is unresolved. The isolated protagonist is subject to successive interrogations. If he is being tested like Job, he does not survive the ordeal. If he is being punished like Prometheus, he retaliates by verbal castigations and assumes the final responsibility for his own victimization.

He can be brought nearer to his Jacobean context if we view him as a malcontent. But malcontents, while cursing their lot, undertake to set things right: to retrieve a princely heritage or avenge a sister's rape. Hamlet wears his antic disposition as a cloak to mask his vengeance. The ingrained malignity of Iago, or of Webster's disgruntled adventurers, seeks to vent itself in action. A closer prototype would be the melancholy Jaques, who cultivates melancholia for its own sake, and whom Hazlitt has described as the sole contemplative personage among the Shakespearean *dramatis personae.* When he retires to a

1. "Some Thoughts on Playwriting," in *American Playwrights on Drama,* ed. Horst Frenz (New York, 1965), p. 58.

house of convertites, one can imagine him finding matter for raillery there. He is not likely to be put out of his humor; nor, on a cruder level, is the low-minded and single-minded Thersites. In comparison, we must remember that Timon did not begin as a Timonist. He was, as one Senator puts it, a phoenix before he became a gull (II.i.31-2). Legend has preserved him in the posture of a reclusive curmudgeon; in his prime he had personified the image of a gregarious prodigal. The problem of recreating that earlier personality, and registering the stages of alienation and decline, was one to overtax the flexibility and resourcefulness of Shakespeare himself. His philanthropist is one man, his misanthropist another, and the transition between them is a sudden recoil rather than a gradual disillusionment.

All this, in bald outline, corresponds well enough with the basic patterns of medieval or Renaissance tragedy. Seldom indeed has a downfall been so precipitate from such lavish prosperity to such crouching adversity. But, whereas the traditional sacrifice was a throne, a high office, or a beloved partner, here the loss is reckoned solely in financial terms. Fortune still is the presiding goddess, although her precipitating symbol is not a wheel but a hill, which the competitive crowd is climbing up or sliding down. The venal allegory of the Poet, which serves as an expository device, is rounded out by his reappearance with a moralistic satire. The barometric references to Timon's *fortune* indicate both his destiny and his affluence. Romeo is "fortune's fool" because he is crossed by fate (*Romeo and Juliet*, III.i.136); Timon's "trencher-friends" are "fools of fortune" because they would do anything for wealth (III.vi.96). The key-words of the play, employed more often than anywhere else in Shakespeare, *friend* and *gold*, almost seem to cancel each other out. Timon learns, from his painful experience with his selfish following, to equate them. Love between the sexes plays no part in either of his two worlds. In the first, though it is Cupid who presents the masque, the dancing ladies are Amazons quickly dismissed. In the second Alcibiades introduces the only two feminine characters, courtesans ungallantly encouraged by Timon to infect mankind with their alleged diseases.

His relations with his fellow men have been predicated upon "a dream of friendship," from which—his steward Flavius perceives—he was bound to be rudely wakened (IV.ii.34). Much of what we hear about his nobility is attested by those who have something to gain from their flattery. While they profit literally from his patronage, he accounts himself metaphorically wealthy in his friends (II.ii.184). However, the arrangement is not reciprocal. His ideal is "to have so many like brothers commanding one another's fortunes" (I.ii.104-5). But he proves to be the lone member of such a brotherhood; as a benefactor he has been a spendthrift. The test of magnanimity on both sides, the process of debasement and undeception, comprises a three-act drama in itself. The opening act is a veritable blaze of overdone hospitality and exploited munificence. The monetary tensions behind this extravagant pageantry come out swiftly in the series of confrontations that follows: the servants shuttling back and forth between debtors and creditors; the sycophants tried and found wanting, each of them fumbling for excuses and disavowals; and, in the dim background, the usurers pulling the ultimate strings. The last scene of the third act, where the fair-weather flatterers are invited to a mock-banquet and told off, is a kind of *dénouement*. We may well then feel, as Melville apparently did, that the curtain of poetic justice has fallen at last. "Served 'em right."

The first three acts attempt to trace, so to speak, the etiology of Timon's malaise. The treatment is somewhat diagrammatic, as in a morality play (or what M. C. Bradbrook would term a "tragic pageant"). Instead of the psychological insight that revealed, step by step, how a Macbeth could become steeped in blood or an Othello corrupted by unworthy suspicions, we are confronted with the overt theatricalism of a Leontes overcome by jealousy in a single instantaneous seizure. As in *The Winter's Tale* likewise, there is a sharp disjunction between the first three acts and Acts IV and V. Yet, insofar as the characterization of Timon is concerned, the real break occurs in Act III. During his absence from the stage, bills have been accumulating and loans put off. One of the servants alerts the others to the fact that an identity-crisis is brewing: "my lord leans wondrously to discontent" (III.iv.70-1). When Timon reappears soon afterward, he is—as the stage direction specifies—*"in a rage."* No longer the easygoing host of Act I or the bewildered patron of Act II, he is abruptly ready to denounce his duns, summon his ever-greedy clientèle to an anti-feast, and emerge as a full-fledged misanthrope: "Henceforth hated be / Of Timon man and all humanity!" (III.vi.104-5). This lightning change from one state of mind to its polar opposite merits the criticism that Apemantus will lodge against Timon himself: "The middle of humanity thou never knewest, but the extremity of both ends" (IV.iii.300-1).

Timon, the man-hater of the last two acts, has hardened into his monolithic attitude. If his prior self seems in retrospect shallow, it is attributable to his thoroughly extroverted disposition. But how much deeper does his embitterment go? In the "better days" of his lordly innocence, he held no mental reservations (IV.ii.27); hence he needed no asides or soliloquies. In his "latter spirits" he continues to speak out directly (V.iv.74). But he cannot be said to have moved from the one extreme to the other through the medium of introspection; nor does he, as an ascetic hermit, engage his thoughts in spiritual meditation. The first scene of Act IV constitutes a soliloquy merely because, for the first time it would seem, he stands alone. This has its counterpart in the climactic episode of *Coriolanus,* where at the gates of Rome the exiled general pronounces his personal decree of banishment against his fellow citizens. Henceforth the speeches of Timon extend and intensify the acrid rhetoric of Coriolanus: the invective vein, the serried style, the pregnant imagery. Timon's farewell to Athens is a baneful prayer that the laws of nature reverse themselves, a litany of curses, "multiplying bans" (IV.i.34). Since obligations to him have not been met, let all sanctions be broken: "Degrees, observances, customs and laws, / Decline to your confounding contraries" (IV.i.19-20). Timon prays for everything that Ulysses warned the Greek generals against. No wonder Karl Marx relished Shakespeare's imprecation against gold.

The discontinuity between the first and second halves of the play is widened further by the shift in locale. A young and lyrical Shakespeare, in *A Midsummer Night's Dream,* had conveyed his characters from Athens to the neighboring woods, where their problems were solved by magical charms. Protagonists of Shakespearean comedy had often found their happiness in one or another part of the forest. Oedipus, on leaving Thebes for Colonus after a much more terrible catastrophe, had found at least a mood of resignation. Timon gives way to his fury even as he relinquishes his Athenian mansion for a cave. The titular epithet, Timon of Athens, has an ironic ring, echoing his bitterness against the Athenians and under-scoring his gesture of self-exile. Like Lear, he exposes man's ingratitude by exposing himself to the barren countryside, by reducing himself to the condition of "un-accommodated man" (*King Lear*, III.iv.106-7). When he looks back to the city from his arboreal retreat, he can accept the paradox of Apemantus: "the commonwealth of Athens is become a forest of beasts" (IV.iii.347-8). It is an additional paradox that, when Timon digs for roots, he discovers gold—now meaningless to him or, rather, fraught with the evil meaning of civic corruption. "The hundredheaded rabble of the cathedral close." Such was Athens for Swift, as characterized by Joyce. "A hater of his kind ran from them to the wood of madness, his mane foaming in the moon, his eyeballs stars. Houyhnhnm, horsenostrilled."

Apemantus performs a unifying function by prefigur-ing the second part during the first, eating roots while the others are banqueting, recognized by them as being "op-posite to humanity" (I.i.273). He strikes the morose note that prepares us for future dissonances: "Who lives that's not depraved or depraves?" (I.ii.140). As a Cynic philoso-pher, in the historical and the etymological sense, he seems to welcome the association with dogs by which he is continually saluted. Timon at one point is constrained to remind him, since his preference for animals is so pro-nounced, that they are quite as predatory as men (IV.iii.327-45). The reunion of these two caitiffs is worthy of Samuel Beckett in its mutual vexation and name-calling, its surly interchange of taunts and gibes. Ape-mantus seems understandably suspicious—and slightly jealous—of Timon in his new role as a carper. Can it be authentic if he has assumed it "enforcedly," if he had no choice but to put on "this sour cold habit" as a response to misfortune (IV.iii.241, 239)? Timon, in his turn, feels better qualified to scorn the world because he has known its amenities. "Why shouldst thou hate men?" he asks Apemantus. "They never flatter'd thee" (271-2). Apemantus, the natural misanthrope, for whom the grapes have never been anything but sour, is put down and driven off by Timon, the conditioned misanthrope, for whom life is all the sourer because he has tasted its sweetness.

The scene that reunites them temporarily and disjoins them forever (IV.iii), one of the longest in Shakespeare, is completed by the first scene of Act V, wherein Timon makes his last appearance. Having delivered his curse against gold, and thereupon discovered and renounced it, he alternates between solitary monologue and denunciation of his old Athenian companions, seeking him out to be rebuffed again, in a quick succession of what might be termed non-recognition scenes. Having been more or less continuously onstage, from one encounter to the next, he withdraws and dies offstage. The moribund moment, which figures so importantly in most of Shakespeare's tragedies, is evaded here. This does not even seem to be a suicide, but rather an expected dissolution. After so vocal and long-drawn-out a rejection of existence, what would be left to say? Why should Timon, having learned to abominate his contemporaries, care for the good opinion of posterity? Instead of a rousing death-speech, three different epitaphs are reported. Each of them is a sullen and stilted couplet in fourteeners, and two of them are transcribed from North's Plutarch, one of which is translated from Callimachus: "Here lie I, Timon, who, alive, all living men did hate. / Pass by and curse thy fill, but pass and stay not here thy gait" (V.iv.72-3). Whatever the inscription on his grave, it will soon be washed away by the sea—a quiet consummation and a static conclusion.

As contrasted with this slackening quiescence, into which his lamentations and agonies subside, the underplot has been loudly kept astir by the drum and fife of Alcibiades' army. Alcibiades has his own reasons for looking back in anger at the Athenians. "To be in anger is impiety," he has confessed before the Senators, "But who is man that is not angry?" (III.v.56-7). Hardly Alcibiades, any more than Timon, and the unwanted gold of the passive angry man backs the revenge of his active brother-in-arms. The Senate has ignored his plea for a fellow soldier's life and, when Alcibiades has pressed it, has responded by banishing him. Therefore he has turned against the city-state, which he reenters in military triumph at the end. He is a more attractive, if no more reliable, figure than his Plutarchian parallel, Coriolanus. Shakespeare has individualized Alcibiades, along with Apemantus and Flavius, because they sustain a degree of affinity with Timon himself. All the other members of the cast are merely typified, as if to suggest that these are the sort of men to whom his cynical generalizations apply. As for Flavius, he is the nonpareil, the *raisonneur* whose head-shaking asides give us an early clue to the situation, the faithful servitor whose continuing honesty forces his master to recognize one exception—"but one"—to the general rule of bad faith. "How fain would I have hated all mankind, / And thou redeem'st thyself" (IV.iii.497, 499-500).

The redeeming virtue of Flavius modifies the scope, if not the intensity, of Timon's hatred. Diogenes the Cynic might have been happy to have encountered a single honest man—might have become, in Melville's phrase, "a genial misanthrope." And Melville, who on occasion could out-Timon Shakespeare, sharpens a nice distinction in *The Confidence-Man:* "tell me, was not that humor, of Diogenes, which led him to live, a merry-andrew, in the flower-market, better than that of the less wise Athenian, which made him a skulking scare-crow in pine-barrens? An injudicious gentleman, Lord Timon." It remains an open question whether Timon's experience should be viewed as one man's hard-luck story or as an indictment of the human race. Other tragic heroes have undergone worse tribulations than bankruptcy, and have not arrived at so wholesale a condemnation of their fellow men. Since Timon is the victim of callousness rather than cruelty, his sufferings are not to be compared with those of King Lear. Grief, which has a humanizing effect on Lear, dehumanizes Timon.[2] Should the limitation be ascribed to the character or to the playwright? Could it be that Shakespeare, so adept and far-ranging in his sympathy, was balked at the portrayal of antipathy? It seems clear that he, who empathized with such numerous and varied themes, found this an uncongenial one. It would be significant if his uncertainties over *Timon of Athens* marked his transition from tragedy to romance.

Not that there is much romance about *Timon.* Its subject-matter would, by neo-classical standards, relegate it to the bourgeois sphere of comedy, where parasites and moneylenders flourish and rich men like Trimalchio entertain. Actually it has few comic moments, if any, and its

---

2. This was written before I had seen the interesting comparison of the two plays drawn by L. C. Knights in *The Morality of Art: Essays Presented to G. Wilson Knight,* ed. D. W. Jefferson (London, 1969). It is especially interesting to see the author of *How Many Children Had Lady Macbeth?* reconciling some of the disparities in *Timon of Athens* by tracing a subtle psychological portrait of the protagonist, which emphasizes self-hatred more than misanthropy.

Fool is Shakespeare's dimmest and dullest. Molière's misanthrope has his laughable aspects, which were sorely resented by Rousseau. Timon himself had been a laughingstock of the Old Comedy; he would be mocked again in an eighteenth-century harlequinade. Shakespeare, taking him seriously, focused attention on the object of his grim mockery: not on money itself, but on the colluding attributes of greed and guile. These, of course, are the mainsprings of Jonson's comedies and of many others— though not, on the whole, of Shakespeare's. Living in the same society at its hour of capitalistic emergence, he cannot have been less aware than they were of acquisition and dispossession as a timely theme. They embodied it in the coney-catching of the London underworld. He conceived it as a cosmic projection, when Timon assures the thieves that sun and moon and sea and earth are bent on pilfering and pillaging. This is darker than those occasional glimpses of anarchy which rift the chain of being from play to play. Possibly it is intended to estrange us, like the sardonic harshness of Bertolt Brecht, and unlike the brighter and warmer vistas that we think of as more characteristically Shakespearean. Shakespeare himself was so far from being Misanthropos, so far from hating mankind, that for once his negative capability got in the way of his dramaturgy.

Two Magian Comedies:
The Tempest and *The Alchemist*

Non hic Centauros, non Gorgonas, Harpyiasque
Invenies: Hominem pagina nostra sapit.

If another confrontation between Shakespeare and Jonson is still allowable, then the challenger should be allowed to arm himself with one of his Latin epigraphs. So, on the title-page of *Sejanus,* the author warns the reader not to look for centaurs or gorgons or harpies; these particular pages will savor of man. The distich is quoted from Martial, an acknowledged kindred spirit of Jonson's, and it seems a curious point of departure for a tragedy, since Martial's epigram (X,iv) had also excluded from his lifelike pages such monstrous figures as Oedipus and Thyestes. Jonson cut the quotation conveniently short, yet it hints at the limitations that might emerge from a critical comparison of *Sejanus* or *Catiline* with *Coriolanus* or *Antony and Cleopatra.* For the younger playwright, always more interested in human machinations than in the workings of destiny, tragedy could be reduced

---

Delivered at the thirteenth international conference of The Shakespeare Institute at Stratford-upon-Avon, September 1–6, 1968; published in *Shakespeare Survey,* 22 (Cambridge: Cambridge University Press, 1969).

to conspiracy. Hence it differed from comedy only to the extent that, in the words of the Prologue to *Every Man in his Humor,* crimes may differ from follies. That prologue, introducing a revision which shifted the setting from Italy to England, heralds a more realistic drama by condemning the extravagances and ineptitudes of the popular theater. After casting an invidious glance at such rivals, and appealing for the more judicious laughter of the audience, it concludes by hoping: "You, that haue so grac'd monsters, may like men." [1]

That Jonson should have made so sharp an issue of this distinction might not have been expected from his own work. Most of his critics have stressed his preoccupation with the anomalous. Some of the visitors to Bartholomew Fair strike us as odder than its exhibited oddities, while Volpone and Mosca and their circle of sycophants seem to be even more twisted than their deformed retinue, the dwarf, the eunuch, and the hermaphrodite. But Jonson, as a classicist, was an upholder of norms who specialized in pointing out and pouncing upon abnormalities. He felt especially close in his kinship with Horace, whom he portrays and with whom he identifies in *Poetaster.* As a translator of and a commentator on the *Ars Poetica,* he gave due weight—perhaps too much—to its opening statement: its composite image of the monstrosity that the poet or painter should avoid, a woman's face joined by a horse's neck to a body covered with parti-colored feathers and terminating in a fish's tail. Though his antimasques are rife with queer creatures, these are rather types than

1. Jonson is quoted and cited here from the authoritative edition of C. H. Herford and Percy and Evelyn Simpson (Oxford, 1925–52). Quotation from a modernized text of Shakespeare, even one so sensitively nuanced as the Riverside, might therefore confuse the comparison. Hence my Shakespearean references are to the Folio text, as reprinted in the New Variorum Edition, ed. H. H. Furness (Philadelphia, 1892).

sports, and their prototypes can be traced to folklore if
not to classical mythology. Consequently Jonson was
shocked by the boldness of Shakespeare's invention. How
could he have got away with it, Jonson was constantly
wondering. In the Induction to *Bartholomew Fair,* where
he did his best to come to terms with the public, he expressed his reservations:

> If there bee neuer a *Servant-monster* i'the Fayre; who can
> helpe it? he sayes; nor a nest of *Antiques?* Hee is loth to make
> Nature afraid in his *Playes,* like those that beget *Tales, Tem-*
> *pests,* and such like *Drolleries,* to mix his head with other
> mens heeles, let the concupiscence of *Iigges* and *Dances,*
> raigne as strong as it will amongst you. . . .

Here the attack on *The Winter's Tale* and *The Tempest* is
fairly overt, and the grounds appear to be twofold. Jonson, the official purveyor of masques to the court, remained a purist with regard to the stage; he did not like
to see the dramatist confound his functions with those of
the choreographer. He had aired the same complaint a
few years before, in prefacing the Quarto of *The Alchemist,*
where he appropriately cautioned the reader against
being *"cos'ned . . . in* Poetry, *especially in Playes."* He com-
plained that *"now, the Concupiscence of Daunces, and Antickes*
so raigneth, as to runne away from Nature, and be afraid of her,
is the onely point of art that tickles the Spectators." He also
seemed to be glancing at Shakespeare *vis-à-vis* himself, in
the contrast between an unfettered copiousness and a restrained succinctness, when he concluded by emphasizing
the *"great difference between those, that (to gain the opinion of*
Copie) vtter all they can, how euer unfitly; and those that vse
election, and a meane." The more serious charge, because it
was less subject to the caprices of self-esteem, is that of
affrighting nature—or, as the preface to *The Alchemist*
more fittingly puts it, of being frightened by nature. This

has its all too concrete embodiment in the outlandish person of Shakespeare's servant-monster, and Caliban has his rejoinder when he tells the newcomers to his island (III.ii.144-5):

> Be not affeard, the Isle is full of noyses,
> Sounds, and sweet aires, that giue delight and hurt not.

Shakespeare's "frekelld whelpe, hag-borne" (I.ii.283) requires no defense at this stage. Not only has he been accepted by criticism as the *ne plus ultra* of original characterization, but he has fascinated later writers, who have appended their own variations to the Shakespearean theme. He has become a mouthpiece for cosmic speculation in Browning's *Caliban upon Setebos; or, Natural Theology in the Island,* for revolutionary ideology in Renan's *Caliban: Drame philosophique,* and for a Jamesian commentary on the play itself in *The Sea and the Mirror* by W. H. Auden. He has been interpreted as a test-case for Montaigne's reflections "On the Cannibals," and as a prefiguration of the missing link in Darwin's great chain of being. Jonson was not the first to comment on Stephano's nickname for Caliban. "Seruant Monster?" Trinculo queries at once and, being a professional fool, he proceeds to generalize "the folly of this Iland" (III.ii.5). If Trinculo belongs among Shakespeare's jesters, the butler Stephano is more of a Jonsonian type, with his petty airs and ill-supported pretensions; it is because the drunken Caliban cannot see through them that Trinculo scorns him as a "debosh'd Fish" (III.ii.29). From their first encounter during the thunderstorm Trinculo has been struck, as everyone seems to be, by the amphibious disposition of Caliban. We are suddenly brought home from the island to London, with a rueful allusion to the new world and a moralistic twist of social satire, when Trinculo speculates (II.ii.26-31):

> . . . a strange fish: were I in *England* now (as once I was) and
> had but this fish painted; not a holiday-foole there but would
> giue a peece of siluer: there, would this Monster, make a
> man: any strange beast there, makes a man: when they will
> not giue a doit to relieue a lame Begger, they will lay out ten
> to see a dead *Indian*.

Similarly it occurs to Stephano, arriving shortly afterward, that he could make a fortune by bringing the
mooncalf back to Naples. But Trinculo's pun, "there,
would this Monster, make a man," has a deeper reverberation. As between such freaks on display at Bartholomew
Fair and the uncharitable sightseer who pays his money
to gape at them, which is the monster, which the man?
To press the question much farther would be to trespass
on Jonson's territory. Shakespeare merely sums it up
when Gonzalo, the spokesman for his humorous idealism,
says of the islanders (III.iii.31-4):

> though they are of monstrous shape, yet note
> Their manners are more gentle, kind, then of
> Our humaine generation, you shall finde
> Many, nay almost any.

Again it is a *double-entendre* of Trinculo's which puts Caliban into perspective: "that a Monster should be such a
Naturall" (III.ii.36). Trinculo has the disdain of the artificial fool for a mere simpleton, yet "this demy-divell" is
really not so simple (V.i.272). He has paid for his instruc-
tion from Prospero by instructing him in "the qualities o'
th' Isle" (I.ii.337); his use of the language Miranda taught
him ranges far beyond his imprecations; and he rises to
poetic heights in recounting his dreams. Though we
might not think of him as a highbrow, he makes it clear
that there are worse shapes than his, when he fears that
he and his fellow conspirators will "all be turn'd to Bar-
nacles, or to Apes / With foreheads villanous low"

(IV.i.249-50). Whether nurture will ever stick to his puppy-headed nature remains in doubt, as he is liberated by the *dénouement;* but at least we leave him disabused of his folly and determined to seek for grace.

If the man-monster is "not in Nature," as Dryden argues in his preface to *Troilus and Cressida,* then "of himself" he represents a new species originated by Shakespeare. For, if the Greeks could imagine the centaur by combining the images of a man and a horse, why should not this hybrid—"begotten by an incubus on a witch"— bear witness to the copiousness of Shakespeare's imagination? The argument is subsumed by the dialogue on grafting between Perdita and Polixenes in *The Winter's Tale.* Shakespeare's attitudes toward human nature were animated by sympathetic curiosity, even as Jonson's were by acute suspicion. In the creation of Caliban, Shakespeare seemed to be pushing nature to the verge of her confine; but, though the outcome was a *lusus naturae,* it was by no means unnatural. The paradox is that Jonson, for once, was criticizing Shakespeare from the standpoint of nature rather than art. Later generations might look upon the issue as a debate between a classical sense of decorum and a romantic feeling for grotesquerie, and that difference has probably been widened by the retrospective classification of *The Tempest* as a romance. Insofar as Shakespeare's comedies deal with love, derive their plots from romances, and usually take place in an aura of Romance culture, the term applies to most of them. The later ones are more precisely differentiated by their elaborate staging, their narrative qualities, and their emphasis on tragicomic vicissitude.

But the category is confusing if it obscures the inherent classicism of Shakespeare's technique, which Bernard Knox has evinced in an article relating *The Tempest* to the

Plautine tradition (*English Institute Essays,* 1954). Whatever liberties he may have indulged in, Shakespeare commenced and ended his career by observing "the law of Writ." *The Tempest,* like *The Comedy of Errors,* defers to the unities of time and place. We may view the first scene as a prologue, which conveys us to the island through the storm. The Jacobean stage, with traps for hatches and the upper level for a bridge, was easily transformed into a ship. All that follows moves within the environs of the line-grove surrounding Prospero's cell—where the characters finally come together "Spell-stopt"—and might readily adapt itself to a single set on a modern revolving stage (V.i.61). After the "Poem vnlimited" of *The Winter's Tale,* when sixteen years are leapt across in an *entr'acte, The Tempest* utilizes the "scene indiuidible"—to borrow from the terminology of Polonius. The time-span, something less than the interval between two and six in the afternoon, is announced near the outset, and we hear reminders of its passage. To achieve such unity and compression, only the last three hours of the twelve-year story could be dramatized. This means that a long retrospect must be taken, and places a heavy burden upon the exposition. After the violent action of the shipwreck comes the calm of the second scene and its leisurely narration.

If *Oedipus the King* had been an Elizabethan chronicle-play, it might have begun with the exposure of the infant hero, continued with the slaying of Laius, the outwitting of the Sphinx, and the marriage with Jocasta, and crowded into the last act all the reversals and recognitions that make up the tragedy of Sophocles. Comparably, the younger Shakespeare might have started from the court of Milan, directly presenting the intrigue, the dethronement, and the whole train of events that Prospero narrates. Here instead we relive them vicariously, through his troubled remembrance and through their first-hand impact on Miranda, who has not been aware of them before. The drama begins in its penultimate phase, with Prospero reaching his zenith. His years of adversity, like his initial prosperity, are now behind him. Another hour or two will bring the psychological moment for which he has longed and conjured: "At this houre / Lies at my mercy all mine enemies" (II.i.263-4). At long last they are compelled to recognize his arcane power and to grasp the personal significance of the tempest. "O, it is monstrous: monstrous," exclaims the bemused Alonso (III.iii.95-102).

> Me thought the billowes spoke, and told me of it,
> The windes did sing it to me: and the Thunder
> (That deepe and dreadfull Organ-Pipe) pronounc'd
> The name of *Prosper:* it did base my Trespasse,
> Therefore my Sonne i'th Ooze is bedded; and
> I'le seeke him deeper then ere plummet sounded,
> And with him there lye mudded.

The downward thrust of this confession parallels the mock-dirge, in which Ariel has conveyed to Ferdinand an impression of his father's death by water. It contrasts with the upward movement of the tricksy sprite himself, and with the increasing ascendancy of his master. When Prospero is not an actor, he becomes a spectator, standing *"on the top (invisible)"*—the puppeteer whose "demy-Puppets" enact a "liuing *Drolerie*" (III.iii.15; V.i.36; III.iii.21). He is the stage-manager, the book-holder, the prompter, and everything is worked out under his omnipresent control.

The source of his late-won authority has been carefully analyzed by students of demonology and pneumatology. This could not—in a comedy performed before the learned and superstitious King James—have been the black art of witchcraft, goety, which had led to the damnation of Doctor Faustus. Rather it was theurgy, sacerdotal science or white magic, a command over nature attained through an understanding of its phenomena and an influence over the spirits that link them to their correspondences in the spectral world. Though Prospero's book is a repository of that occult lore, books alone are not all-controlling forces, as he learned by neglecting his dukedom for his library. Caliban naively equates the possession of such books with the exercise of magical powers; but the only spell that works for the clowns is that which is cast by the contents of Stephano's bottle; and their parody is underscored by his toast, "kisse the Booke" (II.ii.145). Among Shakespeare's characters, many of whom are confronted by apparitions and portents, Prospero stands unique as a human being who controls the supernatural, through the agency of his ethereal ministers, notably Ariel. Owen Glendower vainly boasts of calling spirits, while Macbeth's witches are actually Fates. As Prospero's epilogue would make clear, if the consistent capitalization of the noun in the Folio did not, his "so potent Art" symbolizes the art of dramaturgy (V.i.50).

We need not identify the poet with the protagonist to regard the latter as a portrait of the artist or to look retrospectively at his ultimate conjuration as a kind of farewell to the stage. Shakespeare's fondness for dwelling upon theatrical matters happily combined with the metaphors of enchantment. Traditionally the enchanter was a demonic—not to say a diabolic—personage, such as Ariosto's Sacripante or Spenser's Archimago. The University Wits could treat him ambivalently, as a scholar straying after forbidden knowledge, like Marlowe's Faustus or Robert Greene's Friar Bacon, who could "Make storming *Boreas* thunder from his caue." The fact

that "our moderne writers" liked to center their fictions
on "the persons of Enchaunters and Commaunders of
spirits," as Thomas Campion would suggest in describing
his masque for the Somerset wedding, helped to motivate
the transformations and scenic effects. Yet Jonson, who
all but held a monopoly over the genre, needed no such
motivation; it is disenchantment which sets the mood for
the masque of *Mercury Vindicated from the Alchemists.* His
paradoxical talents might be characterized in a phrase
which Auden attributes to Prospero: "the power to en-
chant / That comes from disillusion." *The Tempest* is concerned with illusion, as fabricated by magicians and playwrights and "all which it inherit," the illusory stuff that
dreams and dramas and life itself are made of (IV.i.154).
Jonsonian comedy is concerned with the theory and practice of delusion.

The conjunction of Jonson and Shakespeare was never
closer or more productive than in the successive seasons
of 1610 and 1611, when His Majesty's Servants introduced *The Alchemist* and *The Tempest* respectively. It is
conceivable that the same actor created the parts of Jonson's criminal mastermind and Shakespeare's wonder-
working sorcerer, and it is suggestive that the actors' list
for *The Alchemist* was headed by Richard Burbage. To be
sure, *The Tempest*—which may have been revised for the
royal wedding at Whitehall in 1613—bears marks
suggesting a production at the company's private theater
in Blackfriars. One of the ironies is that Jonson himself
was a resident of that Puritan center of small trade; some
of his respectable neighbors appear as a chorus in Act V.
Shakespeare, who had caught the local color of Eastcheap
years before, was increasingly attracted to remote and exotic locations. His lifelong interest in the sea reached its
culmination with *The Tempest,* where, although the unin-

habited island is located in the Mediterranean, the ambience has been affected by reports of American voyages and the winds are stirred by "dewe / From the still-vext Bermoothes" (I.ii.228-9). Jonson glanced at the transatlantic horizon when he collaborated with Marston and Chapman on *Eastward Ho;* but their title reverses the direction, and their voyage founders on the Isle of Dogs, a rubbish-dump in the Thames. The Prologue to *The Alchemist* proudly announces that the cockney humanist has chosen familiar ground (5-9):

> Our *Scene* is *London*, 'cause we would make knowne,
> No countries mirth is better than our owne.
> No clime breeds better matter, for your whore,
> Bawd, squire, impostor, many persons more,
> Whose manners, now call'd humors, feed the stage.

This may sound like a somewhat ambiguous declaration of civic pride, but it brings into focus the traditionally urban perspectives of New Comedy. The roles that are named could be the typical masks prescribed by ancient convention, but they will be localized with an almost journalistic particularity. Actual dates will be cited, which topically refer to the time of the play's first presentation. That may have been the occasion when the Globe Playhouse and the other public theaters reopened after a visitation of the Black Death, the plague that still hangs so heavily over the play. The unified locale is a house in Blackfriars, presumably around the corner from Jonson's. The doorways and stairways and levels of the stage are exploited with a furtive agility which seems at times to foreshadow the bedroom farces of Georges Feydeau. The framing circumstance—the servant left by the master in charge of his house, which becomes a hotbed of trouble and frolic during his absence—was inherited from the

Mostellaria of Plautus, and would also furnish the underplot for Thomas Heywood's *English Traveller*. The abandoned domicile of Lovewit, under the relaxed surveillance of the housekeeper Jeremie while the epidemic runs its course, provides the ideal "caue of cos'nage" for the interaction of Jonson's coney-catchers and gulls (V.v.115). The basic pattern was laid down in *Volpone:* a household of knaves through which troops a procession of fools.

But Volpone has been a Magnifico, his house is a Venetian *palazzo,* and the gold he worships is genuine; it crams his coffers to dazzle those would-be heirs whom he elegantly defrauds. Whereas Subtle is never more than a charlatan, a seedy and shady practitioner of the various confidence-games unmasked in the cautionary pamphlets of Greene and Dekker, and his frauds are based on no more substantial a lure than fool's gold. It is the extreme disparity between the claims and aspirations of alchemy and the alchemist's mendicant way of life, the glaring gap between the opulent promise and the sordid fulfillment, between a professed disinterestedness and the most avid self-interest, which made the subject so fruitful a premise for satirists—epitomized by Jonson in a brief epigram and expatiated upon at length by Chaucer's Canon's Yeoman. On the one hand, we are tantalized by all we hear about the great work, the mastery, the elixir, the philosophers' stone, "the secret / Of nature naturiz'd . . ." (II.i.63-4). On the other, we are put off by the anticlimax personified in Surly's description of Subtle (IV.vi.46-50):

> he is the FAUSTUS,
> That casteth figures, and can coniure, cures
> Plague, piles, and poxe, by the *Ephemerides*.
> And holds intelligence with all the bawdes,
> And midwiues of three shires?

The Faustian aspect is quickly discredited by the seamy side. Yet the pioneers of science lived under such imputations of quackery and, what is worse, under the statutes against sorcery, which was punishable by death. Hence there is something of the mad scientist or the rejected prophet in Subtle—or, at any rate, in the role he acts with eloquence and conviction, the role of the trickster as mage. Like Prospero, he can confidently speak of "mine owne great art," not admitting its fraudulence to Face even in the privacy of their collusion (I.i.77). Their expository repartee, as contrasted with Prospero's long-drawn-out monologue, constitutes the most vivid of introductions. The quarrel between the cheaters plunges us *in medias res* and alerts us to the worst about both immediately, with a barrage of mutual invective and a crackle of name-calling scurrility. The magian marvels of Shakespeare's isle seem very far away.

Dryden chose *The Silent Woman* to demonstrate "the pattern of a perfect play," doubtless because it anticipated the taste of the Restoration. What he termed the *coup de maître* of Jonson is more evident in *The Alchemist:* the character-sketch that accompanies the entrance of each personage, such as the little genre-picture of Drugger in his tobacconist's shop. This presupposes a static conception of character, and it nearly immobilizes those later plays which Dryden termed "dotages." Shakespeare preferred to let his characters speak for themselves and to let us form our own impressions. But Jonson's approach works perfectly throughout *The Alchemist,* where it is Face's task to introduce the gulls to the cunning man. They arrive singly at first and then in couples, like the animals entering the ark, and the complications ensue when their arrivals are mistimed. Knocks at the door keep heralding new personalities until the fifth act, when

the sudden appearance of Lovewit—in whose suspenseful
shadow the first four acts have proceeded—precipitates
the catastrophe. A diagram of the plot would show a long
line ascending to that point and then dropping almost
vertically. Whereas the plan of *The Tempest* would con-
form to the pyramidal structure that Shakespeare favored, rising to its apex in the third act, where the lovers
plight their troth while the spirits confound both the
royal party and the clownish plotters. The rest of the play
has the falling cadence of resolution, recognition, recon-
ciliation, and celebration.

Shakespeare's habit of parallelism and symmetry, in
relating the two secondary plots to the main one, is con-
summated here. All three are plots in the conspiratorial
sense: the complot of Antonio against Prospero has its
higher and lower counterparts in the intrigue against
Alonso and the mutiny of Caliban. Each of these strata-
gems plays into the hands of the omniscient Prospero.
Order has never been more completely imposed, nor disorder more decisively routed. But poetic justice has depended, we must note, on the sort of metaphysical aid
that Jonson would have disdained. Human contrivance is
bound to be outdone sooner or later by chance, and his
contrivers are alert in adapting themselves to the main
chance. Among them Lovewit's butler is the cleverest of
servants, and Subtle has been teaching him other parts—
not merely the dim-witted laboratory assistant, Lungs or
Ulenspiegel, but Don Face, the insolent captain, the setter
or verser who picks up customers for both Subtle and Dol
Common. As for the heroine, though she has been
Subtle's *"punque,"* she is currently shared with Face, and
shares in their *"indenture tripartite"* (*Argument,* 4, V.iv.131).
The legal phrase has a Shakespearean resonance, when
we remember the compact of the rebels in the first part

of *Henry IV*. Meanwhile Subtle and Face are falling out over the prospect of hooking a match with the well-endowed Widow Pliant, and in the internal conflict *sotto voce* the disciple proves himself less squeamish and more brash than his mentor.

The advent of Lovewit is therefore the cue for Face to change sides, to purchase his master's forgiveness at the price of the widow's hand. In accepting this marital bargain, the easygoing Lovewit lives up to his charactonym; he enjoys a good joke, and condones mischief when it is clever and profitable to himself. But Jonson seems slightly uneasy, when he has Face excuse himself in the epilogue: "My part a little fell in this last *Scene*, / Yet 'twas *decorum*" (V.v.158-9). The demotion of Face to his menial job again is some consolation to Subtle, making his ignominious get-away with Dol, though Lovewit would be well advised in future to keep a sharp eye on his buttery accounts. Whether the stricter interests of decorum have been served is an open question. Jonson could be insistently stern in the imposition of justice; typically his concluding scene takes the form of an arraignment, through which every man is put out of his humor, as it were. In *Volpone* there are two trial scenes; the logical *reductio ad absurdum* in the fourth act leaves roguery so shamelessly triumphant, and virtue so helplessly discomfited, that Jonson had to reverse it with a heavy-handed—and much criticized—manoeuvre in the fifth act. *Volpone* is the only one of his four great comedies to be clouded by this legalistic severity, and it is much grimmer than the others. *The Silent Woman* is genially resolved by a pseudo-disputation between two sham lawyers, while the reforming Justice Overdo is pilloried in *Bartholomew Fair*.

What happens to Surly, the one honest man in *The Alchemist*, exemplifies this triumph of acquiescence over asperity. Significantly enough, he is a gambler by profession; and, though he "would not willingly be gull'd," he is willing to concede "That *Alchemie* is a pretty kind of game, / Somewhat like tricks o'the cards, to cheat a man, / With charming" (II.i.78; II.iii.180-1). His cognomen allies him to Asper, the satirical moralist in *Every Man Out of his Humor,* and to those other *raisonneurs* who stand for the sterner Jonson. Since he gets nowhere as a downright skeptic among the deceivers and the deceived, Surly ventures to play a game of his own: his masquerade in the guise of a Spanish grandee. Thereby he exposes himself to the rogues he is trying to expose, and loses the widow in spite of—or rather because of—his gallantry. "Must I needs cheat my selfe," he ends by asking, "With that same foolish vice of honestie!" (V.v.83-4). His impersonation of the Spaniard is carried through by Lovewit, after unsuccessful attempts by Drugger and Face. The costume for the part, "HIERONYMO'S old cloake, ruffe, and hat," is a reminder that Jonson himself, in his acting days, played Hieronimo on provincial tours of *The Spanish Tragedy* (IV.vii.71). As a sardonic moralist, an unheeded reformer, and a sometime Roman Catholic, Jonson amiably lampooned himself in Surly's interventions. Yet they cannot seem other than surly, when they are juxtaposed to the irrepressible good nature of Gonzalo, Shakespeare's *raisonneur.*

Surly's skepticism presents an ineffectual foil to the expansive gullibility of his companion, Sir Epicure Mammon. He is Subtle's principal customer, and the diurnal timing of the play is set by the imminent maturation of his ill-starred project. "This is the day," he apprises Surly, "wherein, to all my friends, / I will pronounce the happy word, *be rich*" (II.i.6-7). The explosion of the alchemist's furnace could be viewed as a Jonsonian analogue to the

Shakespearean tempest. The "voluptuous mind" that motivates this convenient disaster finds expression through a lyrical voice, the only one in the cast, projecting sybaritic fantasies by means of Marlovian rhetoric as Sir Epicure counts his chickens before they are hatched (IV.v.74). His infirmity—should we call it elephantiasis of the imagination?—gives us an insight into the psychology of the swindler's victim, his ardent desire to be swindled. This massive suspension of disbelief achieves its climax in Sir Epicure's courtship—"all in gold"—of "lord WHATS'HVM'S sister," impersonated by Dol (IV.i.25; II.iv.6). The excruciating irony is to witness all these courtly compliments and arts of persuasion lavished upon a woman who, professionally speaking, is more likely to solicit than to be solicited. Jonson is careful to underline the willful immorality of Sir Epicure's speeches, oozing with lust and glittering with luxury, by drawing upon the imagery of imperial Rome, whose decadent excesses will be surpassed (IV.i.144-5):

> we but shewing our loue,
> NERO'S POPPAEA may be lost in storie!

Dol's mad scene rushes to the other extreme, inasmuch as her ravings are memorized from the Reverend Hugh Broughton's deranged explanations of Biblical prophecies. These compose a poetry of sorts, as Hart Crane recognized when he made them the starting point for one of his own poems ("For the Marriage of Faustus and Helen"), and they bring a final touch of opacity to the competing jargons of the play. The dramatic conflicts have their echo in the verbal prestidigitations. "What a braue language here is? next to canting?" (II.iii.42). It is considerably better than cant, the secret slang of thieves, at impressing and befuddling its hearers. The experiment in alchemy may be a failure, but the bravura of pseudo-scientific language is an overwhelming success, when Subtle lectures to Surly or catechizes Face for the benefit of Deacon Ananias. The Puritans have their own tropes and intonations, to which Jonson's ears were particularly sensitive. Ananias is an adept at casuistry, as his pastor Tribulation attests, and can put a sanctimonious construction on the sharpest chicanery. It is not surprising that Subtle treats him as a professional rival. The auditory humors mount to the highest pitch of calculated misunderstanding during the mock-Spanish interlude. The most remarkable feature of the blank verse is that it pours forth colloquial speech with as little constraint as the prose of *Bartholomew Fair*. Thus the angry boy Kastril, wanting to live by his nonexistent wits, is advised by Face to study with Subtle (III.iv.43-46):

> You cannot thinke that subtiltie, but he reades it.
> He made me a Captaine. I was a starke pimpe,
> Iust o' your standing, 'fore I met with him:
> It i' not two months since. I'll tell you his method.

Jonson's dramatic method is to tell us the respective methods of his *dramatis personae*. He is nothing if not analytic, where for Shakespeare we must use such Coleridgean adjectives as *organic* and *esemplastic*. Where Shakespeare fuses things together, Jonson sorts them out; he breaks them down, where Shakespeare builds them up. Each of Jonson's plays reveals, so to speak, the tricks of another trade. Subtle, the arch-trickster, can hoax the multitude; but Jonson is forever reminding us that, like Surly(?), he himself can never be gulled. When Shakespeare takes a magician for his hero, he himself submits to the mysteries of natural magic, and Prospero becomes their priestly celebrant, a king of the wood, the veritable *magus*. Though the potency of his magical book is reinforced by his staff and robes, he does not engage in abracadabras. His only incantation is a last summons and a promise of release to his agents, who remain invisible. Though it mentions some enchantments borrowed from Ovid's Medea, there is little itemizing and no cataloguing. Since the drama is illusive or dream-like, rather than delusive or misleading, it does not call for Jonsonian exposures. Jonson, who well knew how insubstantial a pageant could be, would hardly have accepted Prospero's masque as a paradigm of reality. Rather, it was what he had meant by antics that *"runne away from Nature"*—modes of escape no less evanescent, to him, than the wish-dreams of Sir Epicure.

Nor will Shakespeare's worldly cynics, Antonio and Sebastian, believe in travelers' tales of unicorns or the phoenix, until they are perforce initiated into the "subtleties o'th'Isle" (V.i.124). Prospero's theatrical-magical art conjures up the masque as a betrothal rite for Ferdinand and Miranda. These two favored spectators will be actors in their turn, when Prospero *"discouers"* them to the others, *"playing at Chesse"*—a game of kings within a game of kings (V.i.171). Ariel, the protean star of Prospero's spirit-troop, has successively figured as a nereid, as a harpy in what might be considered the antimasque, and as Circe to join in the marriage blessing. His characteristic idiom is the rhyming trochaic tetrameter, which Shakespeare reserved for his sprites and fairies (and witches), and which Milton echoes in "L'Allegro" (IV.i.46-7):

> Each one tripping on his Toe,
> Will be here with mop, and mowe.

The play is as full of sound effects as the isle is full of noises. Many of them are evoked by Ariel, from the bark-

ing and crowing refrains of his very first song to the pipe
and tabor with which he invisibly misleads the clowns.
Even the language of Caliban transposes discords into the
harmony of "a thousand twangling Instruments"
(III.ii.146). The general effect is a semi-tropical atmosphere of twittering birds, chirring insects, rustling fo-
liage—above all, vocal winds and beating waves, set aroar
and then allayed at Prospero's behest. His magic is
thereby associated with music, as Ferdinand implies: "This
is a most maiesticke vision, and / Harmonious charm-
ingly" (IV.i.118-9). But the charm is broken, and
the dancing nymphs and reapers vanish into thin air,
after the interruption of *"a strange hollow and confused
noyse"* (IV.i.138). Prospero expounds the object-lesson to
the lovers. So it is with life, that elusive dream-vision. *La
vida es sueño.*

Subtle's charms work on another plane. The closest he
comes to staging a ceremony is the hoax he puts on for
Dapper, the earliest and slightest of the gulls, a lawyer's
clerk who seeks a familiar spirit in order to improve his
chances at gambling. That gift is to be conferred by the
versatile Dol in her most dazzling role, the Faery Queen.
But before the epiphany of Gloriana, her pathetic postu-
lant is blindfolded and pinched and squeaked at, mulcted
of all his cash by Subtle and Face, and stripped of everything on his person that has the least value. "I ha' nothing
but a halfe-crowne / Of gold, about my wrist, that my
loue gaue me," he swears and pleads, "And a leaden
heart I wore, sin' shee forsooke me." Face is not wholly
obdurate to this modest heartcry (III.v.43-9):

> I thought, 'twas something. And, would you incurre
> Your aunts displeasure for these trifles? Come,
> I had rather you had throwne away twentie halfe-crownes.
> You may weare your leaden heart still.

The ritual is interrupted by the knocking of Sir Epicure, and Dapper is led away to bide the interim in the privy. His touching resourcelessness is overmatched by the utter heartlessness of his cozeners; after all, the concession has cost them nothing. What is more, it measures the distance from Shakespeare, from the Shakespearean empathy with which Miranda watches the shipwreck: "Oh! I haue suffered / With those that I saw suffer" (I.i.5-6). Since she is her father's "non-pareill," she is not to be compared with anybody—certainly not with Dol Common, whose surname is the trademark of her total promiscuity (III.ii.108). When Miranda walks the island as its virgin goddess, radiating unaffected innocence, she persuades us to agree with Samuel Pepys, who described *The Tempest* as "the most innocent play that ever I saw." However, the description of Pepys turns into a reflection on the Restoration theater, when we recall that the version he saw six times was the prurient *rifacimento* of Dryden and Davenant.

Wonder is Shakespeare's epithet and synonym for Miranda, and it offers a better clue to the play as a whole than Jonson's catchword, *monster*. Monstrosity is inhumanity, a tragic theme for Shakespeare, welling to the surface when Lear's daughters are likened to tigers and serpents and kites. "Be-monster not thy feature," Albany warns Goneril; if the heavens do not punish such offenses as hers (*King Lear,* IV.ii.63, 49-50),

> Humanity must perforce pray on it self
> Like monsters of the deepe.

True, as the concordance informs us, *monster*—along with *spirit, art, remember,* and *strange*—is one of those thematic words which Shakespeare employs in *The Tempest* more often than anywhere else. Taken together, they virtually outline the story. The strangeness of Prospero's recital, or the later sight of strangers, has its response in Miranda's wonderment, which is not unlike Desdemona's admiration for Othello's adventures. The revelation goes "From strange, to stranger," as Alonso reacts to it (V.i.228); the situation is "as strange a Maze, as ere men trod" (V.i.242). He himself does not drown, as Ariel's lyric has misleadingly predicted, or "suffer a Sea-change / Into something rich, & strange" (I.ii.400-1). But everyone is changed for the better by his island experience. Prospero, through his exile to a state of nature, has been better fitted for a return to society. "In one voyage," Gonzalo rejoices (V.i.208-13),

> Did *Claribell* her husbande finde at *Tunis,*
> And *Ferdinand* her brother, found a wife,
> Where he himselfe was lost: *Prospero,* his Dukedome
> In a poore Isle: and all of vs, our selues,
> When no man was his owne.

Such developments, the change and growth and diversification fostered by Shakespeare's comedy, are at odds with the attempted transmutations of Jonson's alchemy, which leaves its subjects basically unchanged. The striking consequence is that the two plays devoted to such closely related themes, and produced under identical auspices, should stand in such polar opposition as indoors to outdoors or the underworld to the upper air. That *The Tempest* came after *The Alchemist* means, of course, that Shakespeare had the opportunity to reflect and reply, as he is said to have done in the so-called War of the Theaters. He responded to Jonson's brilliant example not through imitation or refutation but, we might opine, through sublimation—remembering that this notion was held by the alchemists long before it was adopted by the psychoanalysts.

III
FURTHER PERSPECTIVES

The Primacy of Shakespeare

My sermon piously begins by citing a text from the literary gospel of our time, Northrop Frye's *Anatomy of Criticism*. "Shakespeare, we say, was one of a group of English dramatists working around 1600, and also one of the great poets of the world," so says Professor Frye. "The first part of this is a statement of fact, the second a value-judgment so generally accepted as to pass for a statement of fact," he goes on. "But it is not a statement of fact. It remains a value-judgment, and not a shred of systematic criticism can ever be attached to it." This, if we accept it, does not sound very encouraging for systematic criticism. Rightly to be great, as Shakespeare himself envisaged it, was difficult and could be illusory, though he never ceased to ring the changes on that theme. That the adjective itself, with its various congeners, has been applied some twenty times by Swinburne to Victor Hugo, during

The first annual Shakespeare Association Lecture, delivered at the Folger Library in Washington on March 11, 1973, and published in the *Shakespeare Quarterly*, xxvi, 2 (Spring, 1975).

the course of one short article in the *Encyclopaedia Britannica,* would make a good point for Mr. Frye: an argument which might be termed, in Shakespearean phrase, "the abuse of greatness." *Great* in the first place, etymologically speaking, had meant something coarse or large, then heavy in the particular meaning of *pregnant,* or on another plane *noble* by virtue of a designated social rank; it was originally an objective and more or less quantitative conception. Greatness in the sense of acknowledged pre-eminence had to come as a later moral refinement, a qualitative and therefore subjective evaluation, yet one arrived at through democratic consensus, and authoritative enough to shape men's lives and claim their persistent attention.

If Mr. Frye wants facts—and he does not always—I wish he could be present at this conference. I don't mean simply in order to take part in our discussions, much as these may contribute to critical understanding; but, even more significantly, to speculate on what is presupposed by the unique existence of a monumental library primarily devoted to the study of a single author whose work forms the main concern of a professional body of scholars, now converging to celebrate it in the capital of a foreign country 357 years after his death. The facts of Shakespeare's universal pervasion need scarcely be attested here at the Folger Shakespeare Library, of all places. The accumulated bibliography of editions, monographs, articles, and translations, not to mention productions, makes Ossa like a wart. Mr. Frye is well aware of all this, and I suppose he must regard it as an incidental phenomenon of cultural history. But German critics might call it *Rezeptionsästhetik.* The fact that Shakespeare furnished more than one out of every eighteen plays for the theatrical repertory of the middlewestern frontier, as statistically investigated by Ralph L. Rusk, might perhaps have less to do with literature than with sociology. Yet if Mr. Frye is bent on practicing value-free analysis, and if *Anatomy of Criticism* is an organon for literary studies in general, why does it draw so many more illustrations from Shakespeare than from any other writer? By my count, and the index makes for fascinating perusal, he gets mentioned on 209 pages. This is far more than the frequency of the next most frequent source, the Bible itself, with a score of eighty-eight, although that figure might be supplemented by the forty entries under "Jesus Christ" and "Messiah."

Mr. Frye, of course, may choose not to examine the complex succession of value-judgments that led him to such an implicit selection. And it is perfectly true that, if we listen to all of the witnesses, we shall be hearing a pentecostal babble of contradictions and distortions, along with other and better things. But do not the very range and volume of the cumulative response to a given writer's work constitute a part of the process with which the critic has somehow to deal? Criticism, at best, has been systematic only in shreds here and there. Its usual pronouncements have intermixed the affective with the analytic, so that, if we exclude the one, we are likely to miss out on the other. Necessarily its observations are approximations to its object, many of them pretty far removed yet sometimes meaningful in their misconstruction. If we admit the possibility of moving past a mistaken interpretation toward a more valid one, then we believe—as Mr. Frye apparently does—in some sort of critical progress. He will allow for no organic connection between criticism and the history of taste, "where there are no facts," he tells us, merely "Hegelian half-truths." Well, *de gustibus non disputandum*. Yet the history of criticism is a virtual battleground of disputes over taste; recorded opinions become historical facts in the light of their origin and impact; quantity is a variable of quality; and Hegelian half-truths are proverbial for being not only soon controverted but also synthesized with their missing halves in the long run. The history of taste is the name we give to criticism after it has become obsolete, and that obsolescence is the measure of progress.

Shakespeare's reputation has undergone all the vicissitudes save neglect. He has been called everything from an upstart crow or a drunken barbarian to a king of men or a god of the theater. Though his first notice was an attempted put-down by his moribund rival, Robert Greene, the curve of recognition has moved generally skyward, much of it on the far side of idolatry. Matthew Arnold's sonnet was conceived on the wings of such exaltation ("Making the heaven of heavens thy dwelling-place"), and this quasi-religious reverence tends to abash the critical temper: "Others abide our question. Thou art free." Arnold, as I have noted elsewhere, had very little to say about Shakespeare; even when choosing his famous "touchstones," he discovered more of them in Homer, Dante, and Milton. Nevertheless he showed no lack of Shakespearean piety; and when he exemplified his concept of "natural magic" he may have been influenced by a couplet from Dryden, even as Dryden had been inspired by *The Tempest:*

> But *Shakespeare's* Magick could not copy'd be;
> Within that Circle none durst walk but he.

It is Dryden to whom we owe the notion of Shakespeare as nonpareil. Neo-classical craftsman that he was, Dryden was bound to retain certain reservations; but he was ready to promote his gigantic predecessor from *primus inter pares* to *facile princeps*. Shakespeare's faults would not be wholly transcended by his beauties until the Romantic Movement. He would by then be transcending the purely dramatic sphere. Coleridge would single him out as "the most universal genius that ever lived" and—within a nimbus of Christlike incarnation—"the greatest man that ever put on and put off mortality." The Coleridgean epithet "oceanic" accords with Shakespeare's inclusion among those visionaries and sages whom Hugo classified, with the natural landmarks of mankind, as *"hommes océans."* According to Keats, "He could do easily Man's utmost." The consequent question that he must abide from us is how or why any writer came to be placed so decisively ahead of all the rest, came to be so definitively regarded as the greatest of all time: "this Presider," so designated by Keats. "The name of Shakespeare is the greatest in our literature,—it is the greatest in all literature," so runs the typical statement of Henry Hallam. "No man can come near him in the creative powers of the mind."

To approach the unapproachable, as I shall try to do in spite of such caveats as Arnold's, is to recognize that few writers ever arrive at the top of the heap without having survived an intense competition. This was the case with Shakespeare *par excellence*. Every national literature has a tendency to reserve its highest pedestal for the bust of some father-figure. The choice is clearest when there happens to be a founding father in view, who played a strategic part in formulating the language and crystallizing traditions, as Homer did in Greece. His primacy as educator of Hellas was confirmed by subsequent writers, by Aristophanes and Isocrates if not by Plato, as it has been by Werner Jaeger in historical retrospect. For many of Shakespeare's contemporaries, like Chapman, Homer remained "the first and best" of all existing books. Writing somewhat in his shadow, Vergil had to achieve his limited supremacy within the Roman sphere, of which he deliberately made himself the unofficial laureate. But in the Middle Ages his authority was extended, by circumstances of language and religion, so that he became Dante's *"altissimo poeta."* Dante himself, so explicit a pioneer in his Latin treatise on the Tuscan vernacular as well as in his own poetic *Summa,* would already be taught in Italian universities by the admiring generation of Petrarch and Boccaccio. No such individual figure dominates the literary history of France, paradigmatic though it is in many ways. Molière has come closest to a central role, and has clearly exerted the widest appeal. Yet he may still be handicapped by the pedantic snobberies that excluded him from the Académie Française.

Since Shakespeare was a playwright—and, what was worse, an actor—he too had been subject to the same handicap. But, though the drama ranked beneath the epic in the neo-classical hierarchy of genres, tragedy had an advantage over comedy in the inherent seriousness of its mien. As for the novel, there were not many critics who deemed it worthy of any status at all. Hence, despite the immediate and widespread popularity of *Don Quixote,* it was not until the post-Romantic generation of 1898 that Cervantes won acceptance as Spain's characteristic voice. In some countries of northern or eastern Europe, where the development of cultural self-awareness has come relatively late, similar protagonists have emerged with the modern period, which they had done much to bring about. During his protean, comprehensive, and incomparably productive lifetime, Goethe must have been paid more personal tribute than has accrued to any other living man of letters. Heinrich Heine, rather too maliciously, accused him of engaging in literary politics to gain "his autocratic sovereignty over German literature." Russian culture, having neglected itself for so long, seems to have been waiting for the advent of Pushkin, whose tragically abbreviated career left both a legacy and a legend. After both had been eloquently enshrined by Lermontov's elegy, a poet of the next generation, Tyutchev, could pronounce their memory as unforgettable as first love. In contrast with most of these culture-heroes, Shakespeare seems to retain the impersonality of his image, and his emergence as the foremost spokesman for English culture seems belated, almost unlikely, and consequently spectacular.

He cannot be numbered among the founders, whom Ben Jonson salutes in his masque of *The Golden Age Restored:* Chaucer, Gower, Lydgate, Spenser. To be sure, he had a shaping influence on the English language at a crucial stage, amply registered in the *Oxford English Dictionary* or in handbooks of quotations. But this was hardly noticed by his contemporaries, though they readily spoke of his "honey-tongued" or "fine-filèd" phrasing. Though he was assigned an honorable place in such catalogues as that of Francis Meres or such anthologies as *England's Parnassus,* he was treated there as one among many. The illuminating monograph by G. E. Bentley charts his rivalry with Jonson through the seventeenth century, and reckons more acclaim for the younger dramatist until the final decade. The testimony that yields the palm to *Catiline* as "the premier English tragedy" must perforce reflect academic and courtly standards. T. S. Eliot has described it as "that dreary Pyrrhic victory of a tragedy," and Jonson himself quoted Horace to the effect that it had not pleased the public. On the popular stage, it was John Fletcher who dominated what was commonly considered a triumvirate. As a personality in his day, Jonson had made the most striking impression; yet the personalities that Shakespeare had characterized—notably Falstaff—attracted more allusions, and Shakespeare seems to have been the most frequently quoted. Moreover, any qualitative reckoning—as opposed to casual mentions—would show an increasingly Shakespearean preference on the part of thoughtful critics surveying the whole situation: not only Dryden from 1668, but Edward Phillips, William Winstanley, Charles Gildon, James Drake, and Sir Thomas Pope Blount.

To follow the course of esthetic opinion concerning Shakespeare, declared the *Times Literary Supplement* on February 5, 1920, would provide "a kind of epitome of the movements of the human mind through three most eventful centuries"—and it is now much closer to four. Augustus Ralli's *History of Shakespearian Criticism*, published twelve years later under the surprising auspices of the Oxford University Press, signally failed to meet that challenge. To call it mediocre would be to overpraise it; to call it pedestrian would be to assume, with inadequate justification, that it covers its chosen ground. Commenting with tactful brevity in *The Year's Work in English Studies* for 1932, Allardyce Nicoll suggested that a juster title might have been "Abstracts from Some Critics of Shakespeare." Ralli's two ponderous volumes, containing some 1,100 pages, do indeed summarize a compendious if not exhaustive sequence of critical documents in English, French, and German. The author disarmingly states that he has depended upon a translator for the German material; and he squeezes one Italian critic, Benedetto Croce, in among the English and a handful of Americans. There is no method except for repeated synopsis, which requires more precise powers of formulation and a

sharper eye for the telling quotation than are evident
here. There are no discernible standards for placing a
critic or tracing an idea or even determining the allot-
ment of space. The book is too repetitious and ineptly
written to be read continuously. The abstracts are much
too blurred and shrunken to be reliably consulted for reference.

To accept Ralli's presentation of the record would be to
fall in with Mr. Frye's assumption—which he himself has
recently questioned, with regard to Milton—that the history of taste is a grubby dustheap of the second-hand and
the third-rate. That the history of Shakespearean criticism is rich in dynamic and luminous episodes we have
learned from such scholars as Friedrich Gundolf, Jules
Jusserand, Fernand Baldensperger, T. R. Lounsbury,
T. M. Raysor, R. W. Babcock, and David Nichol Smith.
We shall be looking forward to the six-volume collection
of English texts that Brian Vickers has been editing for
the Critical Heritage series. Yet the whole story, the *Über-
lieferungsgeschichte* as an epitome of intellectual movements down the centuries, continues to await its George
Saintsbury or its René Wellek. Meanwhile we must take
our bearings as best we can, and revert to the clinching
testimonials of Dryden. Dryden gives Shakespeare historic, as well as esthetic, priority: it was he, according to
the essay on satire, "who created the stage among us."
Jonson may well have perfected it; and when Dryden
compares the two in the *Essay of Dramatic Poesy,* contrasting his love of Shakespeare with his admiration for Jonson, his respective parallels are Homer and Vergil. But
his opening declaration has already swept him beyond
mere parallel, with the tentative implication that Shakespeare may have outdone the classics: "He was the man
who of all modern, and perhaps ancient poets, had the

largest and most comprehensive soul." As for Jonson, Dryden takes more measured views of him elsewhere, and deprecates the "insolent, sparing, and invidious panegyric" that he contributed to Shakespeare's First Folio.

In fairness we might briefly pause to reconsider that eulogy, which is invidious toward other playwrights only to be generous with Shakespeare—and which really, I think, began the game of exalting Shakespeare at Jonson's expense. To be sure, we should make due allowance for the occasion and for the encomiastic conventions, and we should not forget the pungent animadversions in *Timber* and the conversations with Drummond. Yet this is the Poet Laureate speaking *ex cathedra* and self-consciously addressing posterity. He commences in a rather low key, somewhat like the discursive vein of Pope ("And thinke to ruine, where it seem'd to raise"). Momentarily, from what seems a nervous anxiety to avoid misunderstanding, he is almost forced off key:

> These are, as some infamous Baud, or Whore,
> Should praise a Matron. What could hurt her more?

This fleeting glimpse of Shakespeare as a matron is awkward enough, without pursuing the analogy that Jonson posits for himself. After sixteen lines of prolegomenal hesitation, he gets off the ground and quite deliberately soars into poetic flight, sending off showers of exclamation-points.

> I, therefore will begin. Soule of the Age!
> The applause! delight! the wonder of our Stage!

The heroic couplets that hereupon resound cannot fairly be dismissed as sparing.

> My *Shakespeare* rise; I will not lodge thee by
> *Chaucer*, or *Spenser*, or bid *Beaumont* lye
> A little further, to make thee a roome.

Jonson is playing here upon a conceit, and even borrowing rhymes, from a widely circulated poem on Shakespeare's death written by William Basse, though at one point attributed to Donne. But Basse was merely proclaiming that Shakespeare was worthy of such illustrious company, whereas Jonson, by using the device of *paraleipsis,* places him in a class by himself. Shakespeare by now has been buried for seven years—and, after all, not with the other three in the Poets' Corner of Westminster Abbey. Hence the aptness of the Jonsonian dictum: "Thou art a Moniment, without a tombe."

Passing on, the eulogist pays his respects by announcing that Shakespeare has outshone his contemporary peers: Lyly, Kyd, and Marlowe. It is then, proceeding into the classical realm, that he drops the qualifying remark about "small *Latine,* and lesse *Greeke,*" which has been taken out of context as a disparagement. Actually, it is an early blow on behalf of the Moderns, and from an unlikely quarter, in the emergent Battle of the Books. The Greek and Latin tragedians are now conjured up to admire the Shakespearean spectacle, while the ancient comic writers are more explicitly said to have been outdated by it, largely because of its special relation to nature.

> Or, when thy Sockes were on,
> Leaue thee alone, for the comparison
> Of all, that insolent *Greece,* or haughtie *Rome*
> Sent forth, or since did from their ashes come.

Coming from Jonson, this is unqualified in its magnanimity, let alone its boldness and perspicacity, though it might have shocked Dryden into hurling back the charge of insolence.

> Triúmph, my *Britaine,* thou hast one to showe,
> To whom all Scenes of *Europe* homage owe.
> He was not of an age, but for all time!

First apostrophized as soul of the age, the leading spirit of his time, *der Zeitgeist,* he is now exhibited as a timeless figure belonging to all the ages. The shift from the temporal to a spatial dimension must be the very earliest prophecy of the tributes that other lands would pay. In going on to balance the counterclaims of Art against Nature (the prime *topos* of *The Winter's Tale,* and one which Shakespeare dealt with *passim* through *King Lear* and *The Tempest*), Jonson redresses his allegation that Shakespeare wanted art. The interest that other critics would take in the fruitful variety of his *dramatis personae* is likewise adumbrated.

> Looke how the fathers face
> Liues in his issue, euen so, the race
> Of *Shakespeares* minde, and manners brightly shines
> In his well torned, and true filed lines.

The concluding apostrophe, "thou *Starre* of Poets," touches off the conventional train of light-and-shade imagery. Its modern connotation would not be inappropriate among Jonson's numerous puns; for his poem has conferred upon Shakespeare the stellar billing in the world's theater.

Jonson's Horatian trope about a monument without a tomb would supply the theme for the first English poem that Milton published, his commendatory verses in Shakespeare's Second Folio. By that date we have some record of pilgrimages to the grave in Trinity Church at Stratford-upon-Avon, where the doggerel epitaph, which evokes no memories or associations, had been augmented by the Janssen wall-bust, with its Latin inscription alluding to Vergil and other remote prototypes. But it was not until 1741 that Shakespeare was accorded his official niche in the British pantheon, his cenotaph in the Poets'

Corner. "A hundred years are wasted, and another silent century well advanced, and yet what unborn age shall say, Shakespeare has his equal?," Colley Cibber had asked in his *Apology,* which appeared the previous year. Himself an actor, Cibber pointed out a significant linkage, when he went on: "Betterton was an actor, as Shakespeare was an author, both without competitors!" Thomas Betterton, to whom Shakespeare was "godlike," had been his chief reanimator during the Restoration. It remained for another actor, David Garrick, to organize the rituals of devotion with the first Stratford Festival of 1769. Garrick's jubilee, which had drawn ridicule along with publicity, turned out to be not a feckless hobby-horse but a shrewd manoeuvre for both Shakespeare's interests and his own. Not only did it firmly and finally establish Shakespeare's position as the national poet of England, but Garrick in his culminating oration made ever broader claims, the very broadest: "Shakespeare had a Genius perhaps excelling anything that ever appeared in the World before him."

Though literary criticism was more reserved than histrionic ballyhoo, Garrick's friend and mentor Samuel Johnson had promoted Shakespeare to "the dignity of an ancient"—in other words, to standing among the classics—in his epoch-making preface of 1765. Manzoni and Stendhal would borrow Dr. Johnson's arguments exonerating Shakespeare from infractions of the pseudo-classical unities; and the dominant critic of France in 1850, Sainte-Beuve, would ultimately welcome him into a reconstructed temple of taste as *"le plus grand des classiques sans le savoir."* The lingering qualification, the note of unconsciousness, commemorates a long and bitter struggle. Shakespeare had been prominently instanced in its article on genius by the grand *Encyclopédie* of 1747. The difference between the enthusiasms and energies of *le génie* and the rules and laws of *le goût,* it stated, could be summed up in the old antithesis between Homer and Vergil or else in a new one: Shakespeare and Racine. Original Genius was laying the ghost of Correct Taste with the rise of the pre-Romantics in England. The turning point would not be reached in France before Hugo's generation, rallied by the performances of the English actors at Paris. But a crisis had been precipitated in 1776, when the French Academy was confronted with the translation of Pierre Letourneur. This was the debate in which Voltaire, who had patronized and emulated Shakespeare, who had alternated between condescension and jealousy toward him, and who had protested against his growing international renown in an *Appel à toutes les nations de l'Europe,* staged his last and least effective campaign. Voltaire lost his appeal to all the nations of Europe.

Letourneur had set the pitch of Shakespearolatry when he acclaimed his author as *"le dieu créateur de l'art sublime du théâtre."* Dryden had spoken more soberly of creating the English stage. Alexandre Dumas would not limit this divine creativity to the playhouse, though he stopped short of potential blasphemy: *"Après Dieu, il créa le plus."* Coleridge could be counted on to elaborate the metaphysical ramifications: ". . . the Spinozistic deity—an omnipresent creativeness." Whereas Ruskin drew a quantitive distinction between creative and reflective orders of talent: Homer, Dante, and Shakespeare on the one hand, Wordsworth, Keats, and Tennyson on the other. Now the estheticians of the Renaissance, such as Scaliger, liked to look upon the poet or maker as a creator or demiurge, and such latter-day writer-artists as Flaubert and Joyce have sought to recapture that view of artistic creation. If ever there was a human being who lived up to that lofty analogy, surely it must have been Shakespeare, impersonally conceiving the world as a stage and his stage as the world, richly peopling his private microcosm with a continual abundance of characters unmatched in scale or depth, and broadly identifying the Globe Playhouse with the *theatrum mundi.* But today the metaphor is so often taken in vain, so much unimaginative bungling is palmed off as creative writing, that the term is no longer a compliment to Shakespeare. Possibly we should drop it altogether, candidly admitting to ourselves that only God creates *ex nihilo,* that the most lifelike Shakespearean characters are more literally dramatic roles, and that our veneration might more properly be focused on Shakespeare's artistry than on his cosmogony.

The fervent tone of Shakespeare's eighteenth-century worshipers indicates that he still had some detractors among his compatriots. Goldsmith and Hume demurred that he was grossly overrated, while in many judicious minds Addison's *Cato* had succeeded Jonson's *Catiline* as the premier English tragedy. Nor should we exaggerate the opposition to Shakespeare on the other side of the English Channel; somehow or other a copy of the First Folio had found its way into that sanctum of French classicism, the library of Louis XIV. Yet the issue, as Voltaire had raised it, excited nationalistic repercussions. More precisely, it became a *querelle* between the cosmopolitan ascendancy of a gallicized culture and the aspirations toward a national culture fostered by Romanticism in the Germanic countries. It had been Lessing who struck the counterblow against Voltaire. Though his *Hamburgische Dramaturgie* did not discuss Shakespeare very specifically, it used him as a weapon to beat back the Racinian tradition—even as Stendhal would later do for the French

Romanticists. For Lessing, as for Hegel and other German men of letters, Shakespeare represented the summit
("*der Gipfel*," Friedrich Schlegel put it) of modern poetry.
Framing the perspectives of dramatic history in his
Vienna lectures of 1808, A. W. Schlegel discerned three
peaks of nearly equal height, amid many valleys. For
Classical drama the high point was the Greek; the Latin,
French, and Italian were jejune imitations. For Romantic
drama, as he saw it, there were two more or less contemporaneous epochs: Elizabethan England and the *Siglo de
Oro* of Spain, notable chiefly for Shakespeare and Lope
de Vega.

Whereas some of Shakespeare's classical-minded admirers had excused his formal imperfections, A. W. Schlegel perceived that Shakespearean dramaturgy had an
organic form of its own. (I hope I shall not rake up a fes-
tering scandal of literary history by noting that this is one
of the many points on which Schlegel anticipated Coleridge.) The whirligig of taste has come full circle when,
in concluding his lectures with a call for a new German
drama, Schlegel proposes Shakespeare as the ideal
model. That would be a premise for Gustav Freytag's influential handbook, *Die Technik des Dramas,* where Shakespeare offers the same example of craftsmanship that
Sophocles did in Aristotle's *Poetics.* When we turn to
Goethe, we face Shakespeare with the only one of his
readers who has attained a comparable stature in his native literature. Goethe was highly conscious of the con-
juncture, and Shakespeare was a favorite topic with him
from first to last. He told Eckermann that Shakespeare's
greatness, though it owed much to his epoch, had nar-
rowed the possibilities for his successors. Goethe felt himself fortunate to have worked in a language which har-
bored no such outstanding predecessors. If he freely

conceded his own superiority to such German contemporaries as Tieck, then Shakespeare was by the same standard "a being of a higher order" than himself. He fancied that the daemons like to sport with other men by
setting up certain unsurpassable figures: Raphael in
painting, Mozart in music, Shakespeare in poetry. Eckermann might well have retorted by mentioning the names
of Michelangelo and Bach, but he would have been at a
loss to suggest a match in the poetic domain.

The Schlegel-Tieck translation, fairly close yet so much
simpler than Elizabethan diction, completed the annexa-
tion of *unser Shakespeare* to Germany. Heine could boast
of his countrymen that they had comprehended Shakespeare before the English. Certainly, in forming a cult
around him, both theatrical and pedagogical, they lifted
him from England's hall of fame to the world's—"not our
poet but the world's," said Landor. In that extended
arena he soon was receiving more homage than the culture-heroes of any other country. For instance, one of
Dante's interpreters, Francesco De Sanctis, in his admirable *Storia della Letteratura Italiana,* paused to concede that
the English poet eventually would surpass the Italian. (In-
terestingly enough, the late Edmund Wilson ranked
Dante ahead of Shakespeare, though unfortunately he
did not write about either at any length. The habit of critical ranking at that level was reduced to schoolroom absurdity when T. S. Eliot gave equally high marks to both
poets in poetry, but rated Dante much higher than Shakespeare in philosophy, explaining the odds by a dogmatic insistence that Aquinas was more profound than
Seneca. Value-judgments about philosophical systems fall
much farther short of unanimity than those about poets:
pace, Northrop Frye.) The widening repute of an author
is sometimes manifested by attempts at association with it,

and by the claim of foreign cultures to possess his counterpart: thus Chikamatsu has been proudly referred to as "the Japanese Shakespeare." As early as 1671, in an adaptation of *L'Ecole des Femmes* entitled *Sir Salomon, or The Cautious Coxcomb,* the adapter John Caryl revealed his inspiration by referring in his epilogue to *"Molliere,* the famous *Shakespeare* of this Age."

Beatified if not deified by ever-mounting approbation, Shakespeare was destined to be canonized—along with Dante, but even more reverently—by the lay religion of the nineteenth century, hero-worship. So its high priest, Carlyle, asseverated in one of his heaviest rhapsodies. To him Shakespeare was a hero before he was a poet, since heroism consisted of transcendent qualities which were channelized by circumstance into different walks of life. "He too was a *Prophet,* in his way," and he was "a Force of Nature" as well as "the greatest of Intellects." Gradually the consensual judgment of Europe had been reaching the conclusion "That Shakespeare is the chief of all Poets hitherto; the greatest intellect who, in our recorded world, has left record of himself in the way of Literature." Yet Carlyle seemed not in the least concerned to look into that record. He believed that the works, in spite of their flashes of insight, did rather less than full justice to the man, because of the conditions under which he had been constrained to turn them out. The slogan-studded encomium brings home what "the Stratford Peasant" had in common with Carlyle's two exemplars of kingship, Cromwell and Napoleon: all three were self-made heroes. The heroic principle that allies them with the saints and prophets and divinities who march in the Carlylean procession is the scope of worldly success that each of them has commanded in his way. And, in capturing the minds of their fellow men, how many of them have been more successful than Shakespeare? Carlyle ends in a patriotic outburst of self-congratulation: "He is the grandest thing we have yet done."

The variance between Carlyle's title, *Heroes and Hero-Worship,* and that of Emerson's lectures, *Representative Men,* published in 1850 ten years afterward, marks a more democratic approach. The American lectures, more preoccupied with thinkers than with lawgivers and generals, stressed the collective nature of human achievements. Greatness was attained by those individuals who could best express the general mind; it could be viewed, in transcendental terms, as an emanation of the Oversoul. But Shakespeare had eclipsed all other writers: "He is inconceivably wise; the others, conceivably." A "generic catholic genius," working more in the light of tradition than of invention, nonetheless he left his impress upon everything he touched. "Now literature, philosophy, and thought are Shakespearized." He should be credited, and Carlyle would concur, with the spiritual fatherhood of German literature. Emerson hailed Shakespeare elsewhere not just as the "first of men" but as an unrecognized god among men, like Jesus and Socrates. The very realization of his importance was a virtue in itself: "I delight in persons who clearly perceive the transcendent superiority of Shakespeare to all other writers." Yet the lecture concludes with a hint of reservation: "The world still wants its poet-priest. . . ." The catchphrase, "master of the revels to mankind," does not sound altogether genial when it is pronounced by a New England preacher. Emerson could not confer the seal of his unreserved approval on a philosopher-entertainer. "There was never anything more excellent came from a human brain than the plays of Shakespeare," he would write in his journal and thereupon add, "bating only that they were plays."

Emerson repeatedly criticized the Anglo-American universities, as James Russell Lowell would do at Edinburgh in 1883, for not including Shakespeare in the curriculum. However, Lowell had publicly lectured on the subject at Harvard off and on since 1863; and ninety-nine of Harvard's 175 undergraduates had subscribed to the first complete American edition, when it came out at Boston from 1802. Showboat and lyceum, Chautauqua readings and McGuffey readers: such was the attestation of Shakespeare's presence across this continent. The defensive prediction of Maurice Morgann—that the name and language of Voltaire would be forgotten—has not yet been fulfilled, but Shakespeare had no difficulty in gaining the geographical scope that Morgann's essay had projected for him: "When the hand of time shall have brushed off his present Editors and Commentators, . . . the *Apalachian* mountains, the banks of the *Ohio,* and the plains of *Sciota* shall resound with the accents of this Barbarian." An echo from that locution seems to have got involved, ironically, with Melville's declaration of literary independence: "Believe me, my friends, that men, not very much inferior to Shakespeare, are this day being born on the banks of the Ohio." Melville's review of Hawthorne's tales, which was likewise a manifesto for his own fiction, challenged the Shakespearean precedent on behalf of indigenous talent. ". . . Shakespeare has been approached," he argued, and it is un-American to believe that there cannot be advances in every field. Yet in his correspondence Melville envisioned Shakespeare as another Messiah, with Broadway as the scene of the second coming. A later poem proclaims him *ne plus ultra:*

> No utter surprise can come to him
>   Who reaches Shakespeare's core;
> That which we seek and shun is there—
>   Man's final lore.

Melville's sights were set very high by his emulative attitude: *Moby-Dick* was his *King Lear,* *Pierre* his *Hamlet,* and *The Confidence-Man* his *Timon of Athens.* Whitman responded to the same stimulus, and rehearsed for his own declamations by reciting Shakespeare along the seashore. But his ambivalence toward "the Shakespeare cultus" was much stronger, and his ideological convictions ruled out a good deal of the European heritage: "The comedies are altogether unacceptable to America and Democracy." As for the histories, they were "conceived out of the fullest heat and pulse of feudalism." Paradoxically, it was this aristocratic tone which incited more snobbish Americans to deny the Warwickshire butcher-boy the authorship of the Shakespearean canon. Delia Bacon's obsession was preceded by that of Joseph C. Hart, whose *Romance of Yachting* Melville had politely reviewed, while privately asking: "What great national sin have we committed to deserve this infliction?" As scholars with a vested interest in Shakespeare, we are naturally suspect in opposing the anti-Stratfordian theories. Yet, as an amateur psychopathologist, I am rash enough to hold a counter-theory. Persons with delusions of grandeur, when frustrated in their longings for holiness, tend to identify with Jesus; if it is power that they vainly seek, they may conceive of themselves as Napoleon; if it is genius, then Shakespeare might seem the obvious identification. But, whereas Napoleon was exiled and Jesus crucified, thereby leaving grounds for paranoia as well as megalomania in their emulators, Shakespeare's life was modestly successful and blandly uneventful. Bacon's fills the pattern much more aptly, with its tragic fall from a high office, and with the additional injustice of not receiving the credit that is due his pseudonymous works.

Less controversial is the inference that the critical apotheosis of Shakespeare had produced an elusive *per-*

sona, hard to square with the concrete details of a normal biography, and opened up a gap which invited the swarm of pretenders. Furthermore, there were still a few eminent writers who, more like Voltaire than like Goethe, obstinately rejected Bardolatry. The case of Tolstoy, whose destiny would compel him to reenact the drama he most detested, *King Lear,* has been brilliantly analyzed by George Orwell. The perennial efforts of Bernard Shaw to cut Shakespeare down to his own size were characteristic shock-treatments. Shav was half-serious in accusing Shakes of having "no constructive ideas," nothing but fustian platitudes, and in rating *Hamlet* beneath *Peer Gynt.* An optimistic reformer, utterly lacking in tragic sympathies, Shaw was repelled by what he could only interpret as a "barren pessimism." Well abreast of the modernistic currents, harking back to such didactic forerunners as Bunyan and Dickens, he was adept at turning a ploy into a platform. ". . . I despise Shakespeare," he once confessed, "when I measure my mind against his." A somewhat less self-interested assessment of Shaw's mind, considering his tergiversations from Marx to Mussolini or his uncritical worship of Ibsen and Wagner, together with his lifelong self-indulgence in such fads and fancies as vegetarianism and spelling reform, might not bolster his pretensions as a thinker. Yet his commentary on Shakespearean performance was invariably acute and knowledgeable. And the net result of his Shakespeare-bating, he could retrospectively chuckle, was to reconvert "a divinity and a bore" into "a fellow-creature."

"BETTER THAN SHAKESPEAR?" The caption that heads the preface to *Caesar and Cleopatra* is a typically Shavian inversion of a query that each succeeding dramatist has had to ask himself. Their occupational malady—

which is underlined by Shaw's brashness—has been an inferiority complex, the fear of having been overshadowed before they began to write, the feeling voiced by Goethe that Shakespeare had exhausted human nature. Goethe himself disproved that overstatement: even blank verse as a dramatic medium, when transposed to his and Schiller's language, could regain its vitalizing force. But in English, though it would be rigorously tempered into the epic mode by Milton, it already sounded derivative in such Jacobeans as Webster, who named Shakespeare among his literary acknowledgments. This may have been the real reason why Dryden ordinarily preferred the heroic couplet. But the whole apparatus of convention had been so irreversibly fixed that poetic drama was doomed to a frail and fitful continuity in the English-speaking theater. All of the nineteenth-century poets were, to some extent, disappointed playwrights—few of them so imitative as Beddoes, yet not excluding Wordsworth. The history of the closet-drama touchingly documents what T. J. B. Spencer would signalize as "the tyranny of Shakespeare," which in turn is the cardinal example of what W. J. Bate has designated "the burden of the past." A side-effect was the trend toward burlesque that culminated in Gilbert and Sullivan. It is tempting to illustrate by quoting from Max Beerbohm's "Savonarola Brown." Resisting that temptation, I quote the closing dialogue from an authentic quarto of 1658, Gilbert Swinhoe's *Tragedy of the Unhappy Fair Irene:*

> *Daemo*[*sthenes*].   I was inseparable in life,
> And will not be disjoyn'd in death.
> Oh! Oh!
>
> *He stretches himself close by the Corps,*
> *and with the same Dagger kills himself.*
>
> *All.*   Oh! Loyal Servant!
>
> *Dyes.*

This is a Spectacle of like Woe
To that of Juliet, and her Romeo.
Exeunt omnes.

Truly, Shakespeare has proved a dangerous model as Arnold warned too late. One of his glories was, for Victor Hugo, *"son impossibilité d'être modèle."* The total commitment to his uniqueness brought about the canonization of all his plays within the permanent repertory, though their individual fortunes have greatly varied from one period to another. *Othello,* with its oscillations of love and honor, bore the bell away in the Restoration. It took the moody self-interrogation of the Romantics to bring out the fullest appreciation of *Hamlet. Richard III,* though performed occasionally today, throve upon the expansive forces of the nineteenth century. *Richard II,* for so long in abeyance, has touched a responsive chord in the more passive age of Kafka and Camus. We have seen enough of time's revenges to know that they do not always forward the cause of poetic justice. It is a uniquely Shakespearean touch when Lady Macbeth, after having flinched from Duncan's murder, cries out (II.ii.12-3):

> Had he not resembled
> My father as he slept, I had done't.

The alienation is total in the latest play of Eugène Ionesco, *Macbett,* when her opposite number snaps out: *"Mort, il ressemble à mon père. Je n'aimais pas mon père."* As Shakespeare's works have been continually reread and restaged from generation to generation, they have elicited an intermittent series of reinterpretations at both the critical and the theatrical levels. As traditional lines of interpretation have hardened, and audiences have grown all too familiar with them, there have been countermovements toward farther extremes in the unending search for novelty. A revolution in taste accounted for the program of adaptation and alteration that turned out such "improved" versions as Davenant's *Measure for Measure,* Shadwell's *Timon of Athens,* Tate's *King Lear,* Cibber's *Richard III,* and Garrick's *Taming of the Shrew.* But the restitutions and corrections of the modern stage are necessarily relative. Charles Kean made room for a carnival scene in *The Merchant of Venice* and a dance of Amazons in *A Midsummer Night's Dream* by substantially cutting Shakespeare's lines. Beerbohm Tree was notorious for irrelevant pageantry, such as the Magna Carta scene that Shakespeare forgot to present in his script for *King John.* We can take comfort in the thought that the gimmicks of Peter Brook and the happenings of Charles Marowitz are no more than another chapter, by no means the last, in the annals of Shakespearean production.

As for the forthrights and meanders of criticism, they would seem to have brought us progressively nearer to Shakespeare. This does not mean that the latest words are the wisest, but that wisdom accumulates in a continuous enterprise—along with much dead wood and wasted ingenuity. It is analysis rather than revaluation that matters to Mr. Frye, but the analyses would never have taken place without the revaluations. Excellence means the state of having risen higher than others, and Dr. Johnson's empirical test for it was long-range survival. Such a criterion, we keenly realize, is "not absolute and definite, but gradual and comparative." Posterity is not eternity, and we can speak only for ourselves. Yet Shakespeare occupies us as much as he does because he offers a principal key to our capacities for speech, and therewith opens access to experience beyond ourselves and our day. Insofar as the past stays alive, it lives through its firsthand communications, rather than the synthetic reconstructions of history. Balzac did not invent the nineteenth century; Oscar Wilde was exaggerating, as usual, when he said that; nevertheless his paradox is a reminder that the writer's projections and formulations, so long as they last, are the strongest links in the chain of human time. "That which endures is the work of the poet," Hölderlin affirmed (*"Was bleibt aber stiften die Dichter"*). Hence, although our tutelary hero was not one of Carlyle's activists, his extensions of consciousness form a more durable conquest than military victories or colonial possessions. Kings and queens have come and gone, without meaning very much to us any more. "Indian Empire will go, at any rate, some day," Carlyle accurately prophesied, "but this Shakespeare does not go, he lasts forever with us; we cannot give-up our Shakespeare." Forever will be infinitely longer than anything we can foresee, but the story thus far has been absorbing and reassuring.

Reconsidering Marlowe

On his four-hundredth anniversary, as at all other moments of critical judgment, it has been Marlowe's peculiar
destiny to be reconsidered in a Shakespearean context.
His strongest claim is bound to be the fact that he did so
much more than anyone else to bring that context into
existence. This was the high point of A. C. Swinburne's
eulogy in the *Encyclopaedia Britannica:* "He is the greatest
discoverer, the most daring and inspired pioneer, in all
our poetic literature." Yet even Swinburne qualified his
superlatives: "The place and the value of Christopher
Marlowe as a leader among English poets it would be almost impossible for historical criticism to over-estimate."
The implicit qualification is underlined by our realization
that the Victorian poet was far from being a historical
critic. Marlowe must abide the question of history, which
Shakespeare has all but outflown. Yes, he is for all time,
we must agree with Ben Jonson. And Marlowe then, was

Contributed to a quadricentennial symposium in the *Tulane Drama Review,*
VIII, 4 (Summer, 1964).

he primarily for his age? Certainly he caught its intensities, paced its rhythms, and dramatized its dilemmas as no Elizabethan writer had previously done, and as all would be doing thereafter to some extent. Shakespeare, two months younger, could have emerged only by way of Marlovian discipleship. Had he likewise died at twentynine, he would have left us no more than Marlowe's seven plays. Most of Shakespeare's comparable sheaf of erotic poems seem likely to have been composed shortly afterward. In 1593 the Shakespearean corpus probably comprised three or four of the cruder histories and two or three of the lighter comedies, plus *Titus Andronicus*.

Neither of these matchless contemporaries, at twentynine, was a schoolboy; and it would be presumptuous for us to set them in retroactive competition, awarding Marlowe a special palm for higher achievement to date. Yet it is reciprocally poignant that Shakespeare, who retired early and was not destined to live beyond middle age, had at least twenty years left in which to compose about thirty more plays and thereby to round out the full assertion of his uniqueness. One is almost tempted, on sentimental grounds, by Calvin Hoffman's silly theory: that Marlowe was not really killed in a tavern brawl, but was whisked away to a secret retreat wherefrom he proceeded to turn out Shakespeare's plays. As against the other anti-Stratfordian theories, this one has the merit of naming the single alternate who had actually demonstrated a dramaturgic flair. However, such temptations are easily brushed aside, not merely by the documents attesting Marlowe's death and Shakespeare's life, but by the contrasting patterns of their respective careers. Marlowe's was meteoric in its development, and in its expression as well. In that sense his end was not untimely, and it is futile to sentimentalize now over his fragments and unwritten masterworks. Shakespeare needed maturity to express ripeness, although he could never have matured without assuming first the youthful stance that Marlowe has made permanently his own. Insofar as he must seem forever young, we are inclined to feel old as we belatedly reread him. Michael Drayton set the angle for all backward glances at Marlowe, when he described him as having primordial qualities: "those brave translunary things/ That the first poets had."

Drayton went on to amplify this description with a famous chemical formula, which implies again as much as it states: "His raptures were/ All air and fire. . . ." Significantly enough, they are not said to have been compounded of earth or water, which are after all the elements of flesh and blood, and hence are major components for literature. Shakespeare seems to have marked the passing of Marlowe through his own *Richard III,* where he proved himself to be past master of the Marlovian attitudes and tonalities, even while he was ranging on toward richer complexities and subtler nuances of human relationship. To be sure, *Richard II* would be unthinkable without the example of *Edward II,* or *The Merchant of Venice* without *The Jew of Malta.* Speaking more broadly, *Hamlet* owes a certain amount to the precedent of *Dr. Faustus,* and *Coriolanus* still to *Tamburlaine.* Yet, in each of these instances, Shakespeare moves on a wholly different plane—and appeals to a wholly different mode—of experience. *Titus Andronicus* itself, perhaps his most derivative work and surely his least effective, already shows a few of his humanely original touches. The ear that has been attuned to Marlowe, of course, will catch reverberations throughout the whole repertory. Incongruously Barabas, under a balcony, prepares the ground for Romeo's advances (*Jew of Malta*, II.i.41-2): [1]

> But stay: what star shines yonder in the east?
> The lodestar of my life, if Abigall.

Ophelia's madness would have been less plaintive, had she not been preceded by Zabina (1 *Tamburlaine*, V.ii.255-7):

> Let the soldiers be buried. Hell, death. Tamburlaine, hell!
> Make ready my coach, my chair, my jewels. I come, I come, I come!

And Hamlet might not have contemplated the other world so intensively, if it had not been for Mortimer (*Edward II*, V.vi.65-6),

> That scorns the world, and as a traveller
> Goes to discover countries yet unknown.

Nor would Milton's Satan have spanned quite so wide an arc, if Mephistophilis had not declared (*Dr. Faustus*, II.i.122-3):

> Hell hath no limits, nor is circumscrib'd
> In one self place: but where we are is hell.

But the very echo sounded increasingly hollow as the theater gained in depth, and as the histrionic manner of Marlowe's Alleyn gave way to the modulated acting of Shakespeare's Burbage. Within a decade after the prologue to *Tamburlaine* had so proudly vaunted its forthcoming innovations, they were looked upon as old-fashioned fustian, mouthed by such seedy playgoers as Ancient Pistol, and burlesqued by many lesser play-

1. Reference is to the six-volume edition whose general editor was R. H. Case (London, 1930–3).

wrights. Shakespeare and others paid incidental tribute to the Dead Shepherd; gossip about Kit's wild escapades and shocking opinions continued to spread; and the final stab carried with it an obvious moral to be heavily labored. As for the plays themselves, except for the debasement of *Dr. Faustus* into a puppet show, they went unperformed through the latter seventeenth and the eighteenth centuries. They were passionately rediscovered by the Romantics, who saw in Marlowe himself a fellow Romantic, and read him for such purple passages as Charles Lamb extracted in his *Specimens of the English Dramatic Poets.* Signs of growing appreciation included Edmund Kean's revival of *The Jew of Malta,* as well as Alexander Dyce's scholarly edition of the collected works. During the later years of the nineteenth century, Marlowe came into his own—and possibly into something more. His "Best Plays," edited by Havelock Ellis with a general introduction by J. A. Symonds, inaugurated the popular Mermaid Series in 1887. Their artistic novelty, their sensual coloring, their intellectual boldness, along with their underlying legend of genius misunderstood, held an especially powerful appeal for the *fin du siècle* and for the first generation of the twentieth century.

Marlowe was hailed, in Swinburne's panegyric, as "Soul nearest ours of all, that wert most far." We might wonder whether he stands any nearer to, or farther away from, ourselves after his quadricentennial; and we may well ask ourselves what characteristics found so strong an affinity in his admirers of two or three generations ago. The image of the Superman was then in the air, we recall, and it must have seemed more glamorous than it has subsequently become. Symonds and Ellis both talked about *l'amour de l'impossible* as if it embodied an imminent possibility. Ellis was a professional nonconformist, dedicated to sexual reform, French Naturalism, and the iconoclastic side of many other controversial issues of the day. Symonds was the principal English interpreter of the Renaissance, and his interpretations stressed those tendencies which meant most to the advanced thinkers among his contemporaries: neo-pagan estheticism, hedonistic individualism, secularistic liberalism, naturalistic skepticism. Further reinterpretation, influenced in its turn by some disillusionment over such tendencies, has more recently veered toward the other extreme, stressing the heritage of the Middle Ages and the continuity of its orthodox traditions. Consequently the question "How modern was Marlowe?" entails the counter-question "How modern are we?" If we entertain the more conservative view of his period, we can no longer view him as its characteristic spokesman. Douglas Bush would treat him, with some cogency, as a highly idiosyncratic figure. This should not lessen the interest we take in him as a writer, and it should increase his importance as a historic voice, whose dissents from orthodoxy were pioneering affirmations of modernism.

Such may be the most satisfactory placement that we can make for Marlowe's position today, but the anti-modernists would press the argument farther. Not content with turning back the clock on the Renaissance itself, they would reinterpret Marlowe's outlook in conformity with the canons of traditional belief. Unlike Rimbaud's apologists, they can tell no tale of deathbed conversion to invest the poet with an aura of posthumous respectability. Marlowe's heresies, for better or worse, are matters of legal record. We may not altogether trust his accusers; and we must distinguish their hostile testimony from the considered purport of Marlowe's writing; yet the cloud of suspicion surrounding the man lends credence to the more radical impression of his work. Paul H. Kocher has traced his thought through his dramaturgy on the justifiable assumption that he was a subjective dramatist. This is something of a contradiction in terms, since we ordinarily assume that the drama is—or should be—an objective medium. But objectivity, in the presentation of ideas, emotions, and characters, is at best an approximation. Shakespeare seems most unique in his "Negative Capability," his capacity for effacing his own personality behind his varied and vivid *dramatis personae.* Marlowe's more insistent and limited gift might be characterized, by inevitable comparison, as positive capability. Where Shakespeare is everybody, Marlowe is always himself. The critical method suggested by David Masson, the detection of "fervors" and "recurrences," proves elusive and hazardous for Shakespeare. But for Marlowe it works, because he keeps obsessively returning to certain themes, rising to particular occasions, and modifying his material in distinctly personal ways.

Consider what Mario Praz has called the Ganymede complex. Whether or not Marlowe was a homosexual can be no concern of ours; it is somewhat more relevant that his conversations, as reported by Thomas Kyd and Francis Baines, consistently exhibit a preoccupation with homosexuality; and it is of real significance, in the history of western literature, that few writers have so candidly dwelt on that theme, between the ancients and the epoch of Proust and Gide and Jean Genet. Both in *Dido, Queen of Carthage,* and in *Hero and Leander,* the conventionally heterosexual plot is augmented by the interpolation of a homosexually motivated episode. It has not passed without remark that Marlowe's one sustained treatment of amorous passion appears in the love of Edward II for Gaveston—a relation adumbrated in *The Massacre at Paris* with Henry II and his minions. One of the ironies of Marlowe's fate, under the circumstances, has been his repute among casual readers as a sort of laureate for young lovers of complementary sexes. This may be due in part to his premature demise and to the discredited rumors involving a lovers' duel, but it can mainly be traced to that small handful of quotations from him which have circulated very widely: his much anthologized lyric, "The Passionate Shepherd to his Love"; the rapturous invocation of Dr. Faustus to Helen of Troy, detached from its austere context; and, above all, the quasi-proverbial line about love at first sight that Shakespeare echoed in *As You Like It.* More in the distinctive Marlovian vein is the cynical twist of Barabas' response to the charge of fornication, which T. S. Eliot culled for an epigraph, and which has since provided a title for Ernest Hemingway and latterly James Baldwin (IV.i.42-3):

> But that was in another country; and besides, the wench is dead.

Lamb could not, and would not, have gone into concrete details; yet he pointed in the prevailing direction, when he spoke of Marlowe's disposition "to dally with interdicted subjects." His contemporary reputation for "daring God out of Heaven," in Robert Greene's phrase, clearly echoed fervent lines and mirrored recurrent scenes. We need not forget that those heretical speeches and blasphemous gestures were put into the mouths of protagonists on whose heads they brought down the most exemplary damnations. But if Marlowe is not—what Ellis claimed—his own hero, then his typical heroes tend to be committed heretics, as well as self-made moderns; and *Dr. Faustus,* with a black magic still potent in the curses and conjurations of *Moby-Dick* or *Ulysses,* comes perilously

close to prefiguring Marlowe's own tragedy: the cut
branch, the burnt laurel. The playwright not only takes
part in the scholar's blasphemy, but also seems to enjoy
his anathema. True, the pagan vision of Helen dissolves
before the Gothic grotesquerie of the hellmouth. But it is
the perpetual curiosity, rather than the terminal agony,
that survives in our minds as the peculiarly Faustian posture. Similarly, we go on thinking of Don Juan as an
unrepentant libertine, rather than as a sinner burning in
Hell. Since the interdiction is duly scheduled to win out
over the dalliance, *Dr. Faustus* would have the stark outline of a morality play, if an outline were all that we
looked for in it. Neo-orthodox moralists would indeed
reduce the mighty *Tamburlaine* to the abject level of a cautionary fable, as Roy W. Battenhouse has attempted to
do, by emphasizing the dogmatic background at the expense of the dramatic foreground, though the latter expressly flouts the former.

Since every drama is perforce dialectical, there is much
that has to be said on both sides; and where opinion was
strictly regulated, it would be the right thinkers who had
to say the last word; yet though they reaffirm the appropriate taboo, it has been challenged in the process by
more fascinating spokesmen. These unbelievers maintain
a tense atmosphere of moral ambiguity, made explicit by
the theatrical caricature of Machiavelli. The Latin warrant that brings about Edward's murder would make a
suggestive paradigm for the reading of Marlowe as a
whole. It could convey an innocuous piety (*Edward II*,
V.iv.11):

> Kill not the King, 'tis good to fear the worst.

Or, as repunctuated and retranslated by Mortimer, it
could have a subversive and sinister meaning (9):

Fear not to kill the King, 'tis good he die.

So it sounds with Marlowe's ambiguous situations. There is no impiety, from a Christian standpoint, when Tamburlaine burns the Koran; his ensuing death, in any case, might well be regarded as Mohammed's revenge. When the Christian armies break their oath, the Mohammedan leader calls upon Christ, who avenges their just cause against his own adherents. It is in this connection that the infidel Orcanes makes the most elevated of Marlowe's religious pronouncements, affirming the existence of a transcendant God who—like the hell that accompanies Mephistophilis—is not "circumscriptible" (2 *Tamburlaine*, II.ii.50). This is as far from Marlowe's alleged atheism as it is from any theological dogma; and it does not exclude a thoroughgoing anticlericalism, or a skeptical feeling that few religionists live up to the creeds they profess. As a study in comparative ethics, *The Jew of Malta* is more anti-Christian than anti-Semitic. Here again it is the Christians who do the oath-breaking, and their Governor outdoes the Jew in Machiavellian blackmail and double-dealing.

The gods themselves are pantheistically pluralized by Marlowe, with room among them for both Christ and Mohammed under the ultimate deity of Jove. That classical ruler, who coalesces at times with the Old Testament visage of Jehovah, is likewise seen as the Olympian revolutionary who overthrew the Titans. Tamburlaine cites him as an illustrious forerunner in an eternal conflict; and it is revealing to compare this triumphal account of a perpetually dynamic cosmos, where nature teaches men to have aspiring minds, with the hierarchical conception of order and degree that Ulysses elucidates in *Troilus and Cressida*. The individual movement is upward, with Mar-

lowe; the total framework is more balanced, with Shakespeare. Tamburlaine's be-all and end-all (*1 Tamburlaine*,
II.vii.29),

> The sweet fruition of an earthly crown,

becomes, for the Lancastrian kings, the mere beginning
of responsibility (*2 Henry IV*, IV.v.23):

> O polish'd perturbation, golden care!

Marlowe's later heroes, though they are no less mono-
maniacal or megalomaniacal, have more sublimated ambitions—capital, sorcery—than the kingship, which Edward so pathetically loses. Yet even Tamburlaine, in the
midst of his amoral drive to power, can pause to speculate on "What is beauty?" (V.i.160). Though he remains
untouched by his cruel slaughter of the Damascene
virgins, he is finally moved by Zenocrate's tears for her
father, and he expends the utmost Marlovian eloquence
in expressing the problem of poetic inexpressibility. More
pointedly, when Faustus apostrophizes Helen, his esthetic
rapture is framed by the ethical situation. And the de-
lights of music and poetry are frankly envisioned as
snares to be manipulated by Gaveston, whose introductory monologue concludes by describing an ominous
masque, wherein Actaeon will be stricken down for having observed the naked goddess (played, as Marlowe
takes the pains to remind us, by a boy).

Marlowe's chastened and penitential mood, so ambivalently interwoven with his exaltations and exuber-
ances, might be summed up in this distich from a posthumous poem by E. E. Cummings:

> where climbing was and bright
> is darkness and to fall.

These are not the inert and untragic falls of medieval tragedy; for the overriding emphasis is upon the intellectual pride, the extreme *hubris*, the dazzling brightness that went before them and virtually made the price worth paying. Nonetheless it is acknowledged and paid, and herein lies the sharp difference between Marlowe and the Romantics. His psychic pattern is not Titanic, like theirs, but Icarian, since it encompasses both the limitless aspiration and the limiting consequence: both infinitude and fragmentation. His Faust is much less close to Goethe's hero, who gets out of his diabolic bargain with such Romantic casuistry, than to the guilt-ridden genius of Thomas Mann's *Doktor Faustus*. We cannot read Marlowe as naively today as our predecessors could in the nineteenth century; and he might make us happier if we could stick to his bright surfaces; but his stature as a tragic playwright is enhanced by the darker and deeper meanings we may now be finding in his tragedies. The note of triumph that runs through them, Renaissance triumph uncontrolled, rings false already in *Edward II* and takes on an ironic reverberation for us. Among their spectacular properties, which symbolize aspects of the human predicament, Tamburlaine's chariot fascinates us less than Bajazeth's cage. Standing—as we do—somewhat closer to Kafka than to Nietzsche, alas, we comprehend the reaching of limits as well as the testing of potentialities. Capitalism seethes in the self-prepared caldron of Barabas. Science itself is tormented by the flames that Dr. Faustus has conjured up.

Thus Marlowe still has resonance, albeit in an unexpectedly minor key, for a time which terms itself the Age of Anxiety; and it might not be unduly hypothetical to look for a restaging of his drama in the light of what we sometimes term the Theater of the Absurd.[2] Its anti-heroic characters have more in common with the exceptional Edward, standing beardless and bemused in his puddle, than with the more flamboyantly Marlovian figures. It may indeed be no accident that Bertolt Brecht, in his earliest playwriting days, collaborated on a German adaptation of *Edward II*. Marlowe seems to have naturally obtained that effect for which Brecht has been so consciously striving: alienation rather than identification, estrangement and not endearment—and this must be our last and clinching distinction between Marlowe's art and Shakespeare's. Yet we live in a world, and in a universe, where a sense of strangeness may be more pertinent than the illusion of being at home. Every day remote and obscure nations clamor to be heard; vaunts of ever more menacing weapons are thunderously exchanged, while intrepid voyagers are being launched on interplanetary flights. Marlowe, with his insatiable urge to prove cosmography, to confute the geographers, and to transform history into modernity, might have gained more pleasure from such spectacles than many of us may do. To reread him now is to be reminded of the exotic breeds and barbaric hordes that migrate across the poems of St. John Perse, or of those half-forgotten civilizations whose emergences and declines have been so categorically passed in review by Arnold Toynbee. Marlowe is forever the lone explorer.

2. This hypothesis may have found its fulfillment in the production of Jerzy Grotowski.

The End of Elizabethan Drama

> . . . All things have their end:
> Churches, and Citties (that have diseases like to men)
> Must have like death that we have.

Antonio's reflections, at the tomb of the heroine in *The Duchess of Malfi,* reverberate to him from a ruined abbey with an echo of finality: *"Like death that we have."*[1] Yet, strictly speaking, the existence of institutions and communities—let alone historical movements—can never be terminated as readily or as decisively as the individual lives of human beings. Hence the regime of a given ruler, while it sets a somewhat arbitrary *terminus a quo* and *terminus ad quem,* is less problematic than our retrospective arguments over some other beginning or ending of a particular period. It has proved much easier to talk about the reign of Elizabeth I than about the Renaissance in England. We do not speak of Attic tragedy as Periclean, nor do we refer to the theater of the *Siglo de Oro* as Philip-

1. F. L. Lucas (ed.), *The Complete Works of John Webster* (London, 1928), II, 116 (V.iii.19, 20).

Presented *in absentia* to a symposium of the Modern Language Association on "The End of the Renaissance," New York, December 27, 1968; published in *Comparative Drama,* III, 4 (Winter, 1969–70).

pine, and we have better reason to link Molière and Racine with Louis XIV than we have to associate Shakespeare with the Virgin Queen. Nonetheless we are so
impressed by the drama of her career, if not by her own
theatrical interests, that we allow her to exceed its limits
by almost forty years. No cut-off point for any branch of
literature was ever quite so absolute as the closure of the
theaters by order of the Long Parliament in 1642.

Can we justify the presupposition that the English
drama continued to be Elizabethan all the way up to that
point? Are we justified, for that matter, in assuming that
its prior development had been continuous? Father
Harold Gardiner, in *Mysteries' End,* argues for an earlier
discontinuity, blaming Elizabeth for the suppression of
the religious cycles.[2] David Bevington, in *From Mankind to
Marlowe,* has retraced a gradual train of secularization
through the moralities and the troupes of players.[3] More
recently, in *Christian Rite and Christian Drama,* O. B. Hardison Jr. has renewed the attack on an evolutionary conception—an attack which was earlier refuted when Karl
Young put down Oscar Cargill, in a controversy which
Professor Hardison discreetly overlooks.[4] The latter is
fully warranted, of course, in considering the liturgical
drama for its own sake, rather than as a wayside shrine
on some teleological pilgrimage toward Shakespeare. But
he makes a gratuitous appeal to the anti-scientific preju-
dices of humanistic scholars, when he reduces the *évolu-
tion des genres* to a kind of pseudo-Darwinism. Actually the

2. H. C. Gardiner, S. J., *Mysteries' End: An Investigation of the Last Days of the Medieval Religious Stage* (New Haven, 1946).
3. David Bevington, *From Mankind to Marlowe: Growth of Structure in the Popular
Drama of Tudor England* (Cambridge, Mass., 1962).
4. O. B. Hardison Jr., *Christian Rite and Christian Drama in the Middle Ages* (Baltimore, 1965), pp. 1–34; cf. Oscar Cargill, *Drama and Liturgy* (New York, 1930)
and Karl Young, *The Drama of the Medieval Church* (Oxford, 1933), I, 542–3.

origin of biological species is less concretely demonstrable than the genetics of literary form, as they can be observed through the constant interplay of imitation and innovation. Evolution, in the sense of structural unfoldment, has been a serious concern of critics ever since Aristotle looked back from Sophocles to Thespis.

But our present concern is with devolution, and we may be well advised to shy away from the many facile analogies between the life-cycle of plants or mammals or seasons and the history of any given art. The great age of American literature, for Van Wyck Brooks, was *The Flowering of New England;* when he chronicled the late nineteenth and the early twentieth centuries, he called that span *New England: Indian Summer;* and the implication, reflecting his distrust of the moderns and his regional horizons, was that winter was not far behind—indeed is here today. Criticism has been too much bemused by the tropes of vegetation. If drama seems peculiarly organic in its relation to people, it is all the more dependent upon whatever happens to them. The literal concept of the Renaissance was a general revival of classical culture which, insofar as it affected the theater, ended by originating the modern opera. Otherwise, except for sporadic manifestations in Italy, there was little of lasting merit to be seen on the stage until the remarkable series of dramatic performances in England and Spain. Both of those relatively belated cultures might be described, if we could ever agree upon our terms, as having proceeded directly from the Gothic to the Baroque without the intervening phase of the Renaissance itself. However, we can be more precise in our dating.

We have to deal with three successive generations, and with what such historians as John Addington Symonds have labeled germination, efflorescence, and decay.[5] During the first thirty years of the Elizabethan dispensation, as Sir Philip Sidney bore witness, not very much took place in this arena. The vital date is the Armada year, 1588, from which we can roughly count the theatrical début of Thomas Kyd, Christopher Marlowe, other University Wits, and conceivably Shakespeare. Giving or taking a year or two in a sequence where chronology is often vague, we can assume that Shakespeare was active for about twenty-five years, and that they constituted the central epoch of English drama. The year of his effectual retirement, 1613, was marked by the première of *Henry VIII* and by the conflagration of the Globe Playhouse, an unscheduled epilogue to the spectacle. Since *The Two Noble Kinsmen* must have appeared around that time, the rest of the Shakespearean record is silence. And if we allow a few months more for *Bartholomew Fair* and *The Duchess of Malfi,* we conclude that Ben Jonson and John Webster had by then produced their most significant work, and that—as F. S. Boas has stated—the zenith had been reached and passed.[6] Francis Beaumont soon dropped out and died, leaving the indisputable dominance to John Fletcher for the last twelve years of King James's reign.

The season that saw the demise of Elizabeth and the accession of James I in 1603 left no special mark upon the theater, partly because it was beleaguered by the plague. If we look for some dividing line within our twenty-five-year apogee, we are likelier to find it in the last year or

---

5. J. A. Symonds, *Shakespeare's Predecessors in the English Drama* (London, 1900), pp. 3–6.
6. F. S. Boas, *An Introduction to Stuart Drama* (Oxford, 1946), pp. 1–5.

two of the sixteenth century. Most of the University Wits disappeared, just as meteorically as they had emerged, during the previous decade. Marlowe was as dead "as nail in door" when Pistol mouthed his rhetoric, and Nym's current catchword was "the humour of it" (2 *Henry IV*, v.iii.121; *Henry V*, II.i.70). Meanwhile Shakespeare had established himself through his histories and lyrical plays. Shortly before the turn of the century a cohort of new dramatists made their appearance: Ben Jonson, George Chapman, John Marston, Thomas Dekker, and Thomas Heywood. The most important playhouses, the Globe and the Fortune, were forthwith built. Professional rivalries broke out into personal satire with the War of the Theaters. The *fin du siècle* brought its *mal du siècle,* associated less with the moribund queen than with the failure of the Essex conspiracy. If the typical protagonist in an earlier drama had been a conquering hero, he was now a disinherited prince. Thus *Hamlet* foreshadowed the major line of tragedies to come, and the late Elizabethan impetus moved steadily through the first decade of the Jacobean era.

The irony that identifies Shakespeare more closely with Elizabeth is underscored by the fact that James became the official patron of the Shakespearean company. But the great wave, which accumulated its force in her later years, receded at the mid-point of James's kingship. What followed was the hegemony of Fletcher, the master-collaborator, Shakespeare's heir (*sed quantum mutatus ab illo*), who would die the same year as the king. His dramaturgy would be more influential than Shakespeare's or Jonson's or any other, in setting the tone for Restoration comedy and for the heroic play. One of his productions, *The Nice Valour,* is characterized in a prologue by another hand as "a Play well made." [7] This suggests, with some degree of aptness, a Jacobean Scribe. Fletcher standardized a *pièce bien faite* notable for fluent verse, sophisticated intrigue, brittle characterization, surprise effects, and tragicomic reversals. Frequently we hear him sounding variations on a well remembered Shakespearean air. *The Beggars' Bush* might almost be a restaging of *As You Like It* in gypsy costume, or *The Island Princess* another *Tempest* with a dusky Miranda and certain prurient afterthoughts. The most distinctive feature of Fletcher's world is its emphasis on femininity. Here he has taken us a long way from the Elizabethans, with their rampant viragoes and domesticated shrews, and has heralded the surreptitious advent of the actress at mid-century.

Shakespeare gave, at best, a double billing to his heroines: *Romeo and Juliet*, *Antony and Cleopatra*. It is symptomatic that both of Webster's principal tragedies cast a woman in the title role. Middleton's titles are interesting to watch in this respect: e.g. *Women Beware Women*. A glance through the Fletcher canon indicates that some fifteen plays have feminine titles, from *The Maid's Tragedy* to *The Fair Maid of the Inn* or from *The Prophetess* to *The Night-Walker*. Perhaps *The Woman-Hater* should be viewed as an exception which proves a rule. *Women Pleased*, at all events, expresses Fletcher's characteristic gallantry. More and more he addressed himself to the courtly audiences of the private theaters at Blackfriars and Drury Lane. The repertory of the public theaters was increasingly aimed at unrefined tastes, while the popular audiences were dwindling under the attritions of Puritanism. Ties

7. A. R. Waller (ed.), *The Works of Francis Beaumont and John Fletcher* (Cambridge, 1912), X, 144.

between the theatrical establishment and the Stuart court were even closer under Charles I and his stage-struck queen, Henrietta Maria. The drama, in going indoors, had entered a hothouse atmosphere; and, depending upon the Cavaliers for support, it became one of their early casualties. Yet it had been declining for nearly thirty years when the Puritans finally suppressed it. Now that G. E. Bentley's monumental compilation stands complete, it should help us to distinguish this late Jacobean and Caroline stage more clearly from the Elizabethan stage, as extended by E. K. Chambers to the death of Shakespeare.[8]

In spite of the interregnum, Caroline drama seems to have more in common with the aristocratic frivolity of the Restoration. Somehow, over the course of the generation since Shakespeare, the theater had lost its broad social base. Already in 1612, prefacing *The White Devil* with acknowledgments to Chapman, Jonson, Beaumont, Fletcher, Shakespeare, and Dekker (*"wishing that I may be read by their light"*), Webster had voiced a late-comer's mood of bookish self-consciousness.[9] His own contribution was intense but strangely fragmentary. It is painful to contemplate all the waste of spirit that Jonson poured into his masques and "dotages." Less original minds, like his self-styled "sons," merely repeated their masters, hardening into the neo-classic rigidities of academic pastiche or closet drama. When the officious Davenant was buried in Westminster Abbey, his very epitaph was a bare-faced plagiary from Ben's: *"O rare Sir Will. Davenant."*[10] The echo is dissonant; for, though Davenant's entrepreneurial

8. G. E. Bentley, *The Jacobean and Caroline Stage*, I–VII (Oxford, 1941–68); E. K. Chambers, *The Elizabethan Stage*, I–IV (Oxford, 1923).
9. *Works*, ed. Lucas, I, 108.
10. See A. H. Nethercot, *Sir William D'Avenant: Poet Laureate and Playwright-Manager* (Chicago, 1938).

energies did much to maintain a theatrical continuity during the Commonwealth ban, he was anything but a rare talent or an uncommon type; and his Jonsonian pretensions were as precarious as his claim to be Shakespeare's illegitimate son. John Dryden, when he paid his respects to Jonson's last disciple, Thomas Shadwell, would have a word for two other predecessors who had been derivative in their day:

> *Heywood* and *Shirley* were but Types of thee,
> Thou last great prophet of Tautology.[11]

The Elizabethans had explored so many rich possibilities that they all but exhausted the medium they left to their successors. Less resourceful playwrights, catering to a more limited and specialized audience, were constrained by the echoes of everything that had been said before. More audacious talents sought to break the tautological mold by straining after sensational themes and novel devices, just as Tennessee Williams or Jean Genet seeks to outrage us a little more with each play. Among the Carolinians, John Ford kept the tragic flame alive by such desperate measures. He was as deeply involved with Robert Burton's cult of melancholy as some of our contemporaries have been with Freudian psychoanalysis. His heroine in *The Broken Heart* dances while dying; the hero is enthroned and entrapped in a sinister chair (more lethal than the same device used by Milton in *Comus* the following year). *'Tis Pity She's a Whore* is a latter-day *Romeo and Juliet,* wherein the star-crossed lovers are brother and sister. They accept their incest as their fate, whereas Fletcher—in *A King and No King*—had characteristically teased the theme and dropped it in favor of mistaken

11. John Sargeant (ed.), *The Poems of John Dryden* (Oxford, 1929), p. 90 ("MacFlecknoe," 29–30).

identity. After *'Tis Pity She's a Whore,* according to Stuart Sherman, it was "time for the theaters to close." [12] Having written his Harvard thesis on Ford during the heyday of D'Annunzio and Maeterlinck, Sherman was especially concerned with the question of decadence. His interpretation of Ford as its pioneering exponent is largely a moral condemnation.

A further source of deterioration, perhaps the hardest to generalize, was the erosion of language. Though we may argue about T. S. Eliot's theory on the dissociation of sensibility, we can acknowledge his description of Philip Massinger's style: "his eye and his vocabulary were not in co-operation." [13] Therefore Eliot pointed out that Massinger should be ranked in the vanguard of a subsequent movement, rather than among the rear-guard of the Elizabethans, for whom words came so near to the senses. Eliot's observation is also borne out by the stage-history of *A New Way To Pay Old Debts,* one of the few plays to be revived with Shakespeare's during the eighteenth and nineteenth centuries. Sir Giles Overreach, its cruel landlord, anticipates the mortgage-brandishing villains of middle-class melodrama, and its sentimental romance contrasts limply with the classical cynicism of its model, *A Trick To Catch the Old One,* Thomas Middleton's city comedy of a generation before. That interval could again be gauged by the curious circumstance that Dekker, having written the first part of *The Honest Whore* in 1604, waited until 1630 to write *The Second Part.* In order to produce a sequel, he had to reverse the roles, and make the erstwhile reformer try to debauch the prostitute his elo-

---

12. S. P. Sherman, "Ford's Contribution to the Decadence of the Drama," in Willy Bang (ed.), *John Fordes Dramatische Werke* (Louvain, 1908), I, xiii; reprinted in *Shaping Men and Women* (New York, 1928), pp. 203–31.
13. T. S. Eliot, "Philip Massinger," *Selected Essays* (New York, 1932), p. 185.

quence has reformed. Where the first play naively preaches reform, the second does its worst to corrupt its characters.

Wherever we may place the others, our focus is still upon Shakespeare, and that relationship is our main critical problem. Is it really true that his coevals and followers only shine with a luster reflected from his poetic genius, as Bernard Shaw and William Archer asserted, when they were campaigning for a naturalistic theater? [14] Or was he simply *primus inter pares*, preeminent in a constellation of peers? Certainly Marlowe and Jonson would have been eminent, had he never lived. Webster depended admittedly upon an accruing tradition, but advanced toward distinction of his own. Marston chose to give up the stage for the pulpit. Chapman was nobly endowed, but his gifts were primarily meditative and narrative; it seems unlikely that he would have attempted the drama, if his age had not made a specialty of it. Many another part-time playwright, such as Thomas Nashe, would seem to have been drawn in for this reason. Dekker and Heywood, like Robert Greene, were hard-working journeymen who did moderately well in various media. How many swallows, after all, does it take to make a summer? We cannot pursue that metaphor without recognizing that the precondition is a favoring climate. Time and place must adhere, in the phraseology of Lady Macbeth. The poet alone cannot make them. Neither can they make the poet, as we recognize by our qualitative distinctions. But their fitness is his challenge, as Shakespeare best understood.

14. G. B. Shaw, "The Space in Time," *Dramatic Opinions and Essays* (New York, 1910), 38, 39; William Archer, *The Old Drama and the New: An Essay in Revolution* (New York, 1923).

Dramatic Auspices:
The Playwright and His Audience

That acute observer, Alexis de Tocqueville, once observed of the drama: "No part of literature is connected by closer and more numerous bonds with the current state of society." It is indeed the most social of literary forms, and consequently the least literary—that is to say, the most dependent on extra-literary conditions. "Theater is an encounter," says the rigorous Polish director, Jerzy Grotowski. So is painting, whenever an individual goes to an exhibition, or fiction, whenever he or she sits down to read a novel. But, as Thornton Wilder reminds us, "A play presupposes a crowd." Not only is it a collective experience, but its presentation involves human be-

---

Some of the material in this paper was presented to a conference of the Fédération Internationale des Langues et Littératures Modernes, meeting at Cambridge University in August, 1972, and was summarized in the proceedings. The full-length version was first delivered as the Jasper Jacob Stahl Lecture in the Humanities at Bowdoin College, April 8, 1973. With further revision, it has been given at various universities in Great Britain and the United States. Since it was intended for a memorial volume which has not appeared, it is dedicated here to the memory of Irving Ribner.

ings, interacting with other human beings in the front of the house. Moreover, its production is an occasion; and though it may no longer be a celebration, as it originally was, still there should be something festive about it.

Insofar as man's tendency to imitate nature, *mímesis,* is one of his basic instincts, dramatic activity would seem to be universal in some form or other. The "dramatism" of Kenneth Burke, the "psychodrama" of J. L. Moreno, the "role-playing" of Erving Goffman, and the "theatricality" of Elizabeth Burns are merely some of its latest extra-theatrical manifestations. Accordingly, the printed scripts to which we have access constitute merely the tip of a vast and rather mysterious iceberg. Folklore, anthropology, archeology, liturgiology, let alone psychology and the social sciences, all have light to cast upon that mimetic substructure. Stage historians have resurrected gossip about the careers of actors and actresses and debated over the conjectural reconstruction of playhouses, though they have not until recently focused such attention on audiences as is paid in the colloquium edited by Jean Jacquot, *Dramaturgie et société: XVIᵉ et XVIIᵉ siècles* (1968). Here, as elsewhere, Germans have pioneered: *e.g.* the essay on acting by the sociologist Georg Simmel or the monograph by the Berlin critic Julius Bab, *Das Theater im Lichte der Soziologie* (1931).

Since the history of the drama has been written on the basis of its literature, it has been riddled with discontinuities. Critics—in the wake of A. W. Schlegel—point invariably to certain towering episodes: Periclean Greece, Elizabethan England, Spain of the *Siglo de Oro,* France of the *Grand Siècle* (Schlegel would have deprecated the last). Elsewhere and at other times, the major contributions have been more sporadic and single-handed. Critical selection has played a large part in determining the traditional canons: for example, the triad of Attic tragedians and the very limited number of their tragedies that have survived intact (thirty-three out of about 250 titles attributed to Aeschylus, Sophocles, and Euripides). Time and chance have operated too, we must believe, when a newly discovered papyrus yields a whole comedy by the fragmented Menander. We may well wonder about the repertory of those many non-Athenian Greek theaters, and wish that additional texts might enable us to reconsider for ourselves the canonical judgments of the Alexandrians. And what of those lost playwrights who won the prizes lost by Euripides?

It remains an arresting, if negative, fact that Roman drama never approached the distinction of its Hellenic models. Furthermore, it was to be surpassed by much of the vernacular drama modeled upon it. Among its three survivors, Plautus had scored unclassically with the populace by tapping an earthy vein; the more fastidious Terence, patronized by an intellectual coterie, had proved caviar to the general. The first performance of his *Hecyra* (*The Mother-in-Law*) was postponed because they preferred a tightrope-walker, and the second could ill withstand the competition of a gladiatorial show. As for Seneca, it seems probable that his self-conscious tragedies had been intended for private recitation rather than for public enactment. After their academic revival during the Renaissance, as irony would have it, they fostered blood-and-thunder thrillers upon the popular English stage, including *Hamlet* and the even more popular *Spanish Tragedy*.

Thus the drama also has its continuities, which may prove more significant in the long run than its gaps or shifts. What we retrospectively call New Comedy could claim one of the oldest and longest traditions in the history of the arts. Despite the submersion of its prime exponent, Menander, it was crystallized in the Latin of Plautus and Terence, to be kept alive by centuries of schoolboys. These comedies, significantly, were not *fabulae togatae,* not fables in Roman dress; they were *fabulae palliatae,* which retained the names and the locales—as well as the costumes—of their Greek derivation. Yet the *dramatis personae* would be universalized into stock types. When the regional mummers banded together in the troupes of the Commedia dell'Arte, Harlequin from Bergamo was seen to reincarnate the clever servant of ancient Rome, while Pantaloon of Venice coalesced with the perennial *senex iratus,* the heavy elder clutching his moneybags. And it was through the highly successful tours of the Italian comedians in France that such characterizations left an incisive imprint on the casts of Molière and Marivaux.

Literary criticism has not always appreciated the presence of the folk and their contribution. Pope blamed Shakespeare, as Boileau did Molière, for courting popularity by making unseemly concessions. In a well known and question-begging disquisition "On the Influence of the Audience," Robert Bridges sought to find a scapegoat for the alleged excesses of Shakespeare and his contemporaries—for what classical-minded critics had deplored as brutality and vulgarity, inconsistency and confusion, above all "foolish verbal trifling." Bridges, the neo-Wordsworthian poet laureate, who was obviously more at home in the hothouse than in the theater, felt that Shakespeare had compromised his artistry by paying more regard to the immediate audience than to the ultimate reader.

This view could be readily aligned with the position, held by bookish admirers ever since Charles Lamb's ac-

count of *King Lear,* that the study was better than the
stage for a true appreciation of Shakespeare. Walt Whitman, who was more attuned to communion with the common people, had reversed Bridges' argument when he affirmed: "To have great poets, there must be great
audiences, too." Neither the dramaturgy of Shakespeare
nor that of Sophocles, not to mention Molière or Lope de
Vega, would have been conceivable without such a precondition. Our belated realization of it is reflected in the
title of a book by Martin Holmes, *Shakespeare's Public*—or
rather in the subtitle, *The Touchstone of His Genius*. A lecture by H. S. Bennett in the *Proceedings of the British Academy* (1944) solidly refutes the Bridges hypothesis.

The drama is differentiated from the other genres—as
we have recognized—not only through its direct mode of
presentation, in being acted out, but through its commu-
nal mode of reception, in being experienced by a group
simultaneously. Therefore it presupposes the support of,
and expects the feedback from, a community whose attitudes it both enunciates and affects. This has meant pre-
eminently a city, more often than not a metropo-
lis—although given the precedent of the *kōmos,* the local
revel that led the way to comedy, it could likewise mean a
village. The pioneering work of George Thomson published a generation ago, *Aeschylus and Athens: A Study in the
Social Origins of Drama,* traces the *Oresteia* to an "organic
union between the drama and the community out of
which it emerged."

Yet, though the theater seems to be a distinctly urban
phenomenon, a cultural emanation of what "the town"
may signify, few cities have emerged to rival Athens or
London or Paris in that respect. Many would come closer
to Geneva, whose most famous citizen, Jean-Jacques
Rousseau, polemicized so fervently against acting.

Though the Christian Fathers showed the same hostility toward all spectacles except their own, the ritual of the church has traditionally been a matrix for drama—as it continues to be when Leonard Bernstein's latest composition is advertised as *Mass: A Theatre Piece for Singers, Players, and Dancers.* The sponsors of the Dionysiac festivals were priestly as well as civic; their dramatized myths were not too far removed from religious rites, initiating beholders into the mysteries of passion, violence, and death. So it was with the Biblical cycles of the Middle Ages, since the municipal gilds that presented them had originated as ecclesiastical confraternities, and had taken over their duties from the clergy.

The primordial theater of Paris, the Hôtel de Bourgogne, was owned by the Confrères de la Passion, who gave up acting themselves and leased it to actors after the sixteenth century. In Japan a clear distinction was sustained between the austerely classical *Noh*, inherited from Buddhist priests who functioned within the moral sphere of Zen, and the popularly spectacular *Kabuki,* a later and more commercial development undertaken on the initiative of professional entertainers. The impetus of religion had created the *autos sacramentales,* so characteristic of Spanish culture; but the conduct of these was gradually absorbed by performing companies, and profoundly influenced the cloak-and-swordsmanship of their secular *comedias.* Drama, in its typical progression out of the cathedral into the marketplace, and from the liturgy to the vernacular, has been necessarily responsive to such changes of environment.

In considering the dramatic auspices of the church and the city, we should not neglect an institution whose resources for pageantry were even more abundant and colorful, namely the court. Queen Elizabeth would not be the most striking exemplar here, inasmuch as she lends her name to a sequence of playwrights which was far more actively encouraged by her successor, James I, who became the patron of the Shakespearean company. It might be more illuminating to glance at Louis XIV, especially in his relationship with Molière. Now Molière, like Shakespeare, owed a divided allegiance to his courtly and his citizen audiences. The son of a tradesman attached to the court as royal upholsterer, he was well situated to follow Boileau's maxim and acquaint himself with both worlds: *"Etudiez la cour et connaissez la ville."* And it was precisely the interplay between *la cour* and *la ville*, between the enlightened courtier and the educated bourgeois, that would provide him with an ideal audience, as Erich Auerbach has shown in an invaluable article.

Molière had his targets, to be sure, and hence his enemies: the *Cabale des dévots*, evangelical zealots ready to be offended by *Tartuffe*, and the exponents of *préciosité*, the literary affectations satirized in *Les Précieuses ridicules* and *Les Femmes savantes*. Yet he could appeal from them to a broader coalition—to the pit—in the name of common sense: *"Le parterre a du sens commun."* The equilibrium was delicate, and tended to tip now on one side and again on the other. On the one hand, his bourgeois spokesmen for *le bon sens* put down the pretensions of his bluestockings and the fopperies of his *petits marquis*. On the other, *Le Bourgeois Gentilhomme*, which had its première before the King and his courtiers at the grandiose Château de Chambord, is the consummate satire on middle-class social climbing. On the one hand, it took nothing less than kingly intervention to keep *Tartuffe* from being banned through the wiles of the pious pressure-groups. On the other, Molière fell out of the Sun-King's favor, having gradually been supplanted through the intrigues of his musical collaborator, Lully.

In the last analysis, as Goethe pointed out to his confidant Eckermann, Molière—again like Shakespeare—wrote for money, faced a competitive market, and gained a living by addressing himself to the public. There were advantages to this symbiotic relationship, which Goethe understood. He, protected by ducal patronage as director of the court theater at Weimar, could address himself to an élite. He was free to experiment in every medium, and to elaborate through the long course of his lifetime a great philosophical drama, better suited to reading than to acting on the whole. But could he be considered, as a playwright, to have generated anything like the dramatic impact of Shakespeare or Molière? Whereas, in Pope's words,

> Shakespear (whom you and ev'ry Playhouse bill
> Style the divine, the matchless, what you will)
> For gain, not glory, wing'd his roving flight,
> And grew immortal in his own despite.

Shakespeare was never, unlike Molière, a star; yet each of them, having acquired his mastery through a tough apprenticeship, had earned the theatrical insight of the actor-manager; and the latter formulated his principles when he declared, with unclassical bluntness, that the grand rule of all rules was to please. Samuel Johnson would sum the matter up neatly in his epigrammatic couplet, written for a prologue to be spoken by David Garrick:

> The drama's laws, the drama's patrons give,
> For we that live to please, must please to live.

Once more, then, the seat of judgment is located in the *parterre*. This may leave us asking ourselves *cui bono:* who are the patrons in any particular situation, what do they want in the way of entertainment, and what are the most appropriate means of pleasing such proverbially variable constituencies?

Ben Jonson, after his unsuccessful attempt to flatter Queen Elizabeth in *Cynthia's Revels, or the Fountain of Self-Love,* had concluded his epilogue by having the actor quote the playwright's own opinion, an opinion not devoid of self-love:

> I'le onely speake, what I haue heard him say;
> *By God 'tis good, and if you lik't, you may.*

In easygoing contrast with the gruff truculence of "if you like it" (and the implication that, if you don't like it, you know what you can do about it), Shakespeare's concessiveness stood out strikingly when he named a forthcoming comedy *As You Like It,* or when *Twelfth Night* was subtitled *What You Will* and concluded with the Fool singing: ". . . we'll strive to please you every day." The contemporary measure of Shakespeare's success may be gauged from the testimony of Anthony Scoloker that *Hamlet,* a far more challenging work, pleased all.

It is generally assumed that there were varying reasons for such universality of appeal, that some of the witnesses took pleasure in the melodrama and others in the introspection, some in the poetic conceits and others in the antic quibbles. The resulting eclecticism made for a decidedly mixed mode, which the Elizabethans liked to call a gallimaufry, and made Shakespeare subject to the heavy censure of lightweight purists like Robert Bridges. Jonson would learn to relax his intransigence and to live down his *jemenfoutisme* (if he really hadn't cared, which seems unlikely). In his prologue to the more genial *Silent Woman,* he describes himself as a cook, striving to satisfy the many palates to which he caters: nobility and gentry, servant-girls and citizen's wives, vagabonds and prostitutes. Some of his potpourri will

> Be fit for ladies: some for lords, knights, squires,
> Some for your waiting wench, and citie-wires,
> Some for your men, and daughters of *white-Friars.*

Thomas Middleton is even more specific, if somewhat less confident, in his prologue to *No Wit, No Help Like a Woman's:*

> How is't possible to suffice
> So many ears, so many eyes?
> Some in wit, some in shows
> Take delight, and some in clothes:
> Some for mirth they chiefly come,
> Some for passion,—for both some;
> Some for lascivious meetings, that's their arrant;
> Some to detract, and ignorance their warrant.
> How is't possible to please
> Opinion toss'd in such wild seas?

Middleton, Jonson, Shakespeare, and their colleagues were addressing a cross-section of society, which ranged from the apprentice who paid a penny to stand on the ground through the burgher who paid extra for a bench in one of the galleries to the man-about-town who gloried in a seat upon the stage. And that same company, during the Jacobean period, could pass from this pluralistic audience at the Globe Playhouse to its private theater at Blackfriars, where higher admissions were charged for a more select auditory indoors, or in season and on special occasions to the court itself at Whitehall. (With comparable freedom the Spanish troupes could move from their open-air *corrales* to the privileged halls of palaces.) There were differences of tone and substance, to be sure, particularly between the repertories of the public playhouses and those of the more rarefied children's companies—differences which had been evident in the earlier "court comedies" of John Lyly, and would increase with the sophistication and self-consciousness of the later Jacobean and Caroline periods. Nevertheless, Hamlet's "little eyases" were able to exchange acting vehicles with the "common stages," trading John Marston's sardonic *Malcontent* for Thomas Kyd's naive *Spanish Tragedy* in 1604. By 1640 the demarcation had become so sharp that, when James Shirley's *Doubtful Heir* was acted at the Globe, a prologue asserted that this was the wrong house; it should have been the Blackfriars—how could the Bankside rabble do justice to a serious play which had "no clown, no squibs, no devil in't," and where the language was so clean?

It was the most vitalizing aspect of Shakespeare's heyday that the playhouse still had room for the groundlings, that the middle class had not yet been alienated and puritanized, that there was something for everybody. Nominally patronized by some great personage, whose protection kept the players from being prosecuted as rogues or vagabonds or sturdy beggars, Elizabethan drama depended more upon its own free enterprise. The principal inside document that has come down to us, Philip Henslowe's so-called *Diary,* is actually the account-book of a business manager who was equally a pawnbroker and moneylender. Along with its record of box-office receipts are intermingled disbursements lent for Thomas Heywood to buy silk garters or for Henry Chettle to be released from arrest.

What must have saved the companies from the vagabondage of strolling players was their solid anchorage in London real estate. Henslowe was essentially a landlord, with about as much esthetic commitment as the Shuberts

on Broadway. With him as a partner, Edward Alleyn
could stalk through his Marlovian roles at the Fortune
Theater, while the property-owning Shakespeare—as a
"sharer" with Richard Burbage and other fellow actors—
codirected the rival leading troupe at the Globe. Shortly
before those two landmarks were erected, in 1596, the
Dutch traveler Johannes De Witt had already recorded
his awed impression of the five theaters then standing in
London. A century afterward, in 1699, the antiquarian
James Wright could take a nostalgic retrospect, through
an anonymous dialogue entitled *Historia Histrionica*.
There his mouthpiece Truman recalls:

> Before the wars there were in being all these play-houses at
> the same time. The Black-friers, and the Globe on the Bank-
> side, a winter and summer house, belonging to the same com-
> pany, called the King's Servants; The Cock-pit or Phoenix, in
> Drury-lane, called the Queen's Servants; the Private House in
> Salisbury-Street; and the Red Bull, at the upper end of St.
> John's Street: the two last were mostly frequented by citizens,
> and the meaner sort of people. All these companies got
> money, and liv'd in reputation, especially those of Black-
> friers, who were men of grave and sober reputation.

Such was presumably the physical state of the London
theater when the Puritan Parliament closed it down in
1642. Note the degrees of social stratification that had already evolved since Shakespeare's day. The cockneys still
attended, but they had their own second-rate houses,
whereas the court-supported houses were mainly private.
A sixth theater, the Fortune, is not mentioned, though it
had been rebuilt after a fire in 1621. Truman's interlocutor, who bears the Jonsonian appellation of Lovewit,
makes this pregnant comment: "Which I admire at; that
the town much less than at present, could then maintain
five companies, and yet now two can hardly subsist."

These two companies had been set up at the Restoration by royal patent: the King's under Thomas Killigrew at Dorset Garden and the Duke's under Sir William Davenant at Drury Lane. It intensifies Lovewit's point to recall that the two were merged into a single company at Drury Lane from 1682 until 1695, when Thomas Betterton would lead another second group to Lincoln's Inn Fields. It would not be until 1705, when Sir John Vanbrugh built at the Haymarket, that London—now the largest city of Europe—could again boast a third house. Few would be added in the succeeding century, while the Licensing Act of 1737 would confer an official monopoly on the Drury Lane and the Covent Garden for more than a hundred years. (Paris faced an analogous situation during the 1680's when the crown amalgamated the rivals at the Palais Royal and the Hôtel de Bourgogne to bring into existence the Comédie Française, the slightly posthumous *Maison de Molière.*)

The attrition of London's theaters must be further measured against the growth of the population as a whole. As against a census of 1631, which counted 130,178 inhabitants, John Graunt's pamphlet on the death rates ventured several calculations ranging upward from 384,000 for 1661. Seventeenth-century figures, largely extrapolated from christening and burial records, tend to be modest by comparison with the statistical conjectures of modern demographers. Their outside projections seem to run from 200,000 in 1600 to 675,000 in 1700. Perhaps the most useful guide is the observation of Sir William Petty's *Political Arithmetic* that the city doubled its size every forty years—between the accession of Charles I in 1625, for instance, and Charles II's *Annus Mirabilis,* 1666. Over those same years, theatrical activities were reduced to about a third of what they had been at the less populous period.

A recession of general interest is registered further by the fact that playhouses were becoming smaller as well as fewer. According to the sole contemporaneous estimate, De Witt's, those open structures on the Bankside could accommodate as many as 3,000 playgoers. Whereas the Wren-designed second Drury Lane, even when enlarged under Garrick's management in the mid-eighteenth century, held no more than 2,000. A quantitative shift of such proportions underlines a qualitative shift which is still more far-reaching, since it indicates that drama has been moving from the center to the periphery of society. The Merry Monarch himself might set a pattern of enthusiastic attendance for his followers, and Nell Gwynn might personify the ensuing atmosphere of raffish gallantry. But the ordinary citizen had lost the theater-going habit during the interregnum, if not before.

"The complete estrangement of the British middle class from the theatre" would be subsequently lamented by Matthew Arnold. "The City neither likes us nor our wit," announced the prologue to Thomas Shadwell's *Lancashire Witches*. John Dryden, his arch-enemy, could hardly disagree, though he put forth a positive explanation: "the wit of this age is more courtly." In his *Essay of Dramatic Poesy*, he balanced the accomplishments of "the last age" against the refinements of the present one and the neoclassical importations brought back from the King's French exile. Two of the interlocutors in his dialogue, Sir Charles Sedley and Sir Robert Howard, were all too amateurishly representative of the gentlemen playwrights who worked within the limitations of a courtier's theater.

"The spectator of 1590 gave birth to *As You Like It;* the

spectator of 1600 to *Hamlet* and *Every Man in His Humour;* the spectator of 1670 to *The Conquest of Granada* and *The Man of Mode.*" Allardyce Nicoll may overstate the case while he oversimplifies the dating; but he backs with all his authority, as dean of English stage historians, the view that conceives the spectator as the unacknowledged collaborator. John Dennis, at the threshold of the eighteenth century, could look back with some nostalgia to the courtliness of the Restoration audience. "For that was an age of Pleasure, and not of Business," he explains. Hence the auditors had the cultivation to judge the niceties of wit and the felicities of poetry, whereas the rising class of prosperous tradesmen would have ears and eyes for little except "Sound and Show." This strikes a familiar note for observers of Broadway, or Shaftesbury Avenue, which might be exemplified by the contrast between Shaw's *Pygmalion* and its musical adaptation, *My Fair Lady.*

The subject of Restoration morality, in our theatrically uninhibited days, has ceased to be controversial. After the anathemas of Jeremy Collier and Macaulay have been countered by the apologetics of Lamb and Montague Summers, the residual question is that of L. C. Knights: not that these plays are immoral but that so many of them are trivial, artificial, nerveless, and "insufferably dull." Few of them, at all events, have weathered very well; the heroic play could barely survive its burlesque treatment in *The Rehearsal;* and where would Dryden's reputation be, if it hinged on his dramatic writings? It is hard to think of other tragedies than Otway's *Venice Preserved* which merit revival. One could make a better case for Congreve, purely on the grounds of style, than Professor Knights would allow; yet, chronologically speaking, his comedies belong to the limbo after the Restoration;

and his purest distillation, *The Way of the World,* seems to have eluded the spectator of 1700.

Comparisons with the last age—with "the giant race before the flood"—were bound to be invidious, as Dryden fully realized, and to show up the narrowness, superficiality, and *anomie* of an uprooted culture ("The Second Temple was not like the First"). True, there were surviving links between the Restoration and the attenuating Elizabethan-Jacobean-Caroline tradition. It had been chiefly Davenant who stage-managed the transition; and the features he carried over were those of the private playhouse, with its enclosed auditorium and upper-class clientèle, and of the Stuart masque, with its actresses and machines and painted scenes. By setting up the proscenium as a picture-frame for representational scenery, the Drury Lane chose for itself and subsequent English theaters a model which had been developed at the Italian courts of the Renaissance.

In one of the most promising efforts to survey the field at book-length, *Sociologie du théâtre: Essai sur les ombres collectives* (1965), Jean Duvignaud has suggested how the perspective scene could have been used as an esthetic instrument for the self-expression of monarchic societies. When depth is rendered pictorially on a series of flat surfaces, its effectiveness will depend on the location of the viewer. In perspective there is always one central eye-point, just opposite the vanishing-point, where all the lines fall into place without optical distortion. That, of course, is where the most princely spectator would be seated. He, in turn, would be the cynosure of a counter-spectacle, framed by the ranges of seats and boxes curving toward and centering on his box. It may be worth noting that the counterpart of this royal or ducal station in the old Metropolitan Opera House of New York, at the apex of its "diamond horseshoe," was the box of the pre-potent international banker, J. P. Morgan.

Opera, which Davenant introduced into England, has never made much pretense of being other than a privileged diversion, from its inception in a Florentine *palazzo* to the festivals of Bayreuth or Glyndeborne. Ballet, similarly, has required an opulent framework—despite the historical paradox that one of its greatest traditions is currently maintained on behalf of the Russian workers. Through another paradox, we are likely to connect the use of realistic illusion on the stage with the increasing influence of the bourgeoisie, and the parallel has frequently been borne out in the other arts and literary forms. Yet we have noted that theatrical illusionism was devised by the scene-painters of the Italian princelings, and more latterly the Duke of Saxe-Meiningen would anticipate the naturalistic settings of Antoine, Stanislavsky, and Belasco.

The earliest sets contrived in the Renaissance were heavily immovable and unchangeable, aiming at a literal verisimilitude which put blinders on the spectators' imagination. The actual difficulty of shifting them was one of the motives that prompted such critics as Castelvetro to invent and insist upon the pseudo-Aristotelian unities of place and time. It is ironical that two of the most pedantic and iron-clad doctrines of neo-classicism should have been based on sheer material contingency. With the invention of drop-curtains, lighter scenic devices, and sets more easily changed, criticism would be less bound to the *liaison des scènes*. Dr. Johnson would kick the stone in defense of Shakespeare, and the Romantic playwrights would be at liberty to turn from Racinian to Shakespearean prototypes.

For the sixteenth century and long afterward, the standardized depictions of the tragic and comic scene were those which the architect Sebastiano Serlio had vaguely derived from his Roman predecessor, Vitruvius. Serlio's drawings illustrate a social antithesis: temples and palaces loom on the tragic horizon, shops and domiciles huddle together in the comic precinct. Characters were to conduct themselves in accordance with their respective *milieux;* the laws of decorum put every man not so much in his humor as in his place. The fraternization of kings and clowns was demurred at by Sir Philip Sidney as a breakdown of the proper barriers between tragedy and comedy. Francis Beaumont's *Knight of the Burning Pestle* mocked, though with little applause, the aspirations of a grocer's boy to chivalric stature. The line that Ronsard drew between tragedy and comedy is all the firmer because it was unabashedly based upon rank, on the line between the nobility and the people:

> La plainte des Seigneurs fut dicte Tragedie,
> L'action du commun fut dicte Comedie.

Aristotle's distinctions between tragic and comic protagonists had been morally rather than socially grounded, grounded primarily upon elevation of character. When the amphitheater beside the Acropolis was filled with some 15,000 Athenians, a community had gathered in the fullest sense. "Greek tragedy," Professor Thomson has argued, "was one of the distinctive functions of Athenian democracy." The Homeric epic had propounded the elder and harsher code of tribalism. Aeschylus, in Thomson's interpretation, was dramatizing the democratic ideology of the emergent city-state. The Theater of Dionysius harked back to ritual origins; it also looked ahead to political debates. Athens itself is the theme of Old Comedy, with its choric commentaries on war and peace, its agonistic discussion of topical issues, its brazen mockery of fellow citizens, and its uniquely Aristophanic celebration of the endemic values.

With the city itself as its backdrop, the acting space was basically the orchestra (or circular dancing area), wherein the chorus—fulfilling that role of mediation which Schiller would ascribe to it—functioned to draw the actors and spectators together in a kind of mutual participation. This horizontal conception should be contrasted with the distinctly more vertical design imposed on the modern theater under aristocratic sponsorship and incorporated into most of our box-like edifices today. The indoor auditorium was immeasurably diminished; the audience was divided from the action by the dominating proscenium and by what was left to become a mere orchestra-pit; the stage was raised and lighted; the stalls were sunk and darkened; imaginative collaboration gave way to literal representation and passive acceptance. The actor, once a priest, is now an entertainer; the auditor, once a participant, is now a tired businessman; the drama, once a quasi-religious observance, is now "show-business."

This is doubtless much too brief and brutal a trajectory, which relates to twentieth-century theater only in its more commercialized phases. The lag between the Establishment and the *Avant-Garde* might be reckoned by the years it took some of us to catch up with Bertolt Brecht, who lived in the United States through much of the nineteen-forties, scarcely recognized and all but persecuted. The most interesting signs seem to point away from the tired conventions of naturalism toward elements of fantasy and festival, toward techniques of stylized acting and arena staging, with renewed embellishments of poetry, music, and dance, above all toward meaningful rapport between the performers and the beholders. Conceivably, we may be moving back from a vertical toward a horizontal theater.

Meanwhile, our paradigms may help us to understand the pivotal situation that Shakespeare occupied with relation to his audience; for the Elizabethan playhouse, just as it intermixed its moods and styles, combined the horizontal with the vertical approach. It was largely exposed to the open air, though partially roofed; it was theater-in-the-round for three-quarters of the way, so that the players were encompassed by the groundlings below as well as by the three-tiered gallery at higher levels. To these amphitheatrical aspects it joined not a proscenium but a small curtained area for discoveries, an upper stage to add flexible dimensions, some sort of topmost balcony for musicians, and occasional employment of the turret for sound effects. Though the actors were not religious celebrants, they were seriously trained professionals, and the solution they had found in their showplace was a compromise between convention and realism, with some emphasis on both.

This structural accommodation seems in keeping with Shakespeare's mediatory attitude toward society at large, his capacity for entering so many disparate minds, for comprehending such diverse points of view: what Keats would term "Negative Capability," and Coleridge "the wonderful philosophic impartiality. . . ." In an early essay, *"Zur Soziologie des modernen Dramas,"* Georg Lukács reconsidered Shakespeare and discerned an ethical outlook which, while by no means unaware of ranks or classes, comprehends a set of values common to them all—what, in terms of Tudor politics, was known as "commonweal" or *res publica.* Lukács, from a Marxist point of view, was primarily concerned with the bourgeois drama, where conflict is the outcome of class-consciousness and the ethos is more problematic than heroic or tragic.

So long as matters of taste could be legislated into official doctrines, through such authorities as the French Academy, Neo-classicism could prevail within its delimited jurisdiction, and could lay down laws for tragedies by making an awful example out of a play which had no such intention, Corneille's *Cid* in 1636. Taine set a premature date when he declared that the Revolution had swept away tragedy, along with the *Ancien Régime;* for it lagged majestically with Talma, Napoleon's favorite actor. It took the visits to Paris of the English Shakespeareans, the manifestos of Stendhal and Victor Hugo, and ultimately the première of Hugo's *Hernani* to bring about the triumph of Romantic drama in 1830, almost two centuries after *la querelle du Cid.*

Yet a gradual and inevitable change is documented by John Lough's study of *Paris Theatre Audiences* (as it is for London theater audiences in *The Drama's Patrons* by Leo Hughes). The stylizations of tragedy and comedy had become increasingly remote from the norms of life as lived by the middle class in the eighteenth century. Hence the endeavors to domesticate the one and to sentimentalize the other, the breakdown of fixed rules and the incursion of mixed modes. Oliver Goldsmith, fighting a rear-guard action on behalf of what he styled "laughing comedy" as against "sentimental," pointed out that the citizen-playgoer wanted his own image treated with sympathy rather than ridicule. Pieces that the French termed *"comédies larmoyantes"* ("snivelling comedies," in Irving Babbitt's translation) did not markedly differ, after all, from tradesmen's tragedies: the new vogue ushered in by

George Lillo's *London Merchant* and emulated by Lessing and Diderot.

Beaumarchais too experimented with—as he phrased it—*le genre dramatique sérieux*. But he was to move on and strike his most powerful blow, not with *The Barber of Seville,* but with its ampler sequel, *The Marriage of Figaro* in 1784. Therein the barber Figaro, that ingenious jack-of-all-trades whose career resembles Beaumarchais' in some respects, has resumed his old job as *valet de chambre* to Count Almaviva. Now, the master-servant relations in the drama might well be studied as an ideological index of the societies they reflect. Think of the *fallax servus* in Plautus of Terence, cleverer than the amorous youth he serves, helping him to get around the disapproving elders, yet remaining a slave unless manumitted, constantly threatened with the whip or the mill. Think of Harlequin playing the zany to Pantaloon or some other dignitary of the Commedia dell'Arte. Think again of the knightly Spanish hero who has his *gracioso,* his clownish squire. Then consider that subversive monologue wherein Figaro turns against his master and proclaims himself the better man. "It's the revolution already! (*C'est déja la révolution!*)" was the retrospective comment of Napoleon.

For the courtly audience of Molière the very notion of a bourgeois gentleman had been a contradiction in terms. Making people laugh is a strange business, as he had confessed. Curiously enough, his key phrase, "*une étrange affaire*," is repeated in *George Dandin,* where the opening line announces the moral: "Ah! what a strange business is a lady-wife, and what an object-lesson is my marriage for all those peasants who want to rise above their condition and ally themselves with a noble house, as I have done!" Whereupon, for three successive acts, he is cuckolded and confounded by his lady-wife and her fashionable lover. He can console himself only by shaking his head and muttering his *mot de caractère:* "You asked for it *(Vous l'avez voulu, George Dandin)* . . ." That was in the year 1668. In 1854 Emile Augier and Jules Sandeau brought out a play which won instant popularity and is still occasionally performed, *The Son-in-Law of M. Poirier,* subtitled *The Revenge of George Dandin.* Here the middle-aged mercantile protagonist, who is presented as "George Dandin in the part of father-in-law," turns the tables on his daughter's aristocratic husband, who thereupon reforms, goes into business, and is finally certified as "worthy of being bourgeois."

If the bourgeois could not become a tragic hero, he could leave off being a comic dupe, and the misalliance of George Dandin could be avenged by the enterprise of M. Poirier. But, with the decline of manners, where to look for standards? Who would be laughing at whom, Stendhal had asked under the heading "Comedy Is Impossible in 1836." He had been reading a favorite volume of leisurely correspondence, which had evoked some unhappy disparities between the refinement and "the congenial gaiety" of the eighteenth century and "the sullen and heavy seriousness" of the present hour. The upward mobility of the bourgeoisie had broken through the elegant hierarchies of taste and opinion, engendering two publics with differing lifestyles and opposite reactions. If *The Bourgeois Gentleman* were produced today, maintained Stendhal, half of the audience would hiss the title character, M. Jourdain, while the other half would be hissing the young aristocrat, Dorante.

The society that had laughed at *George Dandin* would be bored by the domestic dramas of Scribe. America ("*la morose Amérique*"), tyrannized over by gross mediocrity, must be even worse, and Stendhal saw it as a preview of the future. "In New York the problem is to please my shoemaker and his cousin, the dyer, who has ten children; and to reach the height of the ridiculous, the shoemaker is a Methodist and the dyer is a Baptist." The possibilities for theatrical intercourse were confused and strained by this problem of the multiple audience. Stendhal responded to it by giving up his earlier ambition to write comedies, and by jotting down in his own copy of *The Red and the Black:* "Since democracy has crowded the theaters with crude people, incapable of understanding finer things, I regard the novel as the comedy of the nineteenth century."

On the other side of the English Channel, William Hazlitt had raised a similar inquiry: "Why There Are So Few Good Modern Comedies." Part of his response was historical: so many have been written heretofore that the question answers itself. "Comedy wears itself out— destroys the very food on which it lives"—by repeating the same old tricks. But Hazlitt's reasoning was rooted more deeply in social generalization. Congreve, following Sir William Temple and followed by Steele and Sterne, had attributed the richness of the Englishman's humor to the liberties he enjoyed, which favored idiosyncrasy of character. Now, Hazlitt reasoned, Englishmen were losing their sense of humor because their lives were becoming more and more uniform and bland. "We are deficient in Comedy because we are without characters in real life." As for tragedy, its highest effects had come earliest. Shakespeare himself would find it difficult to make his mark at the moment. Never a believer in progress among the arts, and always an examiner of the *Zeitgeist*, Hazlitt reaffirmed that dramatic poetry was incompatible with "the spirit of the age."

Generations of poets before and since—from Words-worth to Swinburne and far beyond—have confirmed that dictum by composing dramas more compatible with the closet than with the stage. Hazlitt's journalistic col-league, Leigh Hunt, deplored "the exceeding barrenness which the stage has exhibited of late years in the tragic department," and recognized no authentic tragedy in the annals of English drama since Thomas Otway. Otway's contemporary, Saint-Evremond, even then had believed that "the spirit of our religion is directly opposed to that of tragedy." This viewpoint has been amplified by I. A. Richards and others, who argue that a tragedy must take place in a humanistic climate, that any belief in im-mortality turns it into a divine comedy, with hopes of a happy ending in the next world. Yet the neo-Marxist critic Lucien Goldmann, through his studies in Jan-senism, *Le Dieu caché,* has sketched a rationale for the Christian tragedies of Racine.

The fatuity of judging every play by fitting it into the dogmatic alternative of tragic versus comic masks was pretty well demonstrated by Dr. Johnson; two centuries later we ought not to be quarrelling about such cat-egories. Tragedy has died a thousand deaths, by the proclamation of many a critic, and it may go on dying in-definitely, like an actor who plays Hamlet one night and Othello the next. It has been reborn or transmigrated, along with comedy, into something like the problem play or, more lately, the Theater of Cruelty or the Absurd. But, as these very epithets suggest, and as the critics have for once agreed, the resonance and the dimension are not what they have been in an older order. The current formula would seem to be "The mixture, as unusual." Our version of catharsis is to walk out of the theater say-ing, "Well, now I've seen everything." How much farther can our artists go in complying with Diaghilev's command, "Astonish me"?

Drama itself has been superseded as a main literary genre, notably by the novel, which has had the advantage of needing no formal mediation between the writer and his audience, of adapting to more varied situations, of projecting experience more individually, of not having to be acted out. The transference of energies from the one medium to the other becomes plainly manifest when we note how many novelists have, like Stendhal, been dramatists *manqués:* from the interludes of Cervantes and the burlesques of Fielding to the *Scènes de la vie . . .* (the successive episodes in Balzac's *Human Comedy*) and "the scenic method" preached if not invariably practiced by Henry James.

But now the novel too has outlived its greatest epoch, and criticism heralds its obsolescence. And if we have not yet noticed, Marshall McLuhan will tell us about the effects of the electronic revolution, and show us how much ground the reading habit has lost to the oral and visual media. This, however, need portend no loss to the dramatic process, whose primary components are speech and spectacle. Rather, we can regard it as a momentous extension, teeming with fresh potentialities along with recurrent hazards of standardization and commercialization. The remarkable quality of the best films today is that, though they are mechanically reproduced, though we watch them facelessly in the dark, everywhere we perceive the personal touch of the *auteur,* the director, the ultimate playwright. If he does not literally commune with his audiences, his art finds expression through a community of actors, artists, and technicians.

Cinema is vertical theater with a vengeance, yet it has its horizontal compensations. Though it gets projected on an international scale, it familiarizes us with the most telling details of Fellini's Rome or Bergman's Skåne. Ingmar Bergman is a propitious figure, since the scenarios that he writes are readable as prose fiction, and since he periodically renews his Strindbergian inspiration by engaging in theatrical practice. It seems improbable that the theater will ever regain the cultural centrality that it has occupied in its greatest epochs. Nonetheless, though it has been greatly outdistanced by its technological tributaries, it is irreplaceable as the most fertile source of experimentation and training for them.

The statistical facts reveal the erosion. Malcolm Bradbury's suggestive handbook, *The Social Context of Modern English Literature,* counts about two hundred functioning theaters in the United Kingdom during the year of publication, 1971, as opposed to twice that number in 1900. In spite of certain conspicuous recent additions, the same falling-off could probably be recorded for our country. This does not mean that drama has become unpopular as a medium, but that its popularity is now manifested in the vehicles and on the networks of mass communication, which J. S. R. Goodlad surveys in *A Sociology of Popular Drama,* and which are better evaluated by market research than by literary criticism. To be sure, the England of John Osborne and Harold Pinter has the National Theatre it so conspicuously lacked in the heyday of Shaw and Granville-Barker. Shortly before they began their train of endeavors, Arnold had looked about him and pronounced: ". . . we have no modern drama. . . ." To repeat the diagnosis in Arnoldian terms:

> We know how the Elizabethan theatre had its cause in an ardent zest for life and living, a bold and large curiosity, a desire for a fuller, richer existence, pervading this nation at large, as they pervaded other nations, after the long mediae-

val time of obstruction and restraint. But we know, too, how the great middle class of this nation, alarmed at grave symptoms which showed themselves in the new movement, drew back; made choice for its spirit to live at one point instead of living, or trying to live, at many; entered, as I have so often said, the prison of Puritanism, and had the key turned upon its spirit there for two hundred years. Our middle class forsook the theatre. The English theatre reflected no more the aspiration of a great community for a fuller and richer sense of existence.

Arnold's pronouncement, which was inspired by a visit of the Comédie Française to London, ended by conveying a prophetic message from the apparition of Sarah Bernhardt to her English audience: "The theatre is irresistible; *organise the theatre*." After its long-drawn-out interim of disorganization, organization has set in very lately and very lavishly—whether with the spiritual blessing of Matthew Arnold, or with the laying on of Sarah Bernhardt's hands, we need not pause to surmise. But national theaters, though they serve important functions, can be more closely akin to museums than to studios: witness the Théâtre Français itself or the present-day Moscow Art Theater. The Russian instance arouses some apprehension of Soviet propaganda and censorship, the subordination of arts to the state as means of thought-control. Yet the open market in ideas cannot be said to have scaled greater artistic heights, if we measure it by the oscillations of the Lincoln Center in New York.

The truth has long been plain: that a sole and specialized theatrical capital is not enough for a country as large and various as the United States. It is a question, not of just getting off-Broadway, but of getting off Manhattan island more regularly, of diffusing the unwholesome concentration that has almost paralyzed our theatrical culture. And it can be said that the last generation has witnessed hopeful portents of such diffusion here and there: in Minneapolis under the aegis of Tyrone Guthrie, across the border at Stratford, Ontario, on many university campuses, and in other circumstances involving communities. Size is a factor, since the danger is bigness and the need is immediacy. No amount of expensive professionalism can equal a small band of amateurs with a purpose and with the encouragement of their neighbors, such as the Dublin writers who founded the Abbey Theatre or those Americans who converted a rickety wharf at Provincetown into a playhouse. For, if I may conclude where I began, the essence of the drama is human involvement.

APPENDIX

Shakespeare as Shakespeare

The pleasure of seeing the bust of Shakespeare on the cover of *Harvard Magazine* (November, 1974), and of browsing through an issue so richly illustrated by contemporaneous portraits, is mitigated—for Shakespearean scholars—by the article that accompanies those illustrations: "The Man Who Shakespeare Was Not (and Who He Was)" by Charlton Ogburn. There is a silver lining, however, even to that obfuscating cloud. Frequently the anti-Stratfordians (the small but pertinacious band of zealots who will forever argue that Shakespeare's works were written by someone else) have been allowed to make the somewhat paranoid claim that the universities have denied them a hearing. Now they can no longer claim that their heresy—as they like to put it, in an implicit appeal to more liberal views than theirs turn out to be—has been ignored by the vested interests of an academic establishment. It has indeed been heard, at the cost of no little strain on Harvard's Latin motto, and herewith two of "the orthodox professors" are willing to pause for an answer.

Not that the case for Edward de Vere, seventeenth Earl of Oxford,

---

The circumstances that provoked this article, written in collaboration with G. Blakemore Evans, are explained in its opening paragraph. It appeared in *Harvard Magazine*, LXXVII, 6 (February, 1975). Charlton Ogburn's arguments are so typical of a small but persistent fringe of opinion that the two collaborators thought it might be worth while to reprint their counterarguments here.

has gone unstated or unrefuted before. It was first presented more than fifty years ago by J. Thomas Looney, as Mr. Ogburn notes, while enjoining us that the name should not be pronounced the way it looks. Mr. Ogburn himself seems to be rehashing a book of his own, written in collaboration with Dorothy Ogburn, *Shake-Speare: The Man Behind the Name* (1962), as is indicated in the biographical note. No mention has been made of *This Star of England: "William Shakespeare" Man of the Renaissance* by Dorothy and Charlton Ogburn (Senior), a volume of more than 1300 pages, prefaced by and dedicated to (*inter alios*) the present Mr. Ogburn. Academic pieties could scarcely vie with such devout familial commitments. Nor is there the slightest recognition of the various other contenders for—or, as Justice Wilberforce would say, pretenders to—the greatest title in literature: Bacon, Marlowe, the Earl of Derby, Queen Elizabeth, et cetera. The fact that the anti-Stratfordians seldom agree on a rival candidate is itself an argument in favor of the incumbent.

Mr. Ogburn cites the Wilberforce decision (*In re* Hopkins' Will Trusts, 1964), selectively and rather disingenuously, since he does not indicate that the case revolved around Bacon. In ruling upon a bequest to sponsor a search for Shakespearean manuscripts, the judge was quite explicit in foregoing any determination of authorship. Moreover, though he quoted and summarized a methodological caveat from Hugh Trevor-Roper, he made it clear that the Oxford historian was "keeping his own position firmly in the ranks of the orthodox." This is a significant distinction, which Mr. Ogburn blurs into a distortion by including Professor Trevor-Roper on his list of anti-Shakespearean heretics. That list may contain some distinguished names, such as Sigmund Freud and Charlie Chaplin; but no one professionally versed in historical interpretation has ever challenged the evidence as it stands; hence the inclusion constitutes an unwarranted slur against Trevor-Roper's professional reputation. Additional injustice is done to Henry James by a truncated quotation which misses out on his irony.

Mr. Ogburn is candid enough in describing the "scientific method" that staked his claims for the Earl of Oxford: "What Looney did was to identify the characteristics we should expect in the man who was Shakespeare, then comb the records of the period to see who met the requirements." That is a fair description of an irrational procedure. It begins by demanding acceptance for one man's arbitrary reading of an author uniquely notable for the volume and diversity of the critical in-

terpretations—not to say the controversies—that his works have
evoked. It follows the exploded assumption that Shakespeare's plays,
most of them based on preexisting narratives and adapted to the
conventions of the theatrical medium, can be treated as chapters of an
autobiography. Thereupon it undertakes a Cinderella search of
Elizabethan England to find a fit for the slipper. Anyone who knew how
to comb the records of the period would know that they are too sporadic
to cover the probabilities. This further means not only canceling the
records of attribution that we already possess, but also having to explain
them away.

The reasoning, of course, is circular. It actually starts by presuppos-
ing the idealized image of a pseudonymous playwright and ends by
bending a flexible body of work to accommodate the superimposition.
The autobiographical approach is supported by personal comments
from Samuel Butler, Havelock Ellis, Wallace Stevens, and Edward
Albee, all of whom are modern figures writing in a subjective vein.
Albee is the only dramatist among them, and subjectivity may be his
weakness. Drama is traditionally as objective as a literary form can be,
and Shakespeare has been praised by most commentators for his ability to understand all sides of any issue he presents. Whether it be impersonality or a chameleonic empathy or Keats's "Negative Capability," Shakespeare shows the actor's capacity for entering the minds of
his vast and highly differentiated cast of characters. It is worth noting
that Mr. Ogburn chooses Byron as the closest counterpart to Oxford;
for Byron did more than any other English writer to introduce the
Romantic cult of personality. Byron too was a lord—and social snob-
bery is an unspoken shibboleth among the anti-Stratfordians.

Mr. Ogburn's most persistent point is that our playwright had to be
a nobleman; only a courtier could delineate such "a picture of royal
courts." "The characters he considers worthy of his genius are almost
without exception of the nobility." Such overwhelming exceptions as
Shylock and Falstaff spring to mind at once, together with a host of
lesser figures—tapsters, whores, foot-soldiers, sailors, pedlars, rus-
tics—who do not seem unworthy of his genius. It would have been
harder for an aristocrat to catch their intonations than for an up-
wardly mobile writer of middling origins. Tragedies and history plays
were bound to deal with courts and rulers, and nearly all of Shakespeare's fellow playwrights likewise came from the middle class. "The
world of the nobility" was "foreclosed to him," Mr. Ogburn maintains.
Well, Shakespeare's troupe was under the patronage of Elizabeth's

Lord Chamberlain and later King James himself. Court performance is regularly recorded, as well as participation in one other royal occasion. Like many Elizabethans, Shakespeare's father, alderman and bailiff (or mayor) of Stratford for a while, joined the gentry with the award of a coat of arms.

"Literature affords no parallel for what we are asked to believe of Shaksper [*sic*]," Mr. Ogburn declares: that a country-born commoner could write plays which delighted monarchs. Mr. Ogburn should be informed that Terence, an African slave, charmed the high Roman circle of the Scipios with the refinements of his style and wit. Such sweeping generalizations cast more light on the limits of the generalizer's knowledge than on the outer dimensions of the subject at hand. Again: "In the whole history of literature no writer ever wrote more consistently from the point of view of a nobleman than Shakespeare." Even if his ideological leanings were such as are attributed to him here, and we doubt it, could he stand comparison in this respect with—to mention just one name—Castiglione? It is easy to see why Mr. Ogburn has been bowled over by Shakespeare's "enormous erudition." Here we encounter a genuine paradox, as expressed in John Ward's testimony, in Ben Jonson's, in the poem quoted and misquoted from Davies of Hereford, in Milton's tribute, for that matter in *The Winter's Tale* and *The Tempest:* the antithesis of art and nature.

"The evidence is against Will Shaksper's ever having attended school." There is no direct evidence one way or another, the school records not having survived from those years. But the Stratford Grammar School was a good one, and it was free for inhabitants of the town. What was he doing from seven to thirteen, at a time when his father was a leading citizen, if not going to school? There is a fairly well authenticated tradition that he was briefly employed as a schoolmaster. He had "small Latin and less Greek" by Ben Jonson's standards, not by Mr. Ogburn's. In any case, most of his source material was available in translation. Careful assessments of the curriculum and the extent of his learning have been worked out by T. W. Baldwin and V. K. Whitaker. Whoever he was, he had matchless powers of observation and retention of what he had heard and read. His text reveals no "polymath on the order of Leonardo da Vinci," but it does bespeak the "myriad-mindedness" (Coleridge's phrase) of a Renaissance man. Consequently the more scholarly poets who appraised him early, like Jonson and Milton, established the pattern of a *lusus naturae*—a genius who owed more to nature than to art.

With that special animosity which the anti-Stratfordians commonly vent upon their *bête noire*, Mr. Ogburn speaks of him as "a near illiterate." He goes on to reveal his own ignorance of the secretary hand by speaking of "incomplete" signatures, not recognizing abbreviated forms which are standard in that hand. Far from six signatures being "all we know that he wrote," an intensive study of Shakespeare's handwriting would identify his holograph in a scene from the *Sir Thomas More* manuscript, which has been accepted into the canon of two recent editions. Could it be imagined that the Earl of Oxford would have been called in, as Shakespeare apparently was, to doctor so ill-starred a dramatic venture? Mr. Ogburn seems baffled by the earliest allusion to him in Robert Greene's *Groatsworth of Wit*, which is clearly a protest against a mere actor who has presumed to become a dramatist. The important reference from the *Parnassus Plays* (1598–1602), where Shakespeare is specifically saluted in both roles (and as a poet too), is conveniently ignored. We are told instead: "Shakespeare's contemporaries made it quite plain that they did not consider the Stratford man the author." Plain? Where?

Such cavalier misstatements can only be supported by far-from-plain misreadings out of context, and even these ambiguous contortions yield merely the darkest of hints. Typical is the paraphrase of a line from "the author of *Wit's Recreation*." The book is entitled *Wit's Recreations;* being an anthology, it has no author; and Mr. Ogburn confounds the biographical with the theatrical meaning of the keywords, "histories" and "chronicle." It so happens that, for an Elizabethan-Jacobean who was neither a peer nor a prelate, we have a good deal of documentation about the man Shakespeare, wholly apart from his writings. Some of it is purely documentary; much of this has to do with business transactions; and, since this is the only kind that Mr. Ogburn allows, he thereby enables himself to conclude that the man was wholly preoccupied with money. Yet there remains a substantial and more interesting series of literary allusions and testimonials, which Mr. Ogburn snatches away from Shakespeare and bestows upon Oxford, thereby making good the barefaced assertion: "No word of commendation of him has come down to us."

This Solomonic disjunction is sustained by a bold feat of verbal jugglery. Since so many words of commendation plainly allude to Shakespeare, Mr. Ogburn has appropriated the name itself, in its commonest spelling, as a pseudonym for Oxford. Consistently he refers to the stand-in from whom it has been taken—the Stratford bumpkin, the mercenary shareholder—as Shaksper. Now anyone familiar with the irregularities of Elizabethan orthography and punctuation would hesitate to quibble over the spelling of proper names or to draw far-reaching implications from occasionally misplaced hyphens. But, since Mr. Ogburn makes so much of such details, he should scrutinize them with greater care. The villain of his piece is differentiated from its hero under the baptismal designation of "Gulielmus Shaksper (or Shakspere)." The actual entry in the parish register reads "Shakspere," which is the spelling that appears there almost invariably, while "Shaksper" is very uncommon and never used with regard to Shakespeare himself. The spelling in the marriage license is "Shaxpere"—not, as Mr. Ogburn would have it, "Shaxper." (The final *e* makes a phonetic difference; the substitution of *x* for *ks* does not.) The form "Shakespeare" does appear in the christening record for the poet's daughter Susanna.

Mr. Ogburn's handling of Ben Jonson, who is a key witness in this inquiry, illustrates the preposterousness of his tactics. Alleging that Jonson expressed contempt for "Shaksper," he shores up that dubious allegation with a satirical line about a *parvenu* Jonsonian character; Jonson's editors do not accept the conjecture that the satire was aimed at Shakespeare. On the other hand, Jonson's brief remarks in his confidential conversations with Drummond of Hawthornden are not noticed at all, while the judicious appraisal in the notebooks is handed over to Oxford (masquerading as "Shakespeare"), as is the generous encomium that crowns the First Folio with the blessings of the Poet Laureate. Similarly, Mr. Ogburn draws conflicting testimonies from both the Reverend John Ward and the funeral monument in Holy Trinity Church. Accepting the epitaph as "Shaksper's" (the non-dramatist's), he naturally finds the Vergilian parallel (*"arte Maronem"*) "an obscure reference," and he goes out of his way to omit the mentioning of "art" and "wit" in the English inscription. Yet by the end he is citing the allusion to Vergil's art as if the epitaph applied to Oxford.

Mr. Ogburn is unwilling to concede a decent role to his "Shaksper" even on the stage. He has searched for him vainly in the records of Philip Henslowe and the memoirs of Edward Alleyn—the manager and the leading actor of the rival company to the troupe at the Globe. And he sets no store by the actors' lists in the First Folio and in Jonsons's, wherein Shakespeare is prominently named. As for the Quartos, it is stated that the first six of them "—all pirated—appeared with no author named." Unsupported statements that are at once so flat and so fuzzy are a little difficult to pin down. Due recourse to the bibliographical facts, however, informs us that the first six would include a good text of *Titus Andronicus* and another of *Love's Labor's Lost* with Shakespeare's name on the title-page. Again, "in 1598, Shaksper was bundled back to Stratford" to spare Oxford further embarrassment, and to remain there "in affluent but total obscurity until his death." As a matter of fact, he is mentioned among the cast of Jonson's *Sejanus* in 1603, and there is legal evidence for his presence in London on several occasions during his later years.

It is the essence of anti-Stratfordianism to negate any links between "the Stratford man" and the other man with the same name. Yet Caroline Spurgeon's study of Shakespeare's imagery has shown how such poetic sensibilities could have been nourished by the Warwickshire countryside, matching the very eddies under Clopton Bridge with those that swirl in *The Rape of Lucrece;* and there are local traditions, such as the deer-stealing incident, which may well have been reflected in the plays. Mr. Ogburn's arguments hinge upon his belief that the Stratford butcher's boy was not generally linked with the actor-playwright until "the publication in 1680 of a page or so written by John Aubrey." And Aubrey was "a roving and maggotty-pated man," according to his employer (the Oxonian biographer, Anthony à Wood), who "thought little, believed much and confused everything." We cannot but express a certain admiration when a writer in Mr. Ogburn's position is courageous enough to echo such phrases as these. At all events Wood, who relied on Aubrey for biographical fieldwork, has weathered less well than his research assistant. The notes on Shakespeare have the relative authority of coming from the son of a fellow actor.

But they were not published in 1680; they remained in manuscript until 1761. In any case, 1680 would not have been a "turning-point"; Shakespeare the dramatic poet had been associated with Stratford in the First Folio by Leonard Digges (1623), as well as by Lieutenant Hammond in a travel survey (1634), by Thomas Fuller in *The Worthies of England* (1661), and by the parish rector, John Ward (1661–3). Mr. Ogburn cites Ward on the question of Shakespeare's income, which he thereupon transfers to Oxford. But how could Ward, who has just previously borne witness to Shakespeare's artlessness, have become acquainted with the minutiae of Oxford's finances? Mr. Ogburn's arithmetical theory as to how Oxford was subsidized, play by play under the Privy Seal, hardly squares with his basic reason for Oxford's pseudonymity: the political danger in acknowledging the authorship of so highly placed a personage. The notion that it would have been easier for a courtier than a commoner to have penned the admittedly dangerous Deposition Scene in *Richard II* falls of its own weight. The object-lessons of Leicester and particularly of Essex must have served as warnings that the seditious courtier would be caught in the more exposed situation.

It is very wise of Mr. Ogburn not to quote from Oxford's extant poetry. The little that we have gives no indication of either an especially large vocabulary or of any way with language above the conventional range of a court wit. His sonnet in Shakespearean form is markedly inferior to almost any of Shakespeare's. His association with the theater has been misleadingly set forth. He was patron of the child actors at the First Blackfriars between 1583 and 1584; Shakespeare and his partners acquired and rebuilt that house in 1597. Francis Meres, in his critical survey, did not call Oxford "the best author of comedy in his time." Under the heading of "the best for comedy amongst us," he listed seventeen names. Oxford, whose plays are now lost, led all the rest for obvious reasons of protocol, followed by two forgotten academics. The appearance of Shakespeare's name on the same list is damaging to Mr. Ogburn's thesis: that the one name was used to mask the other. Even more damaging is the date of Oxford's death, 1604. Given the general consensus on dating, this would not account for a dozen of Shakespeare's best plays, and would leave out his late collaboration with John Fletcher.

It is said that once a Harvard alumnus (who was, like many anti-Stratfordians, an unfulfilled man of letters) offered his *alma mater* a munificent gift on the condition that Shakespeare be taught as Bacon. To the glory of *Veritas* President Lowell, advised by Professor Kittredge, turned it down. Let us suppose that somehow the Oxford heresy managed to establish itself as a pedagogical dogma. What illumination would it shed upon our students' understanding of Shakespearean drama? Mr. Ogburn gives us a glimpse when he interprets *Hamlet* as a "self-portrait" of Oxford. It is true that the Earl had a stepfather, Leicester; but the analogy can be carried farther only by straining and twisting; and Mr. Ogburn cannot make up his mind whether Oxford's mother or Queen Elizabeth should be cast as Gertrude. Nothing is gained and everything is diminished by such far-fetched charades. *Hamlet,* after all, is not a topical skit. It is the refined end-product of a long sequence of sources, and its powerful resonances of conflict and passion have a mythical origin. Whoever wrote the play did not envisage it as a self-serving letter in code to a puzzled posterity.

We hope that we have not too much wearied the reader with the particularities of the field. We have addressed ourselves to them because so much has been made out of them on the presumption that they would not be subjected to technical scrutiny. We could go on with them indefinitely, but—never fear—we shall not. The tangled tissue of misinformation, garbled quotations, strained explications, *non sequiturs*, wild surmise, fantasy, and fallacy has been sufficiently exemplified. Had the truth been anything like the story that Mr. Ogburn has sketched, the greatest problem would be to unravel the conspiracy of silence that has thus far kept it from coming out. It would have to be taken for granted that Jonson and other literary men, along with Shakespeare's fellow actors and editors, and all who were aware of the glamorous mystery, had to be bribed or browbeaten into covering it up. This would be the hardest thing of all to prove, and the burden of proof must continue to lie with the anti-Stratfordians, while the great weight of the evidence reposes with the Stratfordians. We are confident, in submitting the case to our readers, that they will recognize on which side there has been a *suppressio veritatis*.

Index

Aaron, Stephen, 24
Adams, J. Q., 156
Addison, Joseph, 177, 249
Aeschylus, 200, 286, 288, 301
Albee, Edward, 317
Alleyn, Edward, 79, 264, 295, 320
Allgood, Sarah, 10
Antoine, André, 300
Aquinas, Saint Thomas, 150, 251
Archer, William, 124n., 135, 283
Ariosto, Lodovico, 218
Aristophanes, 166, 239, 301, 302
Aristotle, 34, 78, 94, 172, 250, 276, 300, 301
Arliss, George, 9
Arnold, Matthew, 17, 54, 55, 185, 238, 239, 258, 297, 310, 311
Artaud, Antonin, 32
Atkins, Robert, 11, 163
Aubrey, John, 321
Auden, W. H., 107, 176, 213, 219
Auerbach, Erich, 290
Augier, Emile, 306
Augustine, Saint, 93, 94

Bab, Julius, 285
Babbitt, Irving, 14, 304
Babcock, R. W., 243
Bach, J. S., 251

Bacon, Delia, 91, 255
Bacon, Francis, Viscount Saint Albans, 90, 160, 255, 316
Baker, G. P., 23, 24
Balanchine, George, 25
Baldensperger, Fernand, 17, 243
Baldwin, James, 268
Baldwin, T. W., 93, 318
Balzac, Honoré de, 260, 309
Bang, Willy, 282n.
Barber, C. L., 132, 135
Barthes, Roland, 2
Barton, John, 124n.
Basse, William, 245
Bate, W. J., 257
Battenhouse, R. W., 90-9, 269
Beaumarchais, P. A. Caron de, 305
Beaumont, Francis, 244, 277, 280, 301
Beckett, Samuel, 32, 33, 76, 91, 205
Beddoes, T. L., 257
Beerbohm, Max, 257
Beethoven, Ludwig van, 195
Belasco, David, 9, 300
Bennett, H. S., 288
Bentley, G. E., 241, 280
Bergman, Ingmar, 310
Bergson, Henri, 26, 113
Bernhardt, Sarah, 311
Bernstein, Leonard, 119, 120, 289

Betterton, Thomas, 134, 247, 296
Bevington, David, 275
Bible, 22
  1 Corinthians, 95
  Job, 173, 200
  Luke, 180
  Matthew, 167
  Numbers, 96
Blount, Sir T. P., 242
Boas, F. S., 88n., 277
Boccaccio, Giovanni, 240
Boileau-Despréaux, Nicolas, 287, 290
Boito, Arrigo, 146
Boswell, James, 177
Bowers, F. T., 15, 117n.
Bradbrook, M. C., 203
Bradbury, Malcolm, 310
Bradley, A. C., 17, 92, 149, 159, 160,
  164
Brecht, Bertolt, 46, 165, 209, 273, 302
Breughel, Pieter, 142
Bridges, Robert, 287, 288, 292
Brontë, Emily, 57
Brook, Peter, 32, 34, 259
Brooke, Arthur, 52
Brooke, C. F. T., 125n.
Brooks, Van Wyck, 276
Broughton, Hugh, 226
Brown, Carleton, 123n.
Browning, Robert, 213
Bunyan, John, 56, 256
Burbage, Richard, 219, 264, 295
Burke, Kenneth, 285
Burns, Elizabeth, 285
Burton, Robert, 281
Bush, Douglas, 266
Butler, Samuel, 317
Byron, George Gordon, Lord, 317

Caius, Dr. John, 67
Calderón de la Barca, Pedro, 229
Callimachus, 206
Calvin, Jean, 93
Campion, Thomas, 219
Camus, Albert, 149, 258
Cargill, Oscar, 275
Carlyle, Thomas, 252, 253, 260
Carroll, Lewis (C. L. Dodgson), 154
Caryl, John, 252

Case, R. H., 264n.
Castelvetro, Lodovico, 300
Castiglione, Baldassare, 318
Cervantes Saavedra, Miguel de, 105,
  128, 240, 309
Chambers, Sir E. K., 280
Chaplin, Charlie, 316
Chapman, George, 79, 220, 239, 240,
  278, 280, 283
Chapman, G. W., 51n.
Charlton, H. B., 108n.
Chaucer, Geoffrey, 46, 60, 128, 221,
  241, 244
Chettle, Henry, 294
Chikamatsu, 252
Child, F. J., 16, 20, 23
Cibber, Colley, 247, 259
Coleridge, S. T., 73, 98, 113n., 143,
  147, 153, 156, 160, 182, 194, 227,
  239, 248, 250, 303
Collier, Jeremy, 298
Commedia dell' Arte, 17, 76, 287, 305
Congreve, William, 56, 298, 299, 307
Corneille, Pierre, 304
Craig, Gordon, 9
Craig, Hardin, 36, 37
Crane, Hart, 226
Croce, Benedetto, 242
Cummings, E. E., 271
Curtius, E. R., 106n.

D'Annunzio, Gabriele, 282
Dante Alighieri, 238, 240, 248, 251
Darwin, Charles, 213, 275
Davenant, Sir William, 230, 259, 280,
  281, 296, 299
Davies, John, of Hereford, 318
da Vinci, Leonardo, 318
Dekker, Thomas, 221, 278, 280, 282,
  283
Dennis, John, 298
De Sanctis, Francesco, 251
de Vere, Edward, Earl of Oxford, 90,
  315-23
Devlin, William, 23
De Witt, Johannes, 295, 297
Diaghilev, Serge, 309
Dickens, Charles, 57, 128, 256
Dickey, F. M., 108n.

Diderot, Denis, 305
Digges, Leonard, 321
Donne, John, 36-8, 93, 245
Dostoevsky, F. M., 167
Dowden, Edward, 162
Drake, James, 242
Drayton, Michael, 263
Drinkwater, John, 11
Drummond, William, of Hawthorn-
    den, 244, 320
Dryden, John, 34, 81, 215, 222, 230,
    238, 239, 242-5, 248, 257, 281,
    297-9
Dullin, Charles, 11
Dumas, Alexandre, 248
Durry, M. J., 131n.
Duvignaud, Jean, 299
Dyce, Alexander, 265

Eckermann, J. P., 250, 251, 291
Edwards, Richard, 117
Eisenstein, Sergei, 13
Eliot, T. S., 92, 124n., 131n., 150, 156,
    195, 241, 251, 268, 282
Ellis, Havelock, 265, 266, 268
Ellis-Fermor, U. M., 198
Ellrodt, Robert, 131n.
Elton, W. R., 97
Elyot, Sir Thomas, 44-6
Emerson, R. W., 198, 253, 254
Empson, William, 81, 82, 146
Encyclopédie, 247, 248
England's Parnassus, 241
Etherege, Sir George, 56
Euripides, 286
Evans, G. B., 315-23
Evans, Maurice, 11

Famous Victories of Henry V, 126n.
Farnham, Willard, 92, 198
Febvre, Lucien, 99
Fellini, Federico, 310
Fergusson, Francis, 107n.
Feydeau, Georges, 220
Fielding, Henry, 56, 309
Fitzgerald, Barry, 10
Flaubert, Gustave, 55, 248

Fleay, F. G., 138
Fletcher, John, 241, 242, 277-82, 322
Florio, John, 171
Fluchère, Henri, 131n.
Foakes, R. A., 79n., 121n.
Forbes-Robertson, Sir Johnston, 8
Ford, John, 281, 282
Forman, Simon, 122n.
Frazer, Sir J. G., 22, 142
Frenz, Horst, 200n.
Freud, Sigmund, 113, 149, 281, 316
Freytag, Gustav, 149, 150, 250
Frye, Northrop, 235-7, 243, 251, 259
Frye, R. M., 92, 93
Fuller, Thomas, 321
Furness, H. H., 211n.

Galileo Galilei, 38
Gammer Gurton's Needle, 170
Gardiner, H. C., 275
Garrett, John, 162n.
Garrick, David, 177, 247, 259, 291
Genet, Jean, 267, 281
Gide, André, 149, 267
Gielgud, Sir John, 10
Gilbert, Sir W. S., 12, 257
Gildon, Charles, 242
Giraldi Cintio, G. B., 152
Goethe, J. W. von, 17, 186, 240, 241,
    250, 251, 256, 257, 272, 291
Goffman, Erving, 285
Golding, William, 147
Goldmann, Lucien, 97, 308
Goldoni, Carlo, 24
Goldsmith, Oliver, 249, 304
Goodlad, J. S. R., 310
Gower, John, 241
Granville-Barker, Harley, 4, 17, 20,
    163, 164, 310
Graunt, John, 296
Graves, T. S., 117n.
Greene, Robert, 81, 218, 221, 238, 268,
    283, 319
Greet, Ben, 24
Greg, Sir W. W., 15, 79n.
Grotowski, Jerzy, 32, 273n., 284
Gundolf, Friedrich, 243
Gurovsky, Count Adam, 129
Guthrie, Tyrone, 9, 11, 12

Harari, Manya, 109n.
Harbage, Alfred, 20
Hardison, O. B., Jr., 275
Hardy, Thomas, 174
Harington, Sir John, 66
Hart, J. C., 255
Hatto, A. T., 118
Hawthorne, Nathaniel, 198, 254
Hazlitt, William, 147, 200, 307, 308
Hayward, John, 36
Hegel, G. W. F., 237, 238, 250
Heilman, Robert, 158
Heine, Heinrich, 240, 241
Hemingway, Ernest, 268
Henslowe, Philip, 79, 121, 294, 295, 320
Herford, C. H., 23, 211n.
Heywood, Thomas, 81, 122, 220, 221, 278, 281, 283, 294
Hobbes, Thomas, 171
Hoffman, Calvin, 262
Hölderlin, Friedrich, 262
Holmes, Martin, 288
Homer, 55, 238-40, 243, 248, 301
Hooker, Thomas, 93
Horace (Q. Horatius Flaccus), 211, 246
Hosley, Richard, 116n.
Houseman, John, 7
Howard, Sir Robert, 297
Howells, W. D., 49, 50
Hughes, Leo, 304
Hugo, François-Victor, 130
Hugo, Victor, 130, 159, 160, 235, 239, 248, 258, 304
Huizinga, Johan, 131
Hume, David, 249
Hunt, Leigh, 308

Ibsen, Henrik, 17, 194, 256
Ionesco, Eugène, 32, 258
Irving, Sir Henry, 8, 134
Isocrates, 239

Jacquot, Jean, 285
Jaeger, Werner, 239
James, Henry, 57, 58, 213, 309, 316
Johnson, Samuel, 15, 133, 177, 247, 259, 291, 300, 308
Jones, Dr. Ernest, 148

Jones-Davies, M. T., 131n.
Jonson, Ben, 2, 6, 14, 23, 34, 56, 64, 65, 124, 125, 131, 135, 139, 141, 153, 199, 210-31, 241, 242, 244-6, 249, 261, 277, 278, 280, 281, 283, 292, 293, 295, 318, 320, 321, 323
Joyce, James, 19, 58, 133, 195, 205, 248, 268
Jusserand, Jules, 243

Kafka, Franz, 258, 272
Kean, Charles, 259
Kean, Edmund, 265
Keats, John, 239, 248, 267, 303, 317
Killigrew, Thomas, 296
Kilty, Jerome, 24
Kirchner, Leon, 26
Kirstein, Lincoln, 24
Kittredge, G. L., 13-7, 19-22, 26, 135, 322
Knight, G. W., 52, 54, 55, 58, 92, 198, 208n.
Knights, L. C., 149, 208n., 298
Knox, Bernard, 215, 216
Kocher, P. H., 267
Komisarjevsky, Theodore, 11
Kott, Jan, 32-4, 91
Kozintsev, Grigori, 13
Kyd, Thomas, 6, 82, 110, 122n., 225, 245, 267, 277, 286, 294

Lamb, Charles, 141, 164, 165, 265, 268, 287, 288, 298
Landor, W. S., 251
Laughton, Charles, 11
Laurence, W. J., 122
Le Gallienne, Eva, 10
Leiber, Fritz, 8
Lermontov, M. Y., 241
Lerner, A. J., 298
Lessing, G. E., 177, 178, 249, 250, 305
Letourneur, Pierre, 248
Lillo, George, 305
Livy (Titus Livius), 94
Looney, J. T., 316
Lopokova, Lydia, 11
Lough, John, 304
Lowe, Frederick, 298
Lowell, A. L., 322

Lowell, J. R., 254
Lucas, F. L., 224n.
Lucian, 199
Lucretius (T. Lucretius Carus), 165, 166
Lukács, Georg, 303, 304
Lully, J. B., 291
Luther, Martin, 93
Lydgate, John, 241
Lyly, John, 125, 245, 294

Macaulay, Thomas Babington, Lord, 298
Machiavelli, Niccolò, 147, 171, 269
Maeterlinck, Maurice, 282
Malone, Edmond, 119n., 199
Mann, Thomas, 272
Mantell, R. B., 8
Manzoni, Alessandro, 247
Marivaux, P. C. de Chamblain de, 287
Marlowe, Christopher, 82n., 88, 90, 97, 98, 125, 127, 147, 153, 191, 218, 221, 222, 226, 245, 261-73, 283, 295, 316
Marlowe, Julia, 8
Marowitz, Charles, 259
Marre, Albert, 24
Marston, John, 64, 132, 139, 145, 220, 278, 283
Martial (M. V. Martialis), 210
Marx, Karl, 204, 256, 303, 308
Massinger, Philip, 282
Masson, David, 267
McGuffey, W. H., 254
McKerrow, R. B., 15
McLuhan, Marshall, 309
Mead, Margaret, 118-20
Melville, Herman, 58, 181, 196-8, 202, 207, 208, 254, 255, 268
Menander, 286, 287
Meredith, George, 139
Meres, Francis, 79, 241, 322
Merriman, R. B., 23
Michelangelo Buonarroti, 251
Middleton, Thomas, 81, 279, 282, 293
Miller, Jonathan, 33
Milton, John, 93, 147, 168, 177, 178, 228, 238, 243, 246, 257, 264, 281, 318

Mirror for Magistrates, 174, 175
Molière (J. B. Poquelin), 17, 44, 145, 200, 209, 240, 252, 275, 287, 288, 290, 291, 296, 305, 306
Mommsen, Theodor, 189
Montaigne, Michel Eyquem de, 98, 171, 183
Moreno, J. L., 285
Morgann, Maurice, 16, 149, 254
Monday, Anthony, 79
Mozart, W. A., 251

Nabokov, Vladimir, 199
Nashe, Thomas, 283
Newman, Charles, 29n.
Nicoll, Allardyce, 242, 297, 298
Nietzsche, Friedrich, 272
North, Sir Thomas, 190
Norton, Thomas, 175

Odets, Clifford, 10
Ogburn, Charlton, 315-23
Ogburn, Charlton, Sr., 316
Ogburn, Dorothy, 316
O'Neill, Eugene, 10
Orwell, George, 256
Osborne, John, 310
Otway, Thomas, 308
Ovid (P. Ovidius Naso), 76, 94, 108, 115, 125, 228

Panofsky, Erwin, 13
Parnassus Plays, 319
Parrington, V. L., 19
Pascal, Blaise, 37, 97, 149
Pasternak, Boris, 109
Pater, Walter, 160
Peirce, C. S., 19
Pepys, Samuel, 230
Perse, St. John (A. St. L. Léger), 273
Petrarch (Francesco Petrarca), 109, 240
Petronius, Gaius, 208
Petty, Sir William, 296
Phillips, Edward, 242
Pinter, Harold, 310
Pirandello, Luigi, 133, 134
Plato, 239

Plautus, T. M., 134, 216, 220, 221, 286, 287, 305
Plutarch, 190, 196, 206, 207
Pope, Alexander, 6, 244, 287, 291
Praz, Mario, 267
Proust, Marcel, 10, 167
Ptolemy, 45
Purcell, Henry, 34
Pusey, N. M., 21
Pushkin, A. S., 241

Rabelais, François, 76, 99, 140
Racine, Jean, 17, 97, 248, 275, 300, 308
Raleigh, Sir Walter, 188
Ralli, Augustus, 242, 243
Raysor, T. M., 243
Redgrave, Sir Michael, 12
Reinhardt, Max, 188
Renan, Ernest, 213
Reynolds, G. F., 122
Reynolds, Sir Joshua, 163
Ribner, Irving, 284n.
Richards, I. A., 91, 308
Richardson, Sir Ralph, 11
Richardson, Samuel, 56
Rickert, R. T., 79n., 121n.
Rimbaud, Arthur, 266
Robertson, D. W., 93
Robeson, Paul, 24, 153
Robson, Flora, 11
Rolfe, W. J., 15
Ronsard, Pierre de, 301
Rosenberg, Marvin, 148
Rossiter, A. P., 122n.
Rousseau, J. J., 171, 209, 288
Rusk, R. L., 237
Ruskin, John, 53-5, 58, 248
Rymer, Thomas, 155-7, 160

Sackville, Thomas, Earl of Dorset, 175
Sainte-Beuve, C. A., 247
Saint-Evremond, Charles de Saint-Denis, Seigneur de, 308
Saintsbury, George, 243
Salvini, Tommaso, 148
Sandeau, Jules, 306
Santayana, George, 92
Scaliger, J. C., 248

Schiller, Friedrich, 257, 308
Schlegel, A. W., 129, 168, 250, 251, 285
Schlegel, Friedrich, 250
Schmidt, Alexander, 150
Schoenbaum, Samuel, 78n.
Schücking, L. L., 17, 148
Scoloker, Anthony, 292
Scragg, Leah, 122n.
Scribe, Eugène, 279, 307
Seale, Douglas, 24
Second Shepherds' Play (Wakefield), 81
Sedley, Sir Charles, 297
Segal, Erich, 132
Seneca, L. A., 98, 150, 286
Serlio, Sebastiano, 301
Seyler, Athene, 11
Shadwell, Thomas, 259, 281, 297
Shaffer, Peter, 124n.
Shakespeare, William
  All's Well That Ends Well, 58, 65, 66, 74, 80, 86, 133
  Antony and Cleopatra, 1, 35, 43, 49, 54, 62, 63, 68, 75, 83, 94-6, 123, 124, 160, 163, 165, 175, 189, 210, 279
  As You Like It, 51, 52, 60, 61, 64, 66, 70, 76, 86, 132, 133, 138, 141, 200, 268, 292
  Comedy of Errors, 60, 67, 73, 85, 86, 133, 140, 216
  Coriolanus, 11, 22, 46, 47, 61, 67, 71, 80, 83, 94, 152, 187-96, 204, 210, 263
  Cymbeline, 52, 61, 86
  Hamlet, 1, 8, 10-3, 16, 19, 24, 30, 35, 37, 38, 41, 45, 48, 53, 54, 58, 60, 61, 64, 67, 68, 79, 84, 85, 87, 94-6, 117, 121, 136, 144, 148, 150, 152, 156, 160, 175, 183, 189, 198, 216, 255, 256, 258, 263, 264, 278, 286, 292, 294, 308, 322
  1 Henry IV, 16, 19, 23, 29, 31, 32, 41-3, 53, 57, 62, 69, 70, 72-4, 77, 80-2, 88, 89, 121-30, 125, 126, 131, 148, 151, 191, 218, 223, 224, 242, 317
  2 Henry IV, 1, 16, 19, 23, 29-31, 34, 35, 40, 42, 57, 62, 63, 70-1, 73-6, 79, 124, 127, 128, 131, 141, 242, 264, 271, 278, 317

Index

Henry V, 13, 24, 31, 35, 36, 43, 44, 65, 72, 73, 76, 83, 96, 124

1 Henry VI, 62, 75, 83

2 Henry VI, 31, 40, 48, 49, 64, 70, 71, 73, 83, 123

3 Henry VI, 31, 38, 46, 83

Henry VIII, 59, 73, 88, 277

Julius Caesar, 7, 35, 47, 58, 60, 83, 189, 190

King John, 34, 39, 40, 52, 74, 175, 179, 259

King Lear, 8, 32, 40-2, 46, 48, 67, 69, 76, 77, 85, 91, 95, 97, 136, 145, 147, 160, 162-86, 189, 198, 205, 208, 230, 246, 255, 256, 259, 288

Love's Labor's Lost, 1, 51, 66, 68, 74, 76, 108, 115, 121, 199, 321

Macbeth, 9, 11, 30, 41, 43, 49, 61, 69, 85, 122, 147, 152, 160, 163-5, 177, 189, 218, 258, 283

Measure for Measure, 42, 43, 64, 68, 71, 73, 86, 145, 259

Merchant of Venice, 9, 54, 57, 58, 60, 65, 67, 70, 86-8, 141, 153, 154, 158, 259, 263, 317

Merry Wives of Windsor, 59, 67-70, 76, 77, 85, 128, 131, 152, 242, 317

Midsummer Night's Dream, 13, 26, 57, 66, 67, 71, 74, 77, 79, 87, 133, 204, 259

Much Ado About Nothing, 57, 64, 70, 71, 87, 133

Othello, 19, 20, 24, 38, 39, 53, 68, 80, 84, 95, 143-61, 189, 196, 200, 231, 258, 308

Pericles, 58, 70, 71, 74, 124n.

Rape of Lucrece, 93, 321

Richard II, 24, 30, 35, 36, 42, 43, 59, 79, 88, 124, 175, 258, 263, 322

Richard III, 11, 29, 33, 59, 60, 63, 83, 125, 147, 258, 259, 263

Romeo and Juliet, 38, 40, 41, 51-3, 55, 57, 64, 70, 84, 87, 94-6, 103-20, 125n., 160, 179, 201, 258, 264, 279, 281

Sir Thomas More, 48

Sonnets, 1, 322

Taming of the Shrew, 6, 33, 65, 75, 123, 259

Tempest, 11, 33, 34, 48, 54, 56, 68-70, 73, 74, 76, 77, 86, 175, 210-31, 238, 246, 318

Timon of Athens, 67, 191, 197-209, 255, 259

Titus Andronicus, 32, 35, 61, 65, 80, 123, 153, 191, 262, 321

Troilus and Cressida, 25, 34, 44-6, 69, 70, 73, 83, 123, 199, 201, 204, 270

Twelfth Night, 34, 42, 60, 64, 66, 87, 125, 131-42, 292

Two Gentlemen of Verona, 60, 64, 65, 69, 108, 121, 134

Two Noble Kinsmen, 71, 124n., 277

Winter's Tale, 60, 63, 64, 70, 74, 80, 86, 152, 203, 212, 215, 216, 246, 318

Shaw, George Bernard, 6, 10, 132, 159, 256, 257, 283, 298, 310

Shaw, Glenn Byam, 12

Sheridan, T. B., 56

Sherman, S. P., 282

Shirley, James, 281, 294

Sidney, Sir Philip, 109, 124n., 168, 277, 301

Simmel, Georg, 285

Simpson, Evelyn, 23, 211n.

Simpson, Percy, 23, 211n.

Sitwell, Dame Edith, 166

Smith, D. N., 243

Smith, G. G., 79n.

Sontag, Susan, 2

Sophocles, 94, 165, 173, 185, 186, 216, 250, 276, 286, 288

Sothern, E. H., 8

Spencer, T. B. J., 12, 198, 257

Spencer, Theodore, 20, 37, 97

Spenser, Edmund, 36, 218, 229, 241, 244

Spingarn, J. E., 124n.

Spinoza, Benedict, 248

Spivack, Bernard, 148

Spurgeon, Caroline, 110n., 123n., 126n., 321

Stanislavsky, Konstantin, 148, 300

Steele, Sir Richard, 307

Sterne, Lawrence, 58, 307

Stevens, Wallace, 317

Stirling, Brents, 114n.

Stoll, E. E., 17-20, 148
Strindberg, August, 310
Sullivan, Sir Arthur, 252
Summers, Montague, 298
Swift, Jonathan, 205
Swinburne, A. C., 235, 261, 265, 308
Swinhoe, Gilbert, 257, 258
Symonds, J. A., 265, 266, 276, 277

Taine, Hippolyte, 304
Talma, F. J., 304
Tasso, Torquato, 166
Tate, Nahum, 185, 259
Temple, Sir William, 307
Terence (P. Terentius Afer), 286, 287, 305, 318
Thackeray, W. M., 57
Thomson, George, 288, 301
Tieck, Ludwig, 251
Tilley, M. P., 72
Tillyard, E. M. W., 37
Tocqueville, Alexis de, 284
Tolstoy, L. N., 130, 176, 256
Toynbee, Arnold, 25, 273
Trask, W. R., 106n.
Tree, Sir H. B., 134, 259
Trevor-Roper, Hugh, 316
Trollope, Anthony, 58
Tyutchev, F. I., 241

Vanbrugh, Sir John, 296
Veblen, Thorstein, 19
Vega Carpio, Lope Felix de, 250, 288
Verdi, Giuseppe, 146
Vergil (P. Vergilius Maro), 240, 243, 246, 248, 320

Vickers, Brian, 243
Vitruvius Pollio, 301
Voltaire (F. M. Arouet), 99, 156, 248, 249, 256

Wagner, Richard, 110, 195, 256
Waller, A. R., 279n.
Ward, John, 318, 320, 321
Warfield, David, 9
Webster, John, 18, 144, 200, 257, 274, 277, 279, 280
Wellek, René, 243
Welles, Orson, 7
Whitaker, V. K., 93, 318
White, G. A., 29n.
Whitman, Walt, 288
Wiener, Philip, 150n.
Wilberforce, R. O., Baron, 316
Wilde, Oscar, 260
Wilder, Thornton, 200, 284
Williams, Tennessee, 281
Wilson, Edmund, 251
Wilson, J. D., 127n.
Winstanley, William, 242
Wits Recreations, 319
Wood, Anthony à, 321
Wordsworth, William, 160, 248, 257, 287, 308
Wren, Sir Christopher, 297
Wright, L. B., 121n.
Wright, James, 295

Yeats, W. B., 38
Young, Karl, 275